Finalist, Books for a Better Life Award; Excerpted in O, *Playboy*, and *The Week*; Featured on NPR's *Weekend Edition*, *The Leonard Lopate Show*, and *The Rachel Maddow Show*

Praise for *Brothers*

"Given the connection between wordsmiths and wound, it may be no mistake that most of these poignant stories spread out like blood from a gash. . . . This book is like a big brother reminding you of what is important in life. It will make you want to pick up the phone and call out: Brother, where art thou?"

—Gordon Marino, *The Boston Globe*

"*Brothers* reminds us that the similarities brothers find so infuriating in their youth and, for some, long into their adulthood, ultimately yield to a kind of comfort and consolation they won't find anywhere else. Though the accounts of the battles fought may differ, they've been through the trenches together and shed the same blood. Who else but a brother can understand that?"

—*The Los Angeles Times*

"An endlessly fascinating book. . . . [*Brothers*] will quite likely appeal to readers in their parental roles, to women with brothers, and just about everybody else in one manner or another."

—Steve Weinberg, *The Denver Post*

"An engrossing anthology of brotherly love. . . . brilliant, touching essays, such as Shepard's piece on how growing up with an emotionally disturbed brother has influenced his writing. This is a fine collection that illuminates the highs and lows of the brother-to-brother bond."

—Carole Goldberg, *The Hartford Courant*

"This collection is as nostalgic and intimate as any."

—*Publishers Weekly*

"This intimate collection offers rare insight into brothers' sometimes chummy, often complex relationships with one another. A compelling read that sheds new light on a relationship that is as old as the Bible, yet often overlooked."

—*The Daily Beast*

"A wonderful read dealing with the funny, sad, complex, comforting, competitive relationship between brothers. . . . Highly recommended."

—Harvey Frommer

"Watch the boys in this rich anthology battle and booze, worship, envy, argue, and die, and try not to think of your own brother. *Brothers*, edited by Andrew Blauner, is aptly subtitled *26 Stories of Love and Rivalry*; by the end, you'll wish there were a single word for that fraternal emotion ('lovalry'?). In this sampler with a surprising number of writer brothers (Wolffs, Cheevers, etc.), it's David Kaczynski's tale of recognizing the Unabomber in an older Ted that haunts, and Rooster Sedaris who amuses, while Phillip Lopate nails it, calling his brother 'my personal metaphor for Life.'"

—Jess Walter, *Playboy*

"Editor Andrew Blauner has brought together some amazing literary lions to tell their tales about their brothers, and the result is breathtaking, stunning, moving, more than a little heartbreaking, hysterical in places, and often completely overwhelming. . . . *Brothers* is a remarkable compilation. Nothing quite like it comes to mind. Its force is electrifying and lasts well beyond the reading; the writers' voices resonating long after the book is closed."

—*Blogcritics*

"[*Brothers*] is a wonderful read dealing with the funny, sad, complex, comforting, competitive relationships between brothers. I can't wait for Andrew Blauner to come out with 'Sisters.' Highly recommended."

—*Travel Watch*

"Frank McCourt's rollicking essay detailing each of his brothers' strengths and weaknesses is a fitting introduction to literary agent Blauner's assortment of sibling ruminations. First up is the friendly fire exchanged between Benjamin and Fred Cheever, who take turns volleying their opinions on each other and how they separately perceived their upbringing in the shadow of a Pulitzer Prize–winning father. In 'Secrets and Bones,' *Rolling Stone* writer Mikal Gilmore reflects on the nature of family ties—a 'fidelity born of blood'— during a bittersweet reunion with his 'relinquished' brother Frank. Ethan Canin's 'American Beauty' touches on the frivolity and melodramatic intercourse of family. Tobias Wolff's recollection, one of the best in the compilation, examines the 'shambles of a summer' spent with his brother Geoffrey in the wake of their father's nervous breakdown. David Sedaris offers an amusingly over-the-top, potty-mouthed family fable. Coming to terms with his brother Robert's harrowingly sad mental illness becomes Jay Neugeboren's key to happiness. David Kaczynski dissects life with 'Unabomber' brother Ted as he describes the drastic repercussions of Ted's cumulative psychological deterioration. Insisting it was 'veneration' and not rivalry, Chris Bohjalian describes his motivation in mimicking his brother's younger years, while rivalry certainly propels Daniel Menaker's footnote-laden tale of family dynamics. Blauner closes the anthology with a hilarious interview of Nathaniel and Simon Rich, who animate the push-pull fraternization of close-knit brothers. An accomplished paean to brotherly love."

—*Kirkus Reviews*

"The tones vary from angry to joyful, nostalgic to insightful, and painful to humorous. . . . Whether or not you have a brother, you'll enjoy the entertaining, affecting tales collected here."

—*Penthouse*

"Grown men do most of their living and dying in a relatively peaceful coalition of wives, partners, children, friends, colleagues, and aging parents. But a brother remains a figure of almost mythic proportions: the one mortal with whom the fight for love is never won, never lost, and only partly understood. Now, here are brutally honest war stories from such veteran brotherhoods of contemporary American literature as the scrappy McCourts, the storied Cheevers, the fighting Dunnes, the lovely Lopates, the Wolffs in Brooks Brothers clothing, and the unpaired but no less affecting voices of must-read siblings like Ethan Canin, Richard Ford, Herbert Gold, Pete Hamill, and Daniel Menaker. David Kaczynski's fearless, tender, and almost unbearably painful tale of learning to be the brother of the Unabomber is a searing metaphor for the mystery—and murder—in the heart of every brother, whether you are a Cain or an Abel."

—David Michaelis, author of *Schulz and Peanuts: A Biography*

"How to understand the mysteries in our own families with our siblings, the laboratories of so much of how we play out our lives? *Brothers* is riveting—an important addition to sibling literature. A band of brothers grappling with their triumphs and failures, fierce loyalties and betrayals. Daniel Menaker astonishes with his heartbreaking and searing essay on his brother's death—and his own misplaced sense of personal responsibility. Nathaniel and Simon Rich joust in a hilarious Q and A. Phillip Lopate grapples with the radio fame of his brother Leonard, Tobias and Geoffrey Wolff pay loving tribute to each other. Dominick Dunne celebrates the enigma and complexity of his relationship with his late brother, the writer John Gregory Dunne. Must reading for all brothers—and their sisters."

—Marie Brenner, author of *Apples and Oranges: My Brother and Me, Lost and Found*

"This book choked me up and made me laugh. It also infuriated me, moved me, challenged me, and in the end left me feeling glad, above all else, that it existed. In other words, reading it was almost exactly like how I feel about my own brother. These wonderful stories should be read by anyone curious about this unique, and uniquely shaping, bond."

—Tom Bissell, author of *The Father of All Things*

"Brothers in prison, brothers in fraternities, brothers in rivalry, brothers in arms, and always, brothers in crisis—Andrew Blauner has invited an all-star team of writers to visit an underexplored subject. The results are moving and revealing."

—Peter D. Kramer, author of *Listening to Prozac* and *Against Depression*, and clinical professor of psychiatry and human behavior at Brown University

"The next best thing to not having a brother (as I do not) is to have *Brothers*."

—Gay Talese

brothers

brothers

26 STORIES OF LOVE AND RIVALRY

Edited by
Andrew Blauner

Foreword by Frank McCourt

JOSSEY-BASS
A Wiley Imprint
www.josseybass.com

Published by Jossey-Bass
A Wiley Imprint
989 Market Street, San Francisco, CA 94103-1741—www.josseybass.com

Readers should be aware that Internet Web sites offered as citations and/or sources for further
information may have changed or disappeared between the time this was written and when it
is read.

Limit of Liability/Disclaimer of Warranty: While the publisher and author have used their
best efforts in preparing this book, they make no representations or warranties with respect
to the accuracy or completeness of the contents of this book and specifically disclaim any
implied warranties of merchantability or fitness for a particular purpose. No warranty may
be created or extended by sales representatives or written sales materials. The advice and
strategies contained herein may not be suitable for your situation. You should consult with a
professional where appropriate. Neither the publisher nor author shall be liable for any loss
of profit or any other commercial damages, including but not limited to special, incidental,
consequential, or other damages.

Jossey-Bass books and products are available through most bookstores. To contact Jossey-Bass
directly call our Customer Care Department within the U.S. at 800-956-7739, outside the
U.S. at 317-572-3986, or fax 317-572-4002.

Jossey-Bass also publishes its books in a variety of electronic formats. Some content that
appears in print may not be available in electronic books.

Library of Congress Cataloging-in-Publication Data

Brothers : 26 stories of love and rivalry / edited by Andrew Blauner ; foreword by Frank
McCourt. — 1st ed.

p. cm.

ISBN 978-0-470-39129-7 (cloth)

ISBN 978-0-470-59964-8 (paper)

1. Brothers. 2. Sibling rivalry. I. Blauner, Andrew.

BF723.S43.B774 2009

306.875'2—dc22

2008053154

Printed in the United States of America

FIRST EDITION

PB Printing 10 9 8 7 6 5 4 3 2 1

For my keepers and my brothers

contents

———— ❦ ————

foreword

There are pictures to prove that the four McCourt brothers assembled on the 5th of September, 1996, at Ireland House, Fifth Avenue, for the launch of *Angela's Ashes,* a memoir of our collective miserable childhood in Ireland. There we are, gray and/or white, sliding into the high-maintenance stage of life. There we are, Frank, Malachy, Mike, Alphie in descending order of age and ascending order of common sense. We're with our nearest and dearest, we're in suits and ties, we radiate the well-scrubbed look butter wouldn't melt. After I had read an excerpt from the book each of the brothers says something and we sing "Barefoot Days," a kind of family anthem.

You'd never guess from these pictures that we hadn't all been together at once in the same room since Christmas, 1966. You'd never guess how careful we were to avoid a repeat of that night of hard words that hurt and flying fists that never found their target. A student of racial stereotypes might have said, "Ah, the Irish. They're at it again with the drinking and brawling. Excuse me, is this a private fight or can anyone get into it?"

Only Malachy escaped that fateful evening. He had dropped in earlier with his wife, Diane, and her parents, John and Berenice. They said how nice everything was: the tree topped with a sweet little white angel; the cat wandering around with his little red Christmas bow on his neck; the aroma of a standing three-rib roast beef wafting from the kitchen; my wife, Alberta, dispensing drinks and appetizers; my mother arriving with a Swiss friend, Violet. "Very nice," said John and Berenice to Malachy. "Such a pleasure to see people enjoying Christmas and each other." They were sorry that they had to go to another Christmas dinner. Wished they could have stayed with us, so comfortable, warm, relaxed. Maybe next year.

They left as the Clancy brothers were arriving, the brothers at the height of their fame—Paddy, Tom, Liam. My brother Mike came in with his wife, Donna, and Alphie trailed behind them, alone. It was, Hi, lovely tree, brought you something, have a drink. It was, Hi, God that smells good, I'm starved, yeah, I'd sure love a drink.

I look back on that night and realize that most of our guests had already imbibed on empty stomachs and that might explain the little brotherly brush fires. Certain guests were already snapping at each other (Hunger? Thirst? Christmas?) and my brothers and I began taking sides. Alphie erupted, "I hate all this family fighting, the four of us always fighting. There's always one fighting the other three or two fighting the other two and I'm sick of it, sick of it." It was admirable the way he sorted out the mathematics of the thing and to prove it he brought his fist down on a shelf of precious cargo—Scotch, Irish, vodka, gin— which went crashing to the floor and when I said, "For Christ's sake, Alphie," brother Mike sprang to his defense, told me to get off Alphie's back. I invited him outside, where we were about to go at it when a car filled with jeering Christmas revelers so enraged us we chased it down the street till it went through a red light and we lost it and forgot what we were fighting about and returned to the apartment singing "Silent Night."

My wife, Alberta, barked at me that I had no business leaving the party like that when she was having so much trouble with one of the guests rolling around the floor there in some kind of fit. Brother Mike joked that the guest was probably hungry and I took him seriously and knelt on the floor offering her a roast beef sandwich. Tom Clancy said, "What the hell are you doing giving a roast beef sandwich to someone in the throes of an epileptic fit?" and his brother, Paddy, said, "When did you become an expert on epileptic fits?" and that led to another sibling battle, Clancy style, with Liam strumming away on his guitar and singing "The Leaving of Liverpool."

There was a yelp from the living room and Mike said, "You gotta see this." What I had to see was my mother's friend, Violet, on her back under a fallen Christmas tree, cursing the cat who was in a corner pawing and chewing on the little white angel, which he had captured by somehow knocking over the tree. Mike lifted the tree and I helped Violet back to the couch beside my mother, where Violet said, "Ve don't do this kind of thing in Switzerland. Ve sit under the tree and sing Christmas carols," and my mother said, "We sing Christmas carols, too, and then beat the shit out of each other."

People were already leaving the party, expressing their dismay over our uncouth behavior, all of us, the whole McCourt family, and that other gang, the Clancys. People were saying, Well, I never, and promising never to return and that was okay with me because the apartment looked like a war zone. How was I to know that when Michael left, shaking his head, we four brothers would drift so far apart geographically and every other way that we wouldn't be in the same room again for another thirty years?

Writing about my brothers is a dangerous occupation, dancing through a minefield. They talk about me: I know they do. Alphie was right. Two of us will talk about the other two and three will talk about one. When we learn that Mike drove his car into a wall in San Francisco we say, "What the hell is he thinking of, driving his car into a wall?" Or if we hear Alphie didn't drive his car into a wall anywhere we might say, "What the hell is he thinking of, not driving his car into a wall?"

It doesn't matter what you do or don't do: there will be talk.

In the matter of drink I have to be careful. I could avoid the topic altogether but it's there, like Catholicism and dandruff, and all I want to do is rise up and tell the world I have three brothers who don't touch a drop. I'm saying this and living dangerously, because one or more of said brothers will bark in high dudgeon, "What the hell. We've done other things in life besides not drink," and I whimper because when they don the mantle of dudgeon they can be fearsome.

I touch a drop myself, a little wine with dinner, as they say, not because I love the stuff but because it gives work, keeps people employed, enables decent men and women to buy shoes and birthday gifts for their loved ones. My brothers take a dim view of my philanthropic nature, of course, and ask why I can't bestow money directly, and I can only reply that their sobriety has rendered them clear-headed beyond my understanding.

Malachy and Alphie have lived for decades on the Upper West Side of Manhattan, Mensa plateau, and the neighborhood does things to you. (Disclaimer: I've moved to the Upper West Side myself and await the moment of enlightenment.) My brothers Malachy and Alphie might have a greater appetite for tofu than Mike and I. They've been advocating yoga for years and are drawn spiritually more to the foot of the Himalayas than to the altars of Rome. I'm more of a Rome man myself. I don't know where Mike stands; though I have a feeling he doesn't give a fiddler's fart.

My brother Alphie may be the only Irishman ever to have opened a Mexican restaurant in Manhattan, Los Panchos. That was a time when the Upper West Side was still pioneer territory and panting for the refried beans and enchiladas. Oh, Alphie had a grand time with his Mexican restaurant and he, his own boss, could saunter up the block to see Lynn, his wife, and their baby girl, Alison. When a magazine gave the restaurant a review that was between enthusiastic and rave Alphie didn't know what hit him. Yuppies stormed the place and brought their mothers. Under the awning in the back lovers quaffed their Coronas and plighted their troth. Alphie was riding high and why not? He could have been a solicitor in Dublin but he escaped. All he had to do was pass a few exams and appear before the board which would determine if he was respectable enough and intelligent enough to enter the exalted world of Irish law. But what Alphie quickly realized was, yes, it isn't what you know it's who you know and there's a streak of integrity in my brother that erupts in a kiss-my-arse attitude.

If my brother Michael doesn't hold the record for having served more drinks than anyone in the world then he must be close to it. He polished his craft at various New York bars till he was invited to work at Chez Jay in Los Angeles, a hangout for stars and those who like to gaze. Next stop, San Francisco, Perry's on Union Street, a New York–style bar, trendy, with-it, swinging, none of which could describe Mike, who, if he had a mind to, could turn wine into vinegar with one withering look. Many a customer squirmed under the withering look, people who would ask for those exotic drinks that consume a bartender's time and patience. Mike would tell them the candy store was around the corner. If Herb Caen needed something for his column all he had to do was visit Mike and there was enough material for four columns. After a few years there isn't much you can tell a bartender. He hears all the jokes, all the opinions on politics, religion, sex, the stock market. And he grows weary. Mike was asked where he'd like to be on the last day of the century. "Home," he said. He'd like to have a nice dinner with wife and family, and what more can a man ask?

When my mother had me she must have been dissatisfied, because a year, a month, and a day later she had Malachy. He was gorgeous—and there were pictures to prove it: reddish blond hair, blue eyes, pink cheeks, pearls for teeth, a personality that would charm Joseph Stalin. When he came to America in 1952 he was like the rest of us: he didn't know what to do with himself. But there were smart people around who spotted the power of that personality and when you combine it with the Irish charm (sorry, Malachy, this is for public consumption) what else can you do but open a bar with Malachy's name on the canopy and Malachy at the door or behind the bar greeting, charming, singing? What else? Producers prowl the bars of New York and spot Malachy and in a minute he's on national TV with Jack Paar, Dick Cavett, Merv Griffin, Mike Douglas, Johnny Carson. They're mad for him the way he brightens the screen and every room he enters. Man, the party doesn't start till Malachy roars in, singing. A dinner table is a dull place without his *bon mots*, his songs. He's made a dozen movies, acted in plays, read short stories at Symphony Space in New York, written a book, *A Monk Swimming*, available at all fine bookstores. He's been a father five times and there's no end to the grandchildren popping into the world.

There's no end to anything in this family, especially when we're all talking about each other, two about two, three about one.

Or one about three, which is what I've done here.

Since that long-ago Christmas there have been marriages and re-marriages and children and grandchildren. Brother Mike moved to San Francisco where he runs the Washington Square Bar and Grill. Alphie is married, has one child, has written a memoir. Malachy had five children who, in turn, have given him five grandchildren. He has also written a memoir. Frank has one daughter and three grandchildren and has written a memoir, *Angela's Ashes*, which was turned into a movie. The brothers are all in their golden years and doing very nicely, thank you.

So, that is a glimpse into the lives of one set of brothers. When you read something like this you might recall what Tolstoy said, "All happy families are happy in the same way. All unhappy families are unhappy in different ways." You may agree or disagree but, as you voyage through this book, you have to admit that every family, and every set of brothers are unique.

brothers

Benjamin Cheever and Fred Cheever

civil war

I don't see Fred all that often, because he lives in Denver and I live outside of Gotham. But whose fault is that? Since outside of Gotham is where our generation of Cheevers was raised. Conveniently, he was planning to visit, when I got this assignment to write an essay about brothers. He would sleep under my roof, eat my wife's cooking, and help celebrate my mother's nintieth birthday. I could see Fred's back swimming into the crosshairs. I figured we'd fight. He'd fly back to Denver. I'd get even.

If writers had a flag, it would be the one John Paul Jones fought under: a rattlesnake and the legend, "Don't tread on me."

But—and don't you hate having your expectations dashed?—we got along famously. He brought two gorgeous and immensely talented children, and a splendid wife. My boys were both home, and so we had the mingling of the cousins. I was certain he'd notice my immoderate coffee consumption and scorn me for it. Instead, we drank a gallon together every morning and then ran five miles. His wife, Mary, ran too. Each daughter came one day. Elizabeth, the eldest, had the effrontery to beat me in the final sprint. But then I'm a wonderful guy. Or did I already tell you that? In any case, we all enjoyed ourselves. And each other.

When they left, I missed them. I didn't have nearly enough vitriol to power the essay. So I phoned Fred and asked if he'd be willing to write half of it. "A sort of call and response," I said. "Sure," he said.

We tossed our essay back and forth. We danced a pavane. Then sending me that last version, he wrote, "*I sucker-punch you at the bottom of page five in this version. You are welcome to call a foul and delete it."*

I left it. Remember this when you come to the last line. I'd be interested to know what you think. If I'm a crybaby, making too much of the slights suffered during my childhood, then Fred, my younger brother, is right to point it out. And certainly our childhood was happier than I let on. But also much sadder.

We Cheevers have a tendency to get nasty with one another. Often we're kidding. Like about the crosshairs. (I don't actually own a high-powered rifle with a scope.) But also there is real animus. Partly it's because our accomplished father, John Cheever, won the National Book Award, the Pulitzer Prize for fiction, the William Dean Howells Medal, which my mother has on display in the library of the house he owned and died in. Fame is a corrosive. Especially if it's not your fame. Although I'm sixty, many people still see me as John Cheever's child. I've given readings from my own book, and had women rush up to me afterwards to say, "I just love your father's writing." This might have been all right, if my father had adored me to the exclusion of others and admired my writing above the work of others. But he didn't and he didn't.

Fred will write in Italics, because he was born in Italy, and Italians are like that. *Per presentare la bella figura.*

For thirty years I have lived at least two full time zones away from the house in which I grew up. My brother lives a ten-minute drive away. I am a lawyer and, for a while now, a law professor. Our parents knew less about law than they did about Romanian car repair. My brother writes books, as did his parents before him.

I live in a city where everyone exercises all the time and people invest more money in spandex than in diamonds or books. My brother, Ben, lives on the very edge of the City of Mammon, where the unbridled, conspicuous consumption of everything scarce—from sea urchin bladders to platinum collar bars—is a civic duty. It's also a place where people actually buy hardcover books, even if only to set them on their coffee tables. My brother seems largely immune from the call of the material god. However, he does have shiny cars that talk to him ("go left, go right at the next . . .") and handheld electronic gadgets that would have gotten him burned at the stake in 17th-century Europe.

My brother is a coward because he chose to spend his life with people to whom his parents meant something. My brother is brave because he chose to live with people who read books, some by his parents. I was brave because I went places where my father's name could do me no good. I am a coward because I seek out places where my father's books aren't often read.

We have a word "fratricide" (although not a distinct criminal offense). You don't do extra jail time just because the person you kill was your brother. It's not classified as a hate crime. According to Justice Department statistics, it is rare. You are much more likely to be killed by your parents or your children. You are many times more likely to kill your spouse. In some dark moments, there is something liberating in the idea of killing your siblings. It's like cutting the fishing line snagged on an underwater rock. Brothers don't kill each other more often because brothers leave.

Not all salmon return to their native stream to spawn. It's obvious once you think about it. If it were otherwise, all the salmon on the planet would be spawning in the first river in which salmon evolved. Salmon leave. What's interesting is that we don't want to believe salmon leave. We want eternal cycles. We want the salmon always to return to Redfish Lake. We want the swallows always to return to Capistrano. We want the cobbler's children to be cobblers in the same shop. We want Chelsea Clinton to be president.

My brother Fred has a talent for statistics: fratricide may be rare, but it has a long and distinguished history. Cain and Abel are the first brothers. Cain murders Abel. Which seems to have been forgotten. In Civil War epics they save it for the knock-out blow, after the nation torn asunder, after the 600,000 dead. "Brother fought against brother," they announce as if this were the rough equivalent of Oedipus and his foxy mom. As if it were something unnatural like—I don't know— a dog with a plastic bag cleaning up after his owner. Whereas

I always wonder why you'd want to murder a man who wasn't your brother.

When people in my family talk about brothers and sisters, they usually talk about parents. There are reasons that this is so. It also appears to be so in every other family I know. Adult children are like islands in a coral atoll, anchored to the sea bed in their unchanging relationship to each other as consequence of another relationship with a once brooding volcanic island now sunk beneath the waves, or moved to Florida. I am sure there are families in which relationships forged among siblings evolve to the point that parents no longer matter. I have just never met any of those people.

For most people, it seems, a lifetime isn't long enough to stop talking about your parents. And, of course, when we talk about our parents, we talk about love.

And when we talk about love, we talk about need. My brother, Fred, wasn't born until I was eight, and so my earliest wishes were for the painful death of my older sister. And boy did I ever wish on a star for that happy eventuality. But when Fred did arrive, the little nipper came along nicely in my disregard.

We lived in Rome and I was in love with my mother. I didn't speak Italian and so I wasn't allowed outside alone on the streets. So I moped around inside the palazzo we'd rented, while my own mother took this naked stranger into bed with her. She breast-fed him. I saw it happening. Not the sort of image to excite brotherly love.

But maybe you all don't feel that way about your brothers. Maybe I need to put my life into context. Sometimes, of course, I remember my childhood as a splendid magical time. "Trailing clouds of glory," I came "from heaven that was my home." And sometimes childhood was splendid. Often not.

I didn't speak Italian either. At the time I lived in Italy, I didn't speak at all. I still don't speak Italian, although I am stuck with Federico. When asked (repeatedly) why they named me Federico, my parents would reply that there is no "K" in Italian and hence no Frederick. Okay, the Italians may not use K much, but they are a cosmopolitan people with the Germans just across the border. A perfunctory glance at any Italian keyboard (there are a number of versions) will reveal the presence of "K": so much for parental accuracy. My parents also told me they lost my birth certificate. I am still wondering about that.

I had two different childhoods. Three actually. The two I lived and the one I remember. The one I remember teeters back and forth between a very heaven and a very hell. In the heavenly childhood, Muzzy and Dazzy were always in love. Muzzy left a postcard under my pillow at night that had a penny scotch-taped to it and the words, "Good morning, good boy." That happened. I was five. I remember.

When awaken in the hellish childhood, my bed is wet. And while in first grade at the Todd Elementary School, I suffered from what, years later, a psychiatrist told me was called "a shy bladder." So we'd all be marched into the bathroom in the morning and everybody else would pee and I'd pretend to pee. Then I'd spend a couple of hours hopping around. Then I'd pee in my pants and spend a damp afternoon failing to learn how to read.

No one can rival my bed-wetting stories. Perhaps there really is something to this genetics stuff. Ben and I share certain other physical traits. When you see those murals of human development ("the ascent of man") with the monkey on the left and the "modern" guy on the right, we resemble the figure just right of center: slumped shoulders, exaggerated brows, hair in the wrong places. In some versions we get a club, which is a comfort. I can imagine potty training wasn't a high priority for Neanderthals. Do we drink so much coffee now to show that we can?

My brother and sister have always maintained that my parents loved me best. I have assumed this was their way of saying that they didn't get enough parental love. There were two possible culprits for this tragic state of affairs: my parents or me (the parental love hog).

The "love hog" hypothesis was easier for my siblings to deal with. If I—always inclined to overeat—had somehow sucked all the available parental love out of the family, then any deficiency in the amount of love they received could be blamed on me. The hypothesis is implausible, but since the only people who were interested (my brother and sister) had some reason in believing it, implausibility was no impediment.

I know people who may actually have been love hogs, or at least they show signs of having received an overabundance of parental love. They were convinced by the time they were thirteen that they deserved to be president, commissioner of baseball (why does everyone want to be commissioner of baseball?), and Mick Jagger's eventual replacement. When I tell these people that their academic labors are unlikely to lead to success, they know I cannot be telling the truth. They know that my recitation of their apparent limitations must be part of a monstrous conspiracy. Their mother and father knew best and told them they were perfect. For better or worse, I am not one of these people. Generally, I only trust people who criticize me.

Talk about unconditional parental love makes me edgy. I don't know if it's the shiny tricycle I never had or whether its existence seems a delusion.

Much as I hate to agree with my dastardly brother, I've always known that he wasn't the fabled love hog. Certainly Fred was brandished in front of me as an example of every sort of achievement, and my mother's house is festooned with pictures of himself and his children. While there seem to be no pictures of my own comely children.

Distance having made my mother's heart grow fonder.

It's much easier to have passionate feelings about people who aren't around. It takes much less time and involves fewer presents. People who aren't around rarely fail to meet expectations. They rarely dash your hopes. They have dramatically fewer opportunities to lie to you. Casablanca is really a movie about two people who discover (over just two days) that their legendary passion will not survive their being together. "We'll always have Paris, we lost it for a while (when you showed up). . . ."

My father took the need for distance a step further. He was always falling in love with strangers. Women and—more surprisingly—men. He liked novelty in his relationships. He was a storyteller, and he was fond of people, when he'd just started to make up the story about them, before they'd tangled the plot line with their petty concerns and multiple failings.

Blake Bailey prefaces his excellent new biography of my father, with this quote from William Maxwell, a friend and editor: ". . . it is too much to ask that people who spend very much time in a world of their own, as all writers do, should immediately and invariably grasp what is going on in this one."

The world's very sentimental these days about storytellers. Frank Capra was a great storyteller. But so was Adolph Hitler. Remember that his Reich was going to last 1,000 years? Storytellers make us care about the world. They make the world dramatic. They distort it. Since my father was a storyteller, I was rarely an ordinary child. Sometimes I was a disaster, sometimes—although rarely—I was a success. It was always interesting.

I find myself in the middle of the thing that storytellers do. My brother, Ben, is, by any standard, an accomplished and successful person. During our short visit he took me to the farmers market where he had to judiciously divide his conversational time between the mayor, prominent international historians, and beautiful women. James Bond could not have done better. He actually has New York Marathon Medals hanging off every surface in his kitchen (he runs the thing every year): talk about festooned. He even owns a Vespa. He has two wonderful children and a magnificent and understanding wife. He has an encyclopedic knowledge of modern fiction and modern film. He has many published books to his name; he writes about truth and love. I, on the other hand, write about section 1604(i) of the National Forest Management Act of 1976. The image of himself as a love-starved urchin serves some purpose. I will have to leave it to you, our reader, to figure out what that purpose is.

When I was the favorite, my father would tell me how disappointed he was in my brother. "Disappointed" isn't the word he used. "Worried" is the word he used. "I'm worried about your brother," he'd confide. "He hasn't got any friends."

My brother had difficulty learning to ride a bicycle. And every year for my brother's birthday my father would buy him a bicycle. These were kept on the front porch. Year after year the new bicycles stacked up. "How can somebody who has never mastered a bicycle learn how to drive a car?" my father asked me as my brother came of age.

Fred learned how to drive a car. He has many friends. And now—at fifty—he rides his bicycle to his job as law professor in Denver. No training wheels. So my father's worries were unfounded. But I enjoyed sitting among the virgin bicycles on the porch of the family house with my father and fretting about my brother's failings and inadequacies. Which is fine, as far as it goes.

But my father used also to sit on the front porch of his house with my brother and fret about *my* inadequacies. Fred had a poor sense of balance. But I was stupid. Actually, they didn't call me stupid. What they called me was "a slow learner." I was "possessed of a mediocre intelligence." Fred was smart.

And they had a case against me. I spent two years in the second grade. I had a dreadful time learning how to read. I did finish high school, and even graduated college. I got jobs. I got promotions. I married a brilliant woman. But at my parents' house Bengie is still slow.

"When Bengie learns something he really learns it," they used to say. And also, "Bengie is so religious," which I guess was their way of explaining why it was I looked so long at everything before making up my mind. And for a slow learner, religion is just the ticket. While a scholar needs to master many books, a religious man reads only one.

And I'm still stupid at my parents' home. When—in her eighties—my mother met some new friends of mine, they told her, "We like Ben so much. He's funny and so smart," Mummy paused. "Smart?" she said. "I wouldn't say smart."

So the honors were carefully doled out. I could ride a bicycle. Fred could read. And so you can imagine how pedaling through life, I haven't always wished the very best for my brilliant brother.

Our parents (and many parents of their generation) were willing to share their perception of their children's faults with anyone who would listen, including their children. I still can't throw a baseball accurately. Catch one? Never mind. I cry in bad movies (and not because they are bad). I bicycle hundreds of miles, but I cannot throw my leg over the seat in the jaunty way my father admired and could pull off until a few months before he died. I am really not that smart. I am dyslexic and struggled a great deal before word processing software made me bionic (or Byronic (but nothing in between)).

The thirty-odd binders of my father's journals aren't full of despair about his inadequate children. Nor are they full of expressions of love for me (the few examples have been identified and catalogued by my siblings). Mostly, we children don't appear at all. Dad didn't imagine us taking over the cobbler's shop after he died. He didn't imagine there would be a cobbler's shop after he died.

So, we Cheever children competed with each other for a share of that modest part of our parents' attention that might be devoted to us. Our parents didn't require us to compete, there just wasn't enough— as we saw it—to go around. We saw our failings as the reason they didn't make more of us, act like parents on TV, celebrate us, love us unconditionally. But that was our perception, not theirs.

Their position may have been reasonable. Depression, world war, and the impending threat of thermonuclear obliteration granted them a realistic sense of their own impermanence. The hard-drinking, chain-smoking generation-with-false-teeth were aware of their mortality. It gave them a taste for living they could never satisfy. Not for nothing did they pioneer chemical consciousness. The bourbon, gin, and Nembutal they consumed in America's suburbs in 1967 would have flattened everyone in Haight Ashbury. Children were a duty (and a joy), but there were limits. There were other needs to meet in the gathering darkness.

Parents of my generation, on the other hand, pledge ourselves to "unconditional love." We read books, go to seminars, and watch DVDs about childrearing—examine color graphics from fetal development to teen brain scans. "Parenting" has become both a verb and a competitive sport. There have been parents like this in the past, but they were rare. Douglas MacArthur's mother followed him to West Point and rented an apartment outside the gate. Yes, we say, and her son became Supreme Commander of half the world with those great sunglasses. We lavish praise, and love and exotic enriching activities. The unshakable sense of self-worth we impart to our children seems to make it impossible for them to make their beds. But then, I feel quite sure Douglas MacArthur couldn't sort laundry (the khakis, the whites, the gold braid . . .).

We seem incapable of imagining our own mortality. We eat a "rainbow of foods" (defined and deconstructed every six months) and engage in a structured exercise regime because we are going to live forever. We explain away each new sign of decrepitude (it could have happened to a twenty-year-old!). In a hundred years, if they lose their lovers, apartments, or jobs, we will welcome our children back home. We will keep their bedrooms dusted. We will always love them.

So what is left for us as our parents fade or die or move to Florida and our children begin to reject the concern we lavish? Is there a relationship with our siblings we can salvage? Is it worth the trouble?

My father, when particularly exasperated with my inadequacy at sports or penchant for tears, would instruct: "Remember. You are a Cheever." It seemed ridiculous, even at the time. A few years ago, I was delighted when Antonio Banderas offered a variation in Spy Kids ("Remember. You are a Cortes"). His version made my father's even more absurd. No one ever suggested the Cheevers conquered Tenochtitlan or outsmarted the Texas Rangers.

Only recently, it occurred to me that my father's instruction might have been part commiseration. Being a Cheever might be as much predicament as distinction, as much like athlete's foot as like the Nobel Prize.

Predicament or distinction, Cheever-ness is something I apparently cannot escape. My brother's existence reminds me I am still anchored to the sea bed, locked in relation to my family, alive and dead, whether I like it or not. But my brother's existence also reminds me that this is a predicament we share.

Brothers are people who share problems, not out of choice, but out of shared experience. When Henry V declared his sorry company at Agincourt "we band of brothers," he did so because they shared a problem, the far larger and more formidable French army. This problem (and the blood Henry assured them they would shed) made each of them brothers "be he ne'er so vile."

So Ben and I are brothers through blood (with beetling brows and hairy bodies), we are brothers through memory (because we can both remember almost all the words to "Little Deuce Coupe"), and we are brothers because there are problems we share.

My father, our father, had an excellent eye. Which means—of necessity—he had an eye for flaws. "What can you do with a man like that?" the narrator asks of the horrid brother in "Goodbye, My Brother," the story with which my father led off the collection that won the Pulitzer Prize. Have I mentioned the Pulitzer Prize? "How do you dissuade his eye in a crowd from seeking out the cheek with acne, the infirm hand. . . ." and I could go on and on, "the lonely boy with the piping giggle and a tendency to burst into tears. . . ."

John Cheever wrote fiction, but he saw me with a critic's eye. Fred may have been praised wildly in absentia, but he didn't escape.

So we had that. We've both stepped off in Pickett's charge, taking bullets for the old Dominion. We both learned the lesson of battle: we learned to crouch, we learned how to make ourselves small. In fact we both walk with a pronounced stoop. People sometimes say I'm self-deprecating, but it wasn't self-deprecation I was after. It was self-preservation.

When my first novel came out, I wrote a scathing review of it. I guess this was an attempt to channel my father, and perhaps disarm imaginary critics. When the book was published in England, I went there and the Guardian (I think it was the Guardian) agreed to run my nasty review of myself.

I wrote cheerfully of how after my first marriage had broken up, I'd returned home and been welcomed back.

"I thought of my return as joyous, something approaching the triumphal. In his journals I later learned that my father's feelings were not unmixed. He wrote: 'On Saturday morning our son, after a week in a spiritual retreat where he got fucked, has left his wife and returned home, for it seems only a few hours.'"

That's where I stopped the quote from the journals. Helpful editors at the *Guardian* looked *The Journals* up and lengthened the excerpt.

"When it became clear that I was staying for more than a few hours, he wrote, 'My son is here. I think that we do not know one another; I think it is our destiny that we never will. I observe in a comical way, that he does not flush the toilet. He observes that I snore. Another son returns tomorrow. I feel that I know him better, but wait and see.' And then, a little ruefully, 'Some part of loving one's children is to part with them.'"

And so, if in the course of my life as a writer, any writer ever wants to take a poke at me, they can call in Big John Cheever to lend a hand.

And it's done. But mostly strangers feel that I grew up in a magic kingdom. It was a magic kingdom all right. Watching from the stands—as readers do—we appeared to be in an enviable position. We looked like actors, but we were often props. He'd shake the carpet and we'd all fall to earth. Which was a long way down. And then—if you look in the journals you'll see this—we'd be forgotten. We were busy finding his car keys, trying to catch a ball, starting our own lives, while he whisked above the rooftops.

"Children" he'd say, "you want children in this scene?" and he'd swoop down and snatch one of us up.

There was the trauma of being his prop, the frequent falls, getting the dirt out of your nose. But we did pick up a sense of humor. And while the world outside his stories is a good deal less vivid, it has its compensations. There's work to do. You can make up your own stories. And—to quote from Mel Brooks—"There are ladies here." And there are friends, good friends and there are brothers.

Aw, it wasn't really so bad. But then brothers don't have to agree on everything.

David Kaczynski

---

missing parts

I'll start with the premise that a brother shows you who you are—and also who you are not. He's an image of the self, at one remove, but also a representation of the "other."

In a universe of unlimited spatial and temporal dimensions, you are brought together with your brother in a unique and specific consanguinity. You come from the same womb. Your family has a certain flavor or smell unlike any other. It has an ethos, perhaps even a mythology all its own. You are a "we" with your brother before you are a "we" with any other. Even your parents' "we" can be turned against you.

Your brother, if there are only two of you, is your first peer, thus your template for later, adult relationships.

When your brother ventures out in the world, he represents you. If he is older, he may become your only way of being and appearing vicariously in a world that you are not yet allowed to enter. He represents, in this sense, your possibility of having a future and a wider social presence. Your pride in your brother is, in part, egoistic projection.

Through your brother, you also learn the limitations attached to self: the things you do less well, the meaning of "belonging" as a noun, the need to compete for attention, the space that opens up for you only after it's been vacated by your brother. In a sense, especially if you are the younger brother, you only begin to "own" yourself in your brother's absence. But his absence may haunt your aloneness.

Culturally speaking, I have an idea that I am at liberty to fight with my brother—indeed, it's expected—until someone attacks either one of us. Then we will turn in unison on the attacker as one force redoubled. If there's a significant difference in age, then the older brother protects the younger with his fists and his power. But the younger brother protects the older with his admiration and love. It should be obvious who bears the greater responsibility.

In expansive affirmation of our fellow man, we sometimes call everyone "brothers." To designate a special friendship, or to invoke community and intimacy within a group, we again use the "brother" formula as a foundational myth of male fellowship.

My brother, Ted Kaczynski, once sent a bomb to an airline executive concealed in a hollowed-out copy of a book with the intriguing title *Ice Brothers*.

I don't remember a time when I wasn't aware that my brother was "special"—a tricky word that can mean either above or below average, or completely off the scale. Ted, seven and a half years older, was special because he was so intelligent. In the Kaczynski family, being intelligent carried high value. But at the time of Sputnik and the space race in the late 1950s, intelligence—especially technical and scientific intelligence—had a certain cultural panache as well. Ted was a "brain" to school-age children in our working-class neighborhood, where the word conferred status, but also a vague stigma since being too intelligent was linked to maladjustment, and most kids wanted to fit in.

As a young child beginning to gauge social perceptions, I thought of my brother as smart, independent, and principled. I heard myself described by our neighbors and aunts and uncles as charming, happy, and affectionate—as if those were traits to be remarked on in a child. Even at a tender age, I sensed that adults contrasted me with my brother. Heck, anyone could be the way I was, since it required no effort. But not everyone could be smart, independent, and principled like my big brother. Given a choice, I would gladly have embraced Ted's persona and relinquished my own. I wanted to be like Ted.

Ted could be kind, but also critical.

When I was about three years old, our family moved from a dingy duplex in Chicago's Back of the Yards neighborhood (the "Yards" being the famous Chicago stockyards) to a house in Evergreen Park, a new working-class suburb on the city's south-west side. It was our first house. When summer came, I used to delight in pushing open the screen door and going out to play in our spacious backyard. It never rained that summer (in my memory, at least). I met other small boys and girls my own age. I was discovering a new world and having a ball. The only frustration came when I tried to re-enter the house, because I was too short to reach the door handle to pull open the screen door. I would often stand on the back patio—a tiny exile—calling for someone, Mom, Dad, or Ted, to let me in.

One day I saw Ted fiddling with something at the back door. He was about ten or eleven years old at the time but always an ingenious person. To this day, it somewhat mesmer-izes me to watch someone drawing or performing some careful manual task, which I ascribe to my early interest in my broth-er's activities. He had taken a spool of thread from Mom's sew-ing kit, and a hammer and a nail from Dad's tool kit in the basement. I watched as he removed the last remnant of thread from the spool, leaving only the bare spool. Then he inserted the nail through the hole in the center of the spool and ham-mered it onto the wooden screen door. When he was finished, he said, "Dave, see if this works!" All of a sudden it dawned on me what he had done: he'd crafted a little makeshift door handle for me.

It seems that even after I grew taller and no longer needed it, the spool remained attached to the door for some time—a lingering reminder of my brother's kindness. A few tender mem-ories like this one (and there were more than a few) soothe the stings that inevitably come in a sibling relationship. Growing up, I never doubted my brother's fundamental loyalty and love, or felt the slightest insecurity in his presence.

Which is not to say that I always felt worthy in his presence.

It was never a challenge to win our parents' approval. Although humble about their own virtues and accomplishments, Mom and Dad seemed to glory in their two boys. I'm sure it was Ted who first clued me in that Mom and Dad's approval ratings were not objective. Once I said, "Aren't we lucky that we have the best parents in the world!" and he replied, "You can't prove that."

Sometimes I suspected that Ted was judging me, even when he said nothing. I wondered if I had done something wrong that I wasn't aware of. Once when he caught me in a fib, he said, "You liar!" and stalked off in contempt. I worried that I had disappointed him terribly, perhaps beyond hope of redemption.

Although I had placed Ted up on a pedestal—wanting to emulate his intellectual accomplishments, bragging to my fourth-grade buddies when he went to Harvard on a scholarship at sixteen—there was another part of me that sensed he was not completely OK.

I was probably seven or eight years old when I first approached Mom with the question, "What's wrong with Teddy?"

"What do you mean, David? There's nothing wrong with your brother."

"I mean, he doesn't have any friends. Why's that?"

"Well, you know, David, not everyone is the same. You have lots of friends because you like people and people like you. That's wonderful! You're a sociable person. But Teddy likes to spend more time by himself, reading and working on things. That's wonderful, too. He's different from you, but everyone doesn't have to be the same. It's OK to be different."

"I know but . . . sometimes it seems he doesn't *like* people."

Mom must have sensed that I needed more than reassurance. "Sit down, David, I want to talk to you about something that happened before you were born."

Mom and I sat down side by side on the couch, the same one she used to read me stories on—the Beatrix Potter series, *Wind in the Willows*, *Tom Sawyer*—and teach me about life through her explanations and commentaries. I always treasured this time with Mom for its intimacy and also for the world of imagination it opened for me. Sometimes she told me stories from her own life. But now she told me one about my brother's early life.

"When Teddy was a little baby just nine months old—before he was able to talk or understand us—he had to go to the hospital because of a rash that covered his little body. In those days, hospitals wouldn't let parents stay with a sick baby, and we were only allowed to visit him every other day for a couple of hours. I remember how your brother screamed in terror when I had to hand him over to the nurse, who took him away to another room. They had to stick lots of needles in Teddy, who was much too young to understand that everything being done to him was for his own good. He was terribly afraid, and he thought Dad and I had abandoned him to cruel strangers. He probably thought we didn't love him anymore and that we would never come back to bring him home again."

I really can't do justice to my mother's capacity for drama. Perhaps it was because of the stories and fairy-tales she read to me on that old couch, but Mom had a way of entering into the emotions of the scenes she described. By the time she finished, I was deeply moved. There were tears rolling down my cheeks as I thought about the terrible suffering my brother had endured when he was a little baby.

It was an important teaching moment, and Mom took advantage of it. "David, your brother doesn't remember what happened to him, I'm sure. He was much too young. But that hospital experience hurt him deeply, and the hurt never went away completely. One thing you must always remember is never to abandon your brother, because that's what he fears the most."

I promised Mom that I would never abandon Ted. She went on to describe her and Dad's patient efforts to help their son heal from his hospital trauma—how after they brought him home from the hospital they spoke gently and cuddled him, and tried over and over to get him to smile back at them. It took a long time, she said, before Teddy resembled the happy baby he'd been before he had to go to the hospital.

Often as I grew older, the story of my brother's traumatic hospital experience would come to mind as I struggled to understand Ted's quirks or to forgive his occasional insensitivity. It helped me to realize that you can't understand someone without compassion.

One summer our father, Ted Sr., caught a baby rabbit in our backyard. He placed the little animal in a wooden cage that was covered with a screen top. Several neighborhood kids clustered around to gape at the rabbit, and our father seemed proud to show it off. Our family, after all, had a pronounced educational bent. Dad used to teach us how to identify plants. So it was only natural that he would take pleasure in exposing the neighborhood kids to an "educational" experience—the chance to view a wild animal up close. My friends were jockeying to get a good look.

Ted was the last kid to join the onlookers, evidently curious to see what all the fuss was about. But as soon as he glimpsed the little rabbit cowering in a corner of the cage, his reaction was instinctive: "Oh, oh, let it go!" he said with panicked urgency.

Suddenly, I saw everything differently. Only then did I notice that the young rabbit was trembling with fright. Only then did I realize that we were being cruel.

Dad, realizing that he had caused his sensitive son distress, quickly carried the cage to a wooded area across the street and released the rabbit into the wild.

When I was around seven, Dad finished our attic in beautiful knotty pine so that Ted, now in high school, could have his own bedroom. The change provided us both with space and a measure of independence. But it also afforded Ted an opportunity to isolate himself from the family whenever he wanted, which turned out to be rather often.

Perhaps puzzled by the long hours Ted spent quietly in his room upstairs, I remember approaching Dad with the same question I'd once asked our mother: "What's wrong with Ted?"

My father pointed out that Ted's intellectual interests set him apart from most of his classmates. While Ted read books about relativity theory, they were listening to Elvis and going to sock-hops. Someday, Dad said, Ted would go off to college and meet other young people with similar interests. He would form close friendships, eventually marry and raise a family of his own. Ted would "find himself," Dad predicted—it just might take him a little longer.

Since Ted didn't seem to crave company, I always felt privileged and rewarded whenever he'd invite me up to his room to show me something—perhaps some ingenious mechanical contraption he had invented, or to view his coin collection and hear how he had acquired the more valuable coins, or to play duets he had composed using our cheap wooden recorders, or to hear him read a favorite story or poem. It was my brother who first introduced me to the stories and poems of Edgar Allan Poe. He once showed me a humorous drawing that he'd made of the emperor Napoleon making him appear quite crazed. To my pre-adolescent and later adolescent mind, it was all so wonderfully cool to have a big brother who would take me into his confidence. I treasured those times we spent together even more than I did our family vacations and excursions to the nearby forest preserve, I suppose because they felt more "special." My emotional bond with Ted was unique and very strong.

Ted left for Harvard at the age of sixteen. It never would have occurred to me that my brother would suffer as a result of social isolation there, because I had no idea that he needed anything from people. I thought of him as emotionally self-sufficient. I never imagined that he shared my "weakness" for human companionship, my need for social validation.

In high school, I sort of became my brother—or at least tried to. I made myself into the class "brain," concentrating on math just like Ted. Although I had a few friends, all National Honor Society types, I grew more socially aloof and never dated. Once an all-star second baseman in our local Little League, I dropped baseball to concentrate on academics. I took an overload of courses so I could graduate in three years. On graduation day, I was sixteen, not much older than Ted had been on his graduation day. I even applied to Harvard and felt very disappointed when my application was rejected. But by then I already knew that I was no match for my brilliant older brother. I may have been an intellectual star at Evergreen Park Community High School, but judging from the way the older faculty members swapped stories about my brother's brilliance, it was clear that Ted was one of a kind, an academic legend.

In May or June of my senior year in high school, Ted was home on vacation from his Ph.D. program at the University of Michigan. One afternoon, I showed him a calculus problem that I'd solved after a long, persistent struggle. Ted, who was also a teaching assistant at Michigan, was impressed. "I'd guess that if I assigned the same problem to my upper-level calculus class, probably no one would be able to solve it." I was thrilled by his praise. I felt as if I had just moved into the select company of a few smart people whom Ted would naturally admire. He seemed proud of me.

In many ways, the next ten years or so were our closest as brothers. At least, that's how I experienced them. But I also felt myself gradually drifting away from Ted. We spent a month one summer camping together on Michigan's Upper Peninsula. We spent a summer traveling across western Canada looking for a piece of land for Ted to homestead after he abruptly quit his professor's job at the University of California at Berkeley in 1969. In 1971—after an unsuccessful attempt to get a Canadian homestead permit—Ted followed me to Montana where I had migrated after college. He suggested that we pool our resources to buy a parcel of land, which turned out to be the 1.4 acre plot six miles outside of Lincoln, where he built his now iconic 10' × 12' cabin and where he lived a seemingly inoffensive hermit's life for the next twenty-five years.

Once, invoking his vision of an ideal society, he described to me hunter-gatherer communities based on reciprocity and trust, "you know . . . like our family." If someone had told me that in another five years Ted would be writing letters of bitter recrimination to our parents, I would have been surprised to say the least. As late as the late 1970s, he invited me to join him in a quest for remote land in the Canadian wilderness where we might live together far from the bane of civilization. By then, however, it was clear to me that I would be quite unhappy with my life shrunk to one relationship with my civilization-hating brother.

On one hand, a change in how I saw my brother was inevitable. Most adoring younger brothers take their older brothers off their pedestal at some point. Idols show their clay feet eventually. In a healthy relationship, disillusioned hero-worship is replaced by mature affection—and there certainly were a lot of qualities to like in Ted. He was still smart, independent, and principled. There was also, by this time, a kind of despondency in him that I found very poignant. He didn't want any of the things most people crave: being loved and admired, having money, comfort, or worldly success. In his humility and integrity, he resembled the saints of old—except that his asceticism was completely disconnected from faith, love, or hope. On the contrary, it seemed haunted by a sorry defeatism. I also sensed that he expected me to live the same way and to share his deeply pessimistic views.

When I left Montana to take a job teaching high school English in the Midwest in 1973, my mother asked a typically worried question, "Did you say goodbye to Ted before you left?"

Her question caught me up short, and I answered a little defensively: "Well, he knew I was going." I would have had to drive 180 miles round-trip to see Ted, I told her. In the back of my mind, I was thinking that I couldn't spend the rest of my life shackled to my brother. He never said that he needed me anyway. Mom was expecting too much, I fretted. But I also remembered my early promise never to abandon my brother. Did it feel to him, perhaps subconsciously, that I was abandoning him now?

Ted's angry—well, blistering—letters to our parents started arriving in the late 1970s. The gist was that he was unhappy all his life because Mom and Dad had never truly loved him. They pushed him academically to feed their own egos. They never taught him appropriate social skills because they didn't care about his happiness. These letters were not an invitation to talk, but an indictment, filled with highly dramatized and—in my view—distorted memories. Yet Ted's conclusion, in his own mind, was as rock solid as a mathematical proof.

At first, I thought he had simply lost his temper. After all, he was emotionally intense and spent nearly all his time alone. He'd given up a promising but unfulfilling academic career to live in the woods—and still he wasn't happy. So it was not surprising that he could lose his grip and say some things he didn't really mean. It could happen to almost anyone.

But when I wrote to Ted, hoping that he would appreciate the pain his letter had caused our parents and apologize, I received a series of increasingly disturbed replies that convinced me that he hadn't just lost his temper: every recrimination he'd flung at Mom and Dad was based in a fixed belief system. I was surely Ted's closest human contact, yet I'd never seen any of this coming. And now, nothing I said could shake Ted's judgment of Mom and Dad in the slightest. At one point he warned me that if I continued defending Mom and Dad, he'd cut me out of his life as well. Once he did so, he said, it would be forever.

For the next ten years, more or less, I thought I might persuade Ted to see things differently. There were occasional crises that made me think my brother might be seriously ill. But each time he seemed to recover, more or less. There was a discernible pattern: I never saw any crisis looming, and Ted never wanted to discuss them afterwards. Looking back now, there was also a downward spiral. There were more and more topics we couldn't discuss because discussing them made Ted upset. There was an undertone of stress in the letters we regularly exchanged, based for me in my brother's harsh treatment of our parents. Ted wanted me to agree with him about everything. I wanted to defend my own ego as an independent person. But most of all, I wanted to defend Mom and Dad against Ted's cruel opinion of them. It upset me to realize that I was not going to change my brother's mind.

My marriage to Linda was the proverbial straw as far as Ted was concerned. Maybe he understood—whether consciously or not—the implications of bringing another fresh, intelligent mind into the family. Perhaps, too, it forced him to see his little brother differently. In any case, it was Linda who made me confront the growing evidence that my brother was suffering from a mental disorder. "But that's the way he thinks!" I protested at first. I remember her then pointing to a bizarre passage in a letter I'd just received. "David, read this. People who are healthy in their minds don't think like this."

My feelings toward Ted shifted after I read the "Unabomber's Manifesto" in the *Washington Post* and began coming to grips with the horrific possibility that Ted might be the long-sought serial bomber. Again, it was Linda who pried open my mind; Linda who urged me to read the Manifesto. I never considered that Ted was capable of violence. In fact, my only fear along those lines was the haunting worry that he might someday kill himself.

Suddenly, it felt as if my brother and I were central characters in a grandiose tragedy. I began to discern a frightening symmetry in our lives that led me to the terrible dilemma that Linda and I then faced: do nothing and run the risk that Ted might kill again, or turn him in and accept the likelihood that he would be executed for his crimes.

The alternatives looked too stark to be true, more like literature than life. Looking back over our lives as brothers, I began to see how every step led us to this terrible juncture. Suddenly, I felt trapped inside the narrative of our lives, my identity forever defined by the fate of being Ted Kaczynski's brother. I wanted out of that role. I wanted to make my own choices in life, not have them foisted upon me. I wanted to create my own life's story. And yet to choose to do nothing was itself a choice. There was no escape. I was boxed in by the awful dilemma we faced as well as by my relationship to Ted. Suddenly, and for some time, I felt engulfed in a vision of the universe as dark as Ted's.

At the same time, my resentment of Ted strangely melted away. My ordinary frame of reference in thinking about him no longer made sense. There was just emptiness and deep pity in my heart where my brother had been.

It has occurred to me that Ted and I are almost like disowned parts of each other. Ted the Unabomber represents the violence and pessimism that I reject. David, the semi-famous "moral hero," represents the inauthenticity of hope in a world gone fundamentally awry. Ted's cruelty stigmatizes my good name; but my reputation for goodness comes at his expense. Like all contrived opposites, we reinforce one another. The worst thing he can do to me is deny any opportunity for reconciliation. Hope of reconciliation is something I am bound to maintain, but it costs me little—only the sneaking intuition that an important part of me is missing.

I'm beginning to see the outline of a developmental scheme in this brothers' motif. As a young kid I had lots of boyhood pals, almost like temporary brothers my own age who would come and go out of my life. Unlike my real brother, they turned out to be replaceable. Many of my post–high school friendships, however, endured much longer. I spent four years with the same college roommate, and we've grown even closer over the years. If something ever happened to Joel, I would grieve as much as I would for Ted. Our conversations pick up just where they leave off, even after a gap of years. I discover in my friend much of the openness and reciprocity that I never found in Ted. He was there for me in my worst hour. There is a level of trust and respect between us that makes the whole world seem stable and sane at its core, simply because this kind of relationship is possible. I suppose it's what Martin Buber named the "Thou."

Several months after Ted's arrest, I made contact with one of my brother's surviving victims—Gary Wright, of Salt Lake City, Utah. In one sense, he represented someone whose experience of the Unabomber saga was the polar opposite of mine. Part of me desperately needed to open a door to that "other side"—the victim's side. Ted would not talk to me, and neither—not surprisingly—would most of his victims or their family members. A lot of worlds got shattered by Ted's bombs. Probably it was foolish—even self-indulgent of me—to imagine that I could reassemble any of those pieces in the hope of making my world whole again. But with incredible grace, Gary volunteered to help me. In the ten years since our first awkward phone conversation, we too have become as close and indispensable to one another as brothers.

On the evening of September 11, 2001, I was home alone in Schenectady. Linda was away in Illinois caring for her sick parents. We were terribly worried about Linda's brother and his wife, whose apartment in lower Manhattan was not far from the World Trade Center site; and also about our niece attending college in Philadelphia, cut off from news of her parents because of the telephone outage. I suppose being the brother of a so-called "terrorist" made the events of that day more disturbing, if possible, than they otherwise would have been for me. I learned from Linda that our sister-in-law had been on the phone with Linda's mother when she saw the second tower fall. Then the phone line was cut off. I managed to reach my niece at her dorm room and found her as sane and sensible as always, somehow managing to give back more reassurance than she took. I couldn't bear to watch the news. But the silence felt equally unbearable. I wondered what my brother might be thinking about all of this.

The phone rang again. "Hey Dave, it's so good to hear your voice! I know you take a lot of trips to New York City. I'm so glad to know that you're OK."

It was Gary Wright.

On a night when just about everyone in America was checking in with their closest family and friends, Gary Wright made a call to the brother of the man who'd tried to kill him. It was reassuring to know that I lived in a world where such a call was possible. In that moment, I knew that Gary would be my friend for life.

Gary and I are virtual "blood brothers." Our bond forged through violence is as powerful and deep as any other. We also share a base of values. Our bond is a bond of choice as much as a bond of happenstance. Tragedy has given us both an unexpected gift. My life is infinitely richer because of Gary's friendship. Nothing can compensate me for losing Ted, but I find a poetic balance in having gained a new brother in Gary. Our choices end up reshaping the universe—at least the universe we know.

No one lives a life without loss. Loss of loved ones. Loss of innocence. Loss of dreams and hopes. Loss of each precious moment as quickly as it passes. Loss of our own lives in the end.

Sometimes, I'll be driving down the road, glance in the mirror, and for a split second I'll see Ted driving the car behind me. A moment later, I realize it's just another guy with a beard. A guy with a completely different mind and a life all his own. Anyone could be my brother, I realize, if fate had just arranged things a little differently. No matter—a flood of memories rushes in. So many memories: some sad, some anxious, some happy and loving, but all of them hauntingly poignant. What happened to those two little boys who grew up together in a different, more hopeful world in 1950s America? Or to the young men who spent an entire summer camping together in western Canada in 1969? Back then, I never could have imagined my life without Ted.

As we were driving back from Canada to Illinois in August 1969, I was feeling eager to return home, thinking about regular baths, Mom's home cooking, an opportunity to catch up on the world's news, perhaps even a chance to see Linda before she returned to school. I wanted to rejoin the stream of my life after this memorable detour. Ted and I were camped out in a county park in the grasslands of Nebraska, lying on our backs side by side, gazing up at the immense, starry sky as warm summer breezes stirred the tall grass around us.

"I wish we were home," I said.

"Really? I wish we didn't have to go back," Ted said.

It was a defining difference. But now I agree with him, wishing we could live that moment again.

the sensations of jim

One sweet November football Saturday, my brother Jim stood outside the gates of Pratt Field at Amherst College and waited for me to arrive with my pal Jimmy Warren. We had come up to western Massachusetts from Washington that morning ostensibly to take in the season finale against archrival Williams. The "biggest little game in America" that season had the bonus attraction of a Cajun quarterback who wore No. 4—our very own "little Favre" leading the way for the Lord Jeffs. But mostly we were there just to hang out with my big brother, who had been Warren's Spanish professor decades ago at Amherst. The game was incidental. "Daaave!" Jim said when our eyes met, sounding exactly like our father, Elliott, who had a way of greeting family and friends as though he were surprised and overjoyed every time. My brother and I adored our dad, but Jim was more overt about it; to him, everything seemed to have a family subtext. Then, when he saw who was with me, he smiled and lowered his voice to acknowledge "Jimmmee!"

He had been stationed outside the stadium for quite a while before we got there, warmed less by the autumn sun than by the constant recognition of former students who had flocked back to campus for game-day reunions. Jim had been a tenured professor at Amherst since the early 1970s (when he was in his mid-twenties), was consistently voted one of the most popular professors on campus, and had a well-known soft spot for students from Wisconsin, anyone who took his classes, and most jocks. As the unofficial gatekeeper at Pratt Field, he was in his element, although putting it that way leaves room for

misinterpretation. This was not Bill Clinton working a cam-
paign rope line as a means of self-gratification. My brother is
the furthest thing from a glad-hander or striver. But the game,
the setting, the students, our arrival—all combined to make
him contagiously happy. Jimmy and I brightened at the sight of
him, rocking slightly on his spindly legs, his pants riding high
above his waist, his pale, bespectacled face protected by a wide-
brimmed hat.

The secret about Jim is that he is too cool to care about appear-
ances. Or, as one of his Amherst colleagues recently described him,
at once joking and accurate, "He's so laid back, he's prone."

We had special seats awaiting us up in the rickety press box,
but as much as Jim looked forward to watching the action from
there, he seemed in no hurry to abandon his pre-game position.
"Life is sensations," he explained, as the three of us loitered outside, chatting. "I'm just soaking in the sensations."

Warren cast a quick glance my way, and we shared an unspoken appreciation that I can't fully explain. It's not just that you
never know what Jim is going to say, it's more that whatever he
says will have several levels to it. In this case, it helps to know
that Jim is a Calderon and Cervantes scholar who wrote his doc-
toral thesis on *Life Is a Dream* and is now working on a translation of *Don Quixote*. Whatever I might say about those seminal
works of Spanish literature would sound embarrassingly superficial
compared to Jim's deep understanding of them, but I sensed that
my brother, as he luxuriated on a Saturday afternoon outside Pratt
Field, was in a frame of mind to blissfully mistake a barber's basin
for a knight's helmet or an innkeeper's hunchbacked daughter for
a princess—or a kid named Marsh Moseley for Brett Favre. Of
course, I don't mean that literally. Jim is rarely literal. I mean it
in the sense that at that moment he was ready and able to experience the illusions of life with two loyal Sancho Panzas at his side.

Life is sensations, he said. The sensation of life with Jim
takes me back to another story, a few years earlier, with Jimmy
Warren again bearing witness along with my wife, Linda, and a

few other relatives and me. On the evening of January 30, 2000, 130.7 million Americans were at home watching the broadcast of Super Bowl XXXIV between the St. Louis Rams and the Tennessee Titans. But in Cambridge, Massachusetts, we plodded through the slush and snow to join a sports-snubbing scrum of literati and music devotees, most of them gray-haired, elegant, and sophisticated, for a singular operatic performance of *Life Is a Dream*. Twenty-two years earlier, Jim had written the libretto for the work by his Amherst friend Lewis Spratlan, a professor of composition, and now it was being performed for the first time. Many in the audience arrived an hour early to hear Jim lead a discussion on Calderon and the meaning of the play on which the opera was based. I forget everything he said except one line that I'll remember the rest of my life. Someone in the audience asked a question comparing Pedro Calderon de la Barca to William Shakespeare. Without missing a beat, Jim rummaged through his massive and eclectic brain to dredge up an apt quote from that famed literary critic George (Sparky) Anderson, former manager of the Detroit Tigers and Cincinnati Reds. "As Sparky Anderson said when asked to compare Carlton Fisk to Johnny Bench . . ."

This was not a crowd expected to know its major league catchers, but for those few of us who followed the allusion, it was classic Jim. He can talk Golden Age literature and minor league prospects for the Tampa Bay Rays; New Wave French Cinema and 1970s pro soccer players from the Netherlands; World War II fighter planes and linemen from the Coach Bart Starr era of Green Bay Packers football. It is typical of Jim that he would focus on Starr as the coach of mediocre teams rather than as the legendary quarterback of the glory years Packers. As for those anonymous linemen from the lost years between Lombardi and Favre, his favorite was Ezra Johnson, who once was delayed lumbering onto the field because he hadn't finished eating a hot dog—or was it bratwurst? Jim was certainly the only member of his Harvard class who, for an alumni magazine in which they were asked to provide capsule summaries of their lives after college, wrote not about himself but about Sweet Lou Whitaker, an African-American Tigers second baseman who had declined to stand for the National Anthem because worshipping the American flag contradicted his religious beliefs as a Jehovah's Witness. That essay, in its own poetic and indirect way, said more about Jim than any account of his advanced degrees and book translations.

James Elliott Maraniss is my only brother, four and a half years older than me, and he skipped a grade in elementary school, so he was gone to college by the time I reached seventh grade. We shared a bedroom until then, but we were not uncommonly close. He was redheaded and skinny, and his ankle and knee joints snapped, crackled, and popped loudly when he walked up the stairs. I was even skinnier and noisier, an asthmatic who wheezed all night, not only keeping him up, but drawing more attention from our mother. I was a little tattle-tale who squealed on him and his friends when I spotted them stealing a baseball from a variety store. One of my strongest memories as a five-year-old in Detroit is of Jim playing the role of a Nazi SS interrogator, sitting on top of me, my arms pinned to the ground by his legs, as he assumed a German accent and asked me what my name was and where I lived and slapped my face, shouting "Oh, you lie!" after every answer. A few years later, when we were at our grandparents' farm outside Ann Arbor, he fired his BB gun at me from about forty paces. I was facing the other way, down past the peach trees. He hit me behind the right knee. I presume he was shocked by his accuracy, and more shocked by the fact that our dad happened to be looking out the picture window and saw the whole thing and came running out to punish him while I whimpered in disbelief. The BB didn't penetrate the cloth of my pants, as I remember it, but still I had a story forever. The time my brother shot me!

During Jim's college years, when he was coming home to Madison from Harvard for the summers, I was at my adolescent worst, a brainless borderline delinquent who read little beyond the sports pages and knew nothing about the wider world. Jim got migraine headaches and listened to Sonny Terry and Brownie McGee and read Garcia Lorca and had an exotic Radcliffe girlfriend named Pamela and wore cool jeans and herringbone sports coats and must have thought he had a loser of a little brother. "Dave, don't be a boor," he admonished me one day, in front of my friends, who mocked me, and I suppose him, by repeating that line for years.

My brother was so much smarter than me that I didn't know how to handle it. On the surface, utterly outmatched academically, I stopped trying to compete with him, and pretended that I was happy to be a dumb jock, even though I was better at playing dumb than at being a jock. But deep inside, at some point I started to feel proud and lucky that he was my brother. The taunts of our early days left no lasting trauma. I knew that he did not want to kill me with that BB gun, and that the rest of it, the slapping and the condescending, was just what big brothers tend to do at certain stages, and by age sixteen I was bigger than he was in any case. If family circumstances and my own laziness had left me trapped in a persona I didn't want, I came to realize as I approached adulthood that Jim was showing me the way out. I couldn't do it his way, by succeeding in academia, but I could draw on the traits we had in common, especially a shared sense of feeling different. He instructed me in what he thought it meant to be a Maraniss, apart from the crowd, not brazenly or predictably nonconformist but nonchalantly so, and made me feel that I could live up to the name as much as he did. For the last thirty years, that is something we talk about between ourselves, but rarely with anyone else, because even to talk about it is to do it a disservice.

A few years ago, at a wedding reception in Washington, a guest in his late twenties came up to me and said he had been one of my brother's students at Amherst. "Man, I love Jim," he said. "In fact, I always wanted to *be* Jim." This well-dressed black guy who had played intercollegiate sports at Amherst always wanted to be Jim? What was that about? I can't imagine that he wanted to have Jim's fragile body—his chronically wobbly legs and various psychosomatic ailments. And there are a lot of people who look bolder and more self-assured. But Jim, he said, seemed so easy, natural, unburdened by the normal pressures of success, so different from the other professors and the white upper-class ambiance of Amherst. "Jim, man, he was the coolest."

Actually, I had heard it many times before. Jim's former students had been coming my way for more than three decades with some variation of that pronouncement. Part of it is easy to explain. Jim didn't abide by routines. He lectured for as long as he had something to say, then stopped and dismissed class, ignoring the standard schedule. He played pool with his students, and talked football with them, or movies, or small towns in the Upper Midwest, or church suppers, or Slovakian surnames. He knew something about everything. He taught what he wanted, his classes ranging from Spanish to Cervantes to the Spanish Civil War to French cinema to Nazi propaganda. He was a notoriously lenient grader. He had a fantasy baseball team called the *Rojos*, and was always inquiring about American League prospects. He was incessantly curious, constantly learning something, and then never forgetting it. His big white house, overloaded with books and newspapers, dirty dishes in the sink, kids everywhere, classical music or reggae playing, and amazing wife Gigi offering wisdom and a sympathetic ear to anyone who dropped by, became a sort of off-campus student union. Who wouldn't want to be Jim?

But part of it is more complex. He hides his vulnerabilities in plain sight. As the oldest of four children, Jim had the most complicated relationship with our mother, Mary, who was brilliant, beautiful, musical, gentle, frustrated, mildly depressed, and the most sensitive person I've ever known. I don't fully understand the dynamics of their relationship, but it seems that her hypersensitivity was difficult for him because he felt it tamped down his ability to enjoy life. I won't go any further than that; it's something he should write about, if he wants to, not me. In the old Smothers Brothers routine, Tommy always complained that Mom liked Dick best. In our family, partly because of my childhood asthma, and partly because I lacked the intellectual powers of Jim and my older sister, Jean, I had to find some other means of parental approval, so I became the child most sympathetic to our mother. I've never been quite sure how Jim felt about that, but she is gone now and all love is equal in memory.

The affection of our dad, a crusty old newspaper editor, was more easily shared. On the surface, he could seem as insensitive and crude as our mother was sensitive and refined. He smelled of bermuda onions and hard salami. He rarely ate without a piece of food sticking to his chin or mustard spotting his shirt. He once slammed a car door on his hand and didn't feel it until someone told him his hand was caught in the car door. But Elliott was equally positive with all his children, he saw the best in each of us, and you always knew where you stood with him. While Jim inherited our mother's intellect, he and I both got our love of sports and journalism, and in some sense our life force, from our dad. Bending the nepotism rules slightly, we both worked at his newspaper, the Madison *Capital Times*, during the summers of our college years, though Jim did it more as a diversion and I saw it as my lone way out. We worshipped the P.M. daily of the precomputer age—the copy paper and pneumatic tubes, the cigarette butts on the linoleum floor, the smell of ink and paste, and the lineup of old-fashioned newspapermen. One of the many things that Jim and I share is a love of names—place names, given names, surnames. To us, names are poetry, evoking more feeling and memory than any adjective.

Few things give Jim more pleasure than to recite the names of the old newspapermen at the *Cap Times*: Art Marshall, Irv Kreisman, Cedric Parker, Frank Custer, Harry Sage, John Sammis, Aldric Revell, John Patrick Hunter, Elliott Maraniss.

The defining story of his summers at the paper involved a tragedy at the Henry Vilas Zoo in 1966, when Winkie the elephant seized a three-year-old girl by the trunk, yanked her through the cage bars, and stomped her to death in front of her horrified parents—the sort of unspeakable story that no journalist, no matter how grizzled, could enjoy. Dad, as city editor, looked around his newsroom, saw that Jim was the only reporter available at that moment, and instructed him to go find the grieving mother for an interview.

"Dad! I can't do that!" Jim said, recoiling at the very idea.

Jim recounted this story at our father's funeral, pausing here for the desired effect, before offering the quintessential city editor's punch line:

"Then you're fired!

Another pause.

"And don't call me Dad!"

The love with which Jim told that story is hard to overstate. When Elliott was dying in a Milwaukee hospital, Jim came out and sat by his side for days and read him chapters of *War and Peace*. He would call me up and moan into the telephone: "Dad! Daaad! Dad!" In many ways, Dad was our strongest bond, and still is, the touchstone for our love and our shared sense of being different. Elliott loved nothing more than to lie on the living room couch or a cot on the side porch in his shorts and T-shirt and talk about sports while listening to a ballgame on the radio. It is no coincidence that many of my sweetest moments with Jim are retakes of that scene. For many years, back when I lived in Austin, we would share a hotel room in Washington every April for the annual baseball draft in our *Washington Post* (Ghost) rotisserie league. It was usually the same weekend as the Masters Golf Tournament, and after the draft we'd go back to the room and lie on our beds in our shorts and watch the final round and talk about our players. It was all about Dad. Sometimes my son Andrew would be there, passing it down another generation. It sounds stupid, perhaps, but the glow in the room was spiritual.

With Dad gone, those moments with Jim are even more special. At Andrew's wedding in Nashville last year, a weekend filled with emotion, one of my favorite moments came late one night when Jim and I and two of his sons, little Elliott and Ben, along with our friend Jimmy Warren, gathered in Jim's hotel room and talked. He sprawled on the bed in the style of our father, and announced that his favorite NFL coach was Jack Del Rio of the Jacksonville Jaguars. "Jack Del Rio!" he said, and Jimmy Warren and I looked at each other with the same unspoken understanding we shared that day outside the gates of Pratt Field. Though I must say I'm still trying to figure out the connection—and I know there must be one—between Jack Del Rio and Calderon and Cervantes.

One final story about my big brother brings this full circle. On April 14, 2000, Jim hosted a conference on Spanish literature at Amherst. Attendance was paltry, and Jim's spirits were even lower as he left for home that night. He felt out of it. Over the hill. Out of the zeitgeist. No one cared about what he did. The world seemed mean, empty, superficial. If life is sensations, this was a sensation he could do without. Inside the big white house, the message light was blinking on his telephone answering machine. It was full of messages—from me, from Jimmy Warren, from our father. All ecstatic. All saying versions of the same thing. Hey, Jim! You won't believe it! The opera. You and Lew Spratlan. Performed only that one Super Bowl weekend up in Massachusetts twenty-two years after you guys wrote it. It won the Pulitzer Prize!

Life is a dream.

Phillip Lopate

———— ·ɷɞ· ————

my brother, life
(with apologies to pasternak)

We are quite a lot alike. Whenever we don't see each other for a while and then reunite and compare notes on movies, books, music, current events, we find we have almost always come to the same conclusions. In our adolescence he was my mentor, introducing me to Billie Holiday and the Dadaists; so it is hardly surprising, my mind having been formed to an extent by his, that we continue to share so many tastes.

When we were growing up, we indulged in that Corsican Brothers fantasy: that whatever happened to one, the other would feel, however much distance separated us.

The narcissism of small differences: he is three years older, yet more ardent, youthful, risk-taking, still chasing happiness. I always act like the older, graver, more prudent one, giving advice. He likes fine wines and fancy food, is something of a sensualist and an epicurean. I, a stoic, can appreciate a well-cooked meal but will not go miles out of my way for one.

He is bolder, more reckless. He acts, I watch. Bicycling around Europe in his mid-sixties, he had an accident and fell off the bike and was taken to a hospital, where he received several stitches. When he phoned from abroad to ask me to pick him up at the airport and drive him home, it gave me great pleasure to run that errand. I waited for him at the receiving entrance and he had a dazed look, a bandage on his head, looking around and not recognizing me at first. It disturbed me, as only a younger sibling can be, to see him so vulnerable; yet also made me proud that I could take him in hand.

When we were teenagers, people would say I was the better-looking. Now, in our middle-aged years, he is probably the more handsome. He has retained a full head of hair, while I have lost mine, following our father's tendency to baldness. He wears a full beard and has a commanding stare, no longer hidden by spectacles, thanks to laser surgery.

One of the ways we differ most is that my brother identifies with our mother, and I with our father. Both our parents are dead, but they continue to rule our psyches and orient our moral compasses. Our mother was a flamboyant, lusty, histrionic personality, for whom the term "larger than life" applies; she had wanted to sing and act, was thwarted for many years by having to work as a clerk and raise a family, but in the last decades of her life she did perform on stage, acted in TV commercials, sang in supper clubs. Our father was a rather withdrawn, self-taught intellectual who wanted to be a writer; he lived what Matthew Arnold called "the buried life," toiling as a factory worker and textile clerk. The taciturn scapegoat of our family, he eventually was divorced by my mother and exiled or abandoned to a nursing home. While they lived together they made an odd couple: Eros and Thanatos, you might say. I felt sorry for my father; our fates were permanently entwined on my assumption of his literary ambition, by which I was both honoring and replacing him. My brother, on the other hand, did not get along with my father and retains very little fondness for him. He drew his strength from the example of my mother, who threw herself, with bravado, into the fray as an entertainer.

My brother is a radio personality, heard every weekday in the New York metropolitan area on a mid-day interview show. Being a generalist and a quick study, he ranges widely, questioning novelists, politicians, scientists, film directors, actresses, car mechanics, chefs, etc. I listen as often as I can, not only because he is my brother but because he has, in my opinion, the best show on radio—the most informative, the most discerning. Even knowing him as I do, I am still amazed at how astutely he can shape a fifteen-minute or half-hour interview. Of course, knowing him as I do, I also am aware when he is bluffing about a subject he has only vague notions about, and I sometimes catch him making errors, confusing, say, T. H. White (whose book about King Arthur, *The Once and Future King*, we read in our household growing up), with the political pundit Theodore White. Or I will yell at the radio, "No no no, Lenny!" when he makes an asinine comment. I am more tolerant of his bad puns; those we love should be permitted their puns.

My secret pleasure in listening to him is that I can still hear the unsure but learning-eager adolescent he was at our dinner table, imparting his latest discovery, inside the smooth tones of the all-knowing radio personality. Though he always had a euphonious voice, he has done considerable work on that instrument, shaping its baritone, losing the family's Brooklyn regionalisms. The only aspect of his radio persona that dismays me is when he comes across as dripping with empathy for some guest who is telling her sob story (usually it's a woman); and I sense a blip of insincerity in that momentary delay or vocal catch that has become a signature tic in his delivery. Maybe I'm too conscious of how sardonic and unsentimental he can be in real life, and how much of a constructed artifact his radio persona is. But that is part of what makes him a professional.

We are both proud of each other's success—he no less than I. Sometimes I am listening to his show and will be brought up short by a reference to his brother the writer. I register that I am in his thoughts as much as he is in mine.

Are we competitive? Of course. But the roots of our sibling rivalry go so far back, and have been overlaid with so much self-conscious discussion between us about our competition, and each of us has gotten so much public approval since, that in truth I don't (consciously) experience competing in his presence anymore. The times I do experience a twinge of sibling rivalry are when he is not around, and others bring him up. People are constantly pitting us against each other, either for their own sadistic amusement or experimental curiosity, to see what reactions they can elicit. Lenny is the more well-known of the two: a radio personality cannot help but have more fans than an essayist. And the bond that a talk-show host has with his regular audience goes deep: not seeing the person but only hearing his mellifluous, sympathetic voice each day invites them to fantasize and idealize him. . . . Nevertheless, even understanding this dynamic, I do not like it when I am giving a reading at a bookstore and someone comes up to me and the first question he or she asks is about my brother: that seems to me a lapse in tact, especially at that moment, when I am trying to project an outsized, authorial persona. I forgive the zhlubs their need to connect with celebrity through me. The ones I have a harder time forgiving are my fellow authors, often with bigger names than mine, who should know better but only want to talk to me about Lenny, and the last time they were on his show or saw him socially. I have the urge to say to them: Look, I've written a dozen books, why not spare a word or two for my literary output? But with typical writer's narcissism they are much more grateful to Lenny for publicizing their latest; he nurses carefully his relationships with big-name authors, and they regard him as a useful extension of their egos.

It's also a source of minor chagrin when I am introduced to someone who says "Oh, I love what you do on the radio." I should laugh it off, the way John Ford did when people told him their favorite film of his was *Red River*; he would say thank you with modest politeness and never correct them by mentioning that particular western was directed by Howard Hawks. My brother tells me that many people have the mistaken impression he has written my books. We laugh at this notion that either one of us could be expected to hold down a demanding radio show while writing book after book.

I also laugh at him a lot, because his renown has given him a touchy sense of self-importance. If we go to a party together and people do not seem to recognize or acknowledge him sufficiently, he will sulk. His way of sulking is to stare high into the middle distance with a frown. He has an elephant's memory, and resents for years those celebrities who by-passed an interview with him or those guests who canceled. I kid him a bit: "So, Abraham Lincoln refused to go on your show? What a pompous jerk."

A trickier side to having a brother who is a public personality (not just on the radio: he emcees countless panels and interviews authors and public figures around town) is that I find myself at times wary of him, sensing, rightly or wrongly, that he is not talking to me so much as (still) to his listeners. If I catch him making pedantic pronouncements, or explaining something he should know I already know, it will put me on my guard. I keep cocking an ear for that intimate, private tone that ought to ensue from a lifetime of brother-relationship; and if it is not forthcoming, or is only intermittent, I judge him severely. I suspect it is hard for him to come down from his public persona. (Then again, I should talk: after teaching a seminar or giving readings on tour, I do not always have the easiest time descending to the domestic requests of my wife and daughter.)

When he is at home and we are talking on the phone, which we usually do about once a week, I sometimes sense that he is making a remark to me for the benefit of his mate, who is within earshot. It can be a flattering remark about her, meant to keep the peace—perfectly understandable, but I resent being used that way as a straight-man. In short, I am very jealous of our unique tie, and do not like to see it diluted in any way. I would rather get together with him alone than share him *en famille*. Those times, all too rare, when we do see each other alone, either going to a play or a preview screening to which he generously invites me, usually because the director or performer will be appearing on his show, we are apt to have a terrific conversation that recaptures the rapport of old. There is something so deeply satisfying and sweet about these occasions, I can only surmise that if they do not happen more often, it may be because we both pull back from an idyllic intimacy which would almost be too threatening to sustain, or painful to see diminished through frequency.

I should point out that, for all my antenna-attuned mistrust of my brother's outer-directed personality, it is Lenny who will finally become much more open about his emotional problems or confusions of the moment, whereas I am more reserved and tend to use shorthand in those matters. I don't know if that's because, being the younger and more easily overwhelmed, I prefer to hold the power of the listener-therapist role, or because Lenny is more given to dramatizing himself, even if it means being seen as the one in crisis.

When we were younger, my brother wanted to be an artist. As a child he painted battleships and self-portraits; then he graduated to abstraction, studied at the university with the arch-purist Ad Reinhardt, as well as such luminaries as Mark Rothko and Robert Morris. His paintings tended in a geometric, color-field direction. They were good, I thought. Had he continued, he would certainly have made a go of it. But he found them lacking in originality, or found he lacked the passion, the "fire in the belly," to pursue painting full-time. Each of the four Lopate children had had artistic ambitions: my brother wanted to be an abstract painter, I, a writer, my sister Betty Ann, a musician, my younger sister, Joan, a painter as well. As it turned out, I was the only one who succeeded in cobbling a career out of my art. It is a situation that looms large in my mind, and fills me with a mixture of gloating and survivor's guilt. (I *said* we were competitive.) Regardless of the greater adulation my brother receives, regardless of the argument that doing radio might be construed as *his* artistic medium, I continue to feel that I hold the edge. My literary works have at least a chance of enduring, while his daily improvised chat, cruel as it may sound, will disappear into the ether. His is a journalist's way of knowing, facts gathered for the occasion and ejected once the occasion is over; mine, I tell myself, is a more arduous, intellectual, serious pursuit of knowledge.

My greatest defect is that much of the time I need to regard myself as superior to those around me, and to position myself in such a way that they will feel it too. Regardless of knowing full well that there are many different kinds of intelligence or that we are all ultimately dust and atoms under the aspect of eternity, I persist in wanting to view myself as the most intelligent person in social situations. That lamentable self-regard undoubtedly colors my relationship with my brother, in less than helpful ways. I insist on holding the "wisdom" and "maturity" cards, or on considering myself a half-step ahead of him mentally. But he forgives me, perhaps because he is the wiser and more ample-spirited one. There is also the difference in our professional practices: he asks questions for a living, whereas I feel called upon, by students, readers and my own didacticism, to give answers.

Together we look forward to sharing all the pleasures of old age: nostalgia, illness, incontinence, senility, abandonment. We will not abandon each other, I hope, because the world is less lonely for me as long as my brother is in it. He has been, if not the most important relationship in my life, certainly one of the most defining ones. I'll say more: he has been my personal metaphor for Life itself, in all its encompassing urgency.

Mikal Gilmore

secrets and bones

I decided to go back to Portland once more—this time to find my brother.

Frank was the last family I had, and I had relinquished him. I had no idea whether he was happy these days or living homeless, whether he was sane or crippled. Too often in my life I had lost those I loved or cared about—sometimes because death took them, sometimes because they gave up their love for me, and sometimes because something in me made it easy to walk away, to withdraw in some irrevocable way from those who might love or need me the most. There were times when it was a frighteningly easy thing to do—something I did almost without thinking—just one of those shameful secrets about myself that I did not fully understand, but now wanted access to.

But the truth is, I missed Frank terribly. I had tried to find him from time to time over the years. I'd get reports that somebody had seen him working someplace, or walking down one road or another in Portland, but I could never track him down anyplace. The last I heard about him had been a couple of years before. A friend had seen him doing some custodial work. By the time I called the employer, Frank had quit and was gone.

I had no idea what I would find when I found my brother, but I did know I wanted to see him. I wanted to talk to him, touch him, see that he was okay and attempt to be fair with him, even if it only resulted in his casting me out of his life for good.

I had been in Portland a season before I finally found Frank. I had done everything I knew to locate him, yet despite a life-time of reading mystery novels, I wasn't proving very good at the

missing person business. I searched death certificates, I went to
homeless shelters, I looked at the face of every man I passed on
the street who could possibly be my brother. Then one night not
long before Christmas, I was having dinner with Jim Redden,
a friend who was a journalist and crime reporter. He offered
to make some calls for me. The next morning, when I got up,
Redden had left a message on my answering machine. He had
found where Frank was living. It was ten blocks from where
I was living, in Northwest Portland.

I got dressed and walked over to Frank's address. It may
have been only ten blocks, but in those few blocks one walked
from one world into another. The area of Northwest Portland
I lived in was an old part of town, filled with Victorian houses
that had been refurbished. It was now an upscale district with
shops, cafés, and bars—just another of those self-conscious,
affluent bohemian neighborhoods that have sprung up in most
American cities over the last decade or two. But as you walk
along 23rd Avenue, you begin to move into the area where
the Victorians have not been refurbished—where old homes
look simply like old homes, and you come closer to the fringes
of northwest Portland's industrial district. It was a part of town
that stood largely untouched and unloved since the 1940s, and
where many older folks and several down-and-outers now con-
gregated, hanging around grocery stores that had iron bars across
their windows, and guard dogs or guns behind the counters.
There were several taverns in the area, and most of them were
rough laborers' hangouts.

Frank lived in the middle of all this, in an old rooming house,
situated above a noisy tavern. I had seen places like this before;
it was like the places my father had taken me as a child, when he
went to find his salesmen. It was the sort of place where new light
or fresh air rarely entered. Instead, you found the accrued smells
of old men who had come to bide out their time, watching TV,
drinking, brooding. The place had a depressing impact on me that
felt unexpectedly primal. For a moment, I wanted to run.

I climbed the stairs and knocked on the door that I'd been told was Frank's. There was no answer. I knocked again, which brought the apartment manager's attention. He told me that the man who lived there had gone to work and wouldn't be back until mid evening.

Waiting until night turned out to be one of the longest waits of my life. I kept thinking about the place where Frank was living. I tried to imagine the reality of his life. Whatever problems I felt I had, I'd known comfort and social interaction. Life had been good to me in many ways—better than to anyone else in my family.

It seemed amazing to me that the lives of two brothers had taken such different courses. It also seemed terribly unfair. Frank had stayed home and taken care of my mother. Indeed, he was the only one of the brothers who had ever really tried to do the right thing. By contrast, I had simply escaped and looked after myself. I had never thought about taking on the burden of my mother and her problems. For his devotion, Frank had ended up with what looked to me like a devastated life, spent in the company of vagrants and other outsiders. Though I may not have ended up with some of the things I claimed to want in life, the truth is, I had not ended up with nothing. I went places, I did things, I had money in the bank. I was not about to end up in a rooming house.

There's no point in flogging myself too much here, or apologizing. I don't believe even now that I would have done anything differently in my life. I think I *had* to run away from my family in order not to be dragged down by its claims. Still, seeing where Frank lived gave me an idea of what his life must have been like in the last decade, and it did not make me feel good about the distance between us. Nor did it make me feel any better about the prospect of walking back into his life.

I spent the rest of the day driving around, thinking about these things. I wondered what the two of us would have to say to each other after such a long time.

At about nine that night, I returned to the place where Frank lived. At the top of the stairs, I nearly bumped into a man who was zipping up a parka jacket and pulling a stocking cap down over his ears in preparation for the cold outside. I studied the face quickly—a habit I'd picked up in recent months—and I saw something I'd seen so many times in my mind's eye over the years: a face deep-cut with the lines that come from bad history. I saw the face of my brother.

"Frank," I said. He looked up. I could tell he didn't know who I was.

"Frank, it's me, Mikal." He stood there, staring at me, his face pulled into a questioning look, as if he didn't believe what I said. I think if he had reached out and shoved me down the stairs I would not have resisted him. I would have thought it was okay.

Instead, he reached out and took me in his arms, and held me. In that moment, the squalor around us didn't matter. In that moment, I felt like I was in the embrace of home.

A half hour later we were seated in the warmth of my apartment. Frank hadn't wanted me to see the room where he lived.

As he entered my place, Frank looked around, taking in the clutter of books and CDs, and the electronic and computer equipment. "Man," he said, smiling, "you're kind of like Mom. It looks like you don't ever throw anything away."

We sat on my sofa, sipping warm drinks, talking. Frank said he had heard I was married, and he wanted to know about my wife. I explained to him that the marriage had been over for a long time, and that it had been one of those honest but sad mistakes that people make. "Geez, man," Frank said, stirring coffee, "I'm really sorry to hear that. No children?" I said no, and lapsed momentarily into silence.

I asked what had happened to him since I had last seen him. He shrugged and cleared his throat. "Oh, I've just sort of drifted around for the most part, spending a few months here, then, there. For a few years after Mom's death, I got into drinking a lot. I felt pretty bad about her dying. I felt responsible in some ways, and I couldn't get it out of my mind. She had hated and feared hospitals. I sent her to one and she died. Maybe if I hadn't, I thought, she would have had a chance. I sold the trailer afterward and just took off. I guess I spent years that way—traveling, working, drinking. I spent a lot of time on the streets. Got into a couple of fights. Had my arms broken twice. Got jumped on once by a bunch of fucking skinheads. They took everything I had."

Frank paused and smiled a gentle smile that was in startling contrast to the litany of horror he had just recited. "I guess I simply went a little crazy during those years. Then I got to thinking about all the other stuff, about Gaylen dying as such a young man, and Gary doing all those horrible things he did . . . had people I barely knew come up to me and ask the most terrible questions, 'Is it true that your brother did those awful things? How could you have lived in the same home with a man like that?' A couple of times, when I was working at a job, somebody would figure out I was Gary's brother. They would want to get in fights with me, like somehow beating me made them bigger or tougher than Gary, or punished him more. A few months ago, I was working a job over in Salt Lake City, and when somebody figured out I was related to Gary, they fired me."

As Frank talked, I felt the past sitting in the room with us. Maybe he felt it too, because he got up and started to move around. He walked around my apartment looking at things, until he came to the dining table, where I had sprawled several of the photos from our family albums. For some reason, I'd become the caretaker of these pictures. They were all I had left of the family's possessions. I'd spent a lot of time recently studying these photos, trying to read them for clues to the riddles of our lives.

"I'd wondered what happened to these," said Frank, picking up one of the pictures and looking at it. "I don't have many of these left. I've traveled so much, had so much stolen or lost. I think about all I have left is a picture of you as a baby, in your playpen with your rubber toad. Do you remember that?"

Frank put down one photo and picked up another. "Do you mind if I sit here and look through these?"

I said he was welcome to look as long as he liked, and I'd have copies made of the pictures he wanted. "That's okay," he said, pulling a chair up to the table. "I don't really want to carry this stuff around with me. It might be fun to look at, though."

We sat together at the table, poring over the old photos. Frank looked at them as somebody who knew a different story about every picture. I looked at them as an outsider. These photos described a certain world, and I had been born at the end of that world.

Frank picked up one of the only color photos from the batch. It was a picture of a Thanksgiving turkey, of all things. Just the cooked bird itself. No people, no smiling holiday faces.

"I remember that turkey," Frank said. "I remember how good it looked sitting on the table while we waited for what seemed like hours to sit down and eat it. I remember Mom and Dad getting into a fight immediately. I remember Mom picking the turkey up and throwing it across the room, and I remember it hitting the floor—SPLAT!—and the dressing bouncing all over the place. I remember that bird sitting there on the floor the rest of the day, because nobody would pick it up, because they were too busy calling each other filthy names. I remember never getting to taste it." Frank put the photo down and sighed. "It had looked like such a nice turkey."

A few photos later, Frank came across the only picture I have of my father and Gary alone together. In the picture, Gary is wearing a sailor's cap. He has his arms wrapped tight around my father's neck, his cheek pressed close against my father's, a look of broken need on his face. It is heartbreaking to look at this picture—not just for the look on Gary's face, the look that would become the visage of his future, but also for my father's expression. In that moment, my father is pulling away from Gary's cheek, and he is wearing a look of barely disguised distaste.

Frank studied the picture quietly for several seconds, then he looked up at me, "Did you know," he said, speaking carefully, "that Gary had a son?"

I told him I had recently learned as much from one of Larry Schiller's last taped interviews with Gary. I told him I had also heard on one of my mother's tapes that the boy hadn't died after all, as Gary thought.

"That's right," Frank said. "The baby never died. That was just something Mom and Dad told Gary. In fact, I think I might have run into Gary's son a couple of years back. It wasn't a very pleasant meeting.

"It was a late summer afternoon. I was walking along Burnside, not far from the park where a lot of the homeless people hang out. There's a little tavern up the street. I was coming from work, and I was heading for the tavern to get a pitcher of beer. Just as I got to the place, this guy comes running up and starts talking to me. He asked me if I was Frank Gilmore, and I said I was. He said, 'Your brother Gary was my father.' I looked at him and said, 'I don't know what you're talking about,' and then I tried to walk on.

"He stopped me. He said, 'Yes, you do. Your brother was my father. Your family fucked me up real good, and now I'm going to fuck you up.' Then he tried to lay me out with a punch. I ducked and grabbed him and slammed his back against a building. Then I saw a dummy stick fall from one of his hands. Those things can hurt you real bad. I kicked it into the street and said, 'Jesus, can't you even fight like a man?' I let go of him and backed off. When I saw that he wasn't going to move on me, I made my way into the tavern and told the bartender what had happened. He said he noticed that the guy had been hanging around there off and on for a few days, like he was waiting for somebody. I sat there and had a beer, and after a while I looked up, and the guy was standing outside, looking at me through the window. I decided I should go out and try to have a talk with him. By the time I got out there he was gone, and I never saw him again."

I asked Frank: "Do you think the man might actually have been Gary's son? Did he look anything like Gary?"

Frank watched me quietly for a moment, then said: "He looked *just* like Gary."

Fucking hell, I thought, if this were true, if the young man Frank faced had in fact been Gary's son, then it might mean something worse than I'd ever imagined. Maybe there was simply no end to a violent lineage or bad legacy. Maybe it just kept spilling over into history, into the world, into our children, into everything that came of our blood.

As I was thinking this, Frank leaned across the table and said to me: "I'm sorry I didn't get in touch with you for all these years. It's not like I didn't know where you were, or didn't know how to find you. I could always have called or written you at the magazine where you worked.

"It's just that . . . I don't know. I thought you were doing fine. Sometimes, I'd be out there, working some dirt job somewhere, or sleeping under a bridge, and I'd think: 'Somewhere, I've got this brother who's doing well. He's a writer, he talks to famous people and people respect him, and he's married and probably has kids now. Yeah, I'm probably an uncle by this time.' And I'd wonder if it was a boy or girl, if it had blond hair and blue eyes like you had when you were a baby. I'd think about all that, and sometimes it would help. Like I said, I was a lost man after Mom died. But I'd think about you and I'd feel proud. And I kind of decided I would never bother you, I wouldn't look you up and embarrass you by making you acknowledge me. I wouldn't be a reminder of the past that I thought was safely behind you. I thought: 'There's one of us—*one*—who has come out all right, who has made it. I think I owe it to him to leave him alone and let him have his happiness. It's good to let him go. There's no reason he should have to stay tied to his family.'"

I didn't say a word. I don't think I could have. I sat there, looking at my brother and thinking: This may be all the family I have left in the world, but it is family enough. I had never truly understood the depths of this man's heart or the expanse of his loneliness, but maybe it wasn't too late. Maybe, just maybe, I was ready to learn something worthwhile about the fidelity born of blood.

Richard Ford

we were men

I wish there'd been a moment in my young life, forty-six years ago, when I could've thought to myself, "What I think I'll do now is join a college fraternity." Because, if there had been, then there *might've* been a moment when I could've said, "No. Wait a minute. I actually think I *won't* join a college fraternity. I'm just not that kind of fellow."

What I did, however, was not give either possibility any thought. I just (mindlessly) joined. *Pledged,* as the saying went and probably still goes. Pledged Sigma Chi—Brad Pitt's, David Letterman's, Grover Cleveland's, even John Wayne's bunch. It's the famous one with the sentimental song, the white cross and the pretty sweetheart who later becomes your wife—like mine.

For a certain kind of uncertain boy, joining a college fraternity is simply a given. I'm talking about a go-along boy who craves ready-made friends. A guy with high standards he can't quite articulate, but who knows 'em when he sees 'em. For this kind of boy, fraternal conformity is a godsend. I was that kind of boy.

In the long run, of course, college fraternities espouse ethical pretensions, but only finally attain the ethical gravity that accompanies, say, having a deep voice, or maybe deciding to try a new hair style, or learning a dance step so perfectly you get praise for knowing it, though you later forget it. There's no use in me feeling truly sorry for having been a member. I was young and far from home, in Michigan, and not very smart. And in any case I'm suspicious of revising my past, and dislike the idea that anything I did and survived and can still remember is completely worthless. (This can alibi for a multitude of sins, of course.)

But still, I'd at least like to have consciously *chosen* to join, to have taken full responsibility for those errant behaviors I exhibited that were not really decided upon. At my current attainment, sixty-four, very little impresses me as much as nervy volition exerted at an early age. But I just missed my chance.

Like all conformists, we Sigs did not think of ourselves as conformists. We were individuals and individualists. We knew what we knew. Alone, we each walked life's lonelier roads, were hard guys to convince about most things. We were stiletto-eyed, serious, even grave. The fraternity, we felt, attracted singular men like us and meant to codify our rare qualities and even add some others—"fairness, decency, good manners." We nodded, rested our chins in our palms while listening, wrinkled our brows, clinched Winstons in our teeth, dealt a fair hand. We meant something, and we knew it.

We also, of course, knew how and when to let down the gates for a good time when a good time was called for. We knew how to treat a woman. We knew how to confide. We were easy in the company of other men. We knew where to draw the line and when to redraw it. We could—at least some of us—hold our liquor. So imagine our surprise at finding an entire group of other guys who felt and believed and behaved as we alone did about practically everything.

"Independents," those sallow fellows who did *not* join fraternities, who stayed back in the dorm and studied or played chess or guitars, and who sculled around the shallows of organized social life—blazerless—these men suffered, we felt, the mark of undesirability, while trying to champion a mean, cast-out status, as if that's what they preferred. Loneliness, unprotectedness, lack of true fraternity seemed to be the features of that glum idea. Independence did not yet have the novelty it would soon come to have. (This was the part of the sixties that were really still the fifties.) Then, it only meant "left out," "passed over."

Anyway, none of us had stomachs for it and chose the brotherhood, instead.

Yes, our group had standards—manners, decency, chivalry,
etc. But to be initiated into Sigma Chi at Michigan State, in
1963, you were still expected to be able to pick a stuffed cock-
tail olive up off the chapter room floor using nothing but the
naked cheeks of your butt—this while many already-initiated
and maturer "actives" cheered and howled and taunted and
wagered and blew nasty cigar smoke at you as you moved, with
difficulty, across the room and deposited the olive into a Dixie
Cup. You also had to sit for six hours straight on the hard front
edge of a hard chair, knees together, arms rigid, blindfolded and
disoriented, while one of the older musically inclined brothers
played Ravel's *Bolero*, fortissimo, directly into your ears. You had
to do many, many painful pushups. You had to let the older men
scream obscenities and insults in your face, and breathe sour
beer breath on you. You had to recite stupid scatological limer-
icks about hermits in caves and men from Nantucket, on and on
until you were sick enough of it to want to go home. You had to
tramp out into the frozen Michigan night in search of nothing
less than a white cross—the fraternity's sacred emblem—which
of course couldn't be found because it wasn't there. (It—and its
absence—were symbolic of our hopeless quest for perfection.)
You had to bray like a donkey, buzz like a fly, bleat like a goat, be
threatened, scorned, scourged and ridiculed until the older men
gave in and let you join. It must've seemed like a good idea.

Exacting calculations, of course, had already been made
about the kind of people who *weren't* being asked in as members. We were, after all—like most high-minded and desirable
sodalities—chiefly in the excluding business. For this important weeding-out process we staged raucous, night-time social
events—"rush parties" as these were for some reason known.
Any male student could attend. Yet many were called but few
were chosen. This guy, it was pointed out, had "the breath of
death"; this fellow had "bad choppers"; this mild-mannered boy

possessed "the handshake of a fish"; this lad apparently thought we were a circus group since he wore his "clown suit" to the party.

And we definitely didn't want Jews, blacks, Orientals, queers, women, big fatties or cripples. Yo-Yo Ma couldn't have been a Sigma Chi at Michigan State. Neither could Steven Spielberg, Woody Allen, Bishop Tutu or Stephen Hawking—who probably wouldn't have wanted to join anyway.

What we did want were "face men," jocks, wild guys, rich guys, guys with class, guys with pretty sisters, guys with "nice threads," "real characters," guys willing to make fools of themselves and others. Guys who did not think all this was bullshit. Good guys, in other words.

I've never seen the movie *Animal House*. I guess I didn't think I needed to. But from old film clips and what people have told me, I've concluded that Sigma Chi, in my day, was a lot like that. We in fact called ourselves by animal names— the "Pigeon," the "Pig," the "Guppie," the "Armadillo," the "Whale." There was also an entire phylum of vegetable names— the "Eggplant," the "Rutabaga," the "Tomato," the "Carrot," the "Root." We put people's heads in toilets. We lit our farts. We dropped our trousers in public. We heaved lots of heavy things out of high windows—TV's, bowling balls, snow tires. We drank a lot and pissed on stuff. We groped girls. We gave the finger. We got sick. We cursed. We wore coats and ties. We were men and knew no bottom line.

A good question to ask of all this business is, I suppose: "Were we *friends*, all of us? Or brothers, of some manufactured kind?" The answer would have to be—not that much, if friendship or being someone's brother are conditions meant to last a long time. I remember detesting some of my fraternity brothers, mocking others, lying to them, disdaining them to their faces, bird-dogging their sweethearts. One boy, now a veterinarian, I punched at a party, reshaping his nostril forever—this, because he'd chided me about being smarter than I was.

It's true that to this day I still hold dear a small cadre of old "brothers." But the fraternity is mostly a matter we now seem embarrassed by, so that our friendship, more than anything, seems to have lasted in spite of all we did together when we were young. You could say we'd have been friends, anyway. It's consoling to think so. Or more truthfully, you could say that friendship, true friendship is a miracle you can't codify, organize, predict or distill. In a sense each precious one is probably a mistake that simply didn't turn out bad, but for some reason, turned out good.

By the time I'd been in a year, I was certain I didn't belong (though neither did I much want to get out). So I became, for a while, aloof with superiority, which I passed off as teasing goodwill. My attitude was that these guys were just children, Goths and Visigoths, barbarians to be brought along for amusement, put on earth for me to observe and occasionally punish. This is also what conformists do.

But what I learned from being a Sigma Chi is enough to make me not regret it completely. I learned that an experience need not be noble or ennobling for good to come of it. This is, after all, the mother soul of satire—whose goal is truth. And I learned that even from a misguided "brotherhood" one could get free—though there might be red-tape, genuine soul-searching and hard feelings expended in the process. Of course, one did have to choose to be free or not. And even if you chose by not exactly choosing, you chose anyway. This lesson is relevant to the nature of all institutions we might subscribe to, whether good or bad.

And I also learned that buffoonery, prejudice, treachery, resentment, pettiness—all the baser instincts—can go hand in hand with earnest efforts toward friendship, trust, affection, honesty and the less base ones. These two categories of impulse may be alien to each other, but I came to know that they are all humors within the larger human dramaturgy. Again, we simply must choose which humor will dominate us.

Can I say that this lesson is what the fraternity always intended us brothers to learn? Is this what the secret *grip* meant? The hooded investiture? The Latin motto? Is this what the worthy forebears knew, and why the white cross wasn't there, and why we'll never be perfect? I don't know. Institutions are always happy to take credit for any good that happens in their neighborhood. The "men" in charge back then would probably say yes—see, we told you. But I kind of doubt it's true. What I think *is* true (now that I'm suddenly so smart) is that it was all a bunch of hooey, as my father used to say. Sigma Chi was like the Shriners or the Masons, the Loyal Order of Raccoons, or the Mystic Knights of the Sea. And its goal was to turn us into a bunch of compliant little Babbits and later on into a bunch of dismal little Meursaults. We were young, okay. But we were phonies, poseurs, bores, joke-meisters, stupids, preposterous boys who wore our untried importance like blue serge uniforms, but who signified nothing but that, and nothing particularly good—me not the least of them. And in truth, if I learned anything at all—and I only learned it later—it might've been that having begun life in this ludicrous, misguided manner, I at least didn't have to stay exactly that way forever.

Ethan Canin

———∼ຈໂ∾———

american beauty

When my brother Lawrence left us to live in California I should have tried to stop him, but I didn't, and I should have been sad, but I wasn't. Instead it was just something happening in our lives. It was like the roof leaking or the electricity going out. I thought of him riding the Trailways bus across the western states, underneath the bubble skylight, sharing cigarettes in station diners, talking with girls he didn't know. I thought of his new life in the Electronics Belt. I imagined going out to see him in a couple of years, heading out to California to stay with him in a split-level ranch with a dark-bottom pool. He was twenty-seven and I was sixteen and computers were booming.

On the morning he left, my mother gave him a Bible. I gave him a watch with a built-in compass, and our sister, Darienne, who was nineteen, gave him a four-by-six foot oil portrait of our family, framed.

"I'm going to have to take it out of the frame," Lawrence said.

"But it's our family."

"Dary, I'm taking a bus." Lawrence looked at me.

"Dary," I said, "he'll break down the frame and roll up the canvas. It's done all the time."

"I worked six weeks on it," she said. She started to cry.

"Don't worry," I said. "He'll be back soon."

Lawrence held up the painting. In it we were sitting together in our kitchen—my brother, my sister, my mother, our spaniel named Caramel and I. Lawrence's wrist dipped below the back of Darienne's collarbone so that his bad hand was hidden around her shoulder.

My father was in the painting also, or at least Darienne's idea of him. He had left fourteen years ago, and not even Lawrence remembered much about him. We certainly never talked about him anymore. But Darienne still put him into her paintings. In them he had a hooked nose, a straight one, the faintly Indian nose and angled cheekbones that I think he really did have; he had thinning hair, full hair; he stared out from canvas, scowled out, held his head turned away from us. He had been a civil engineer. He had stolen some money from his company and left with a woman who was one of my mother's good friends. One of the few times my mother spoke of him after that, years later, she told me that he was looking for something he would never find. In the painting Darienne now gave Lawrence he stood behind my mother. His arm rested on Darienne's shoulder, and he was smiling. He almost never smiled in Darienne's paintings.

"He's smiling," I said.

"He knows Lawrence is going to stay."

"I'm not staying, Dary."

"He's not staying," I said.

"He knows he's coming back soon, then," she said.

Lawrence was leaving because things had reached a point for him here. Although my mother said the good Lord subtracted five years from his age, the five years he spent fighting in black-top lots and driving a car with no hood over the engine, twenty-seven was still old for him to be living where he was, in the basement of our house. He had an engineering degree from Hill Oak College and a night certificate in computer programming. His job, teaching math and auto mechanics at the high school, had ended in June, and on top of that my sister was having a bad summer. In July she had shown me a little black capsule inside a case where she kept her oboe reeds. We were alone in her room.

"Do you know what it is?"

"Cold medicine," I answered.

"Nope," she said. She put it on her tongue and closed her mouth. "It's cyanide."

"No, it's not."

"It is so."

"Dary, take it out of your mouth." I put my hand on her jaw, tried to get my finger between her lips.

"I'm not Caramel."

"Caramel wouldn't eat cyanide." I could feel the tips of her incisors nibbling my fingers. Finally I got my hand into her mouth.

"It's not cyanide," she said. "And get your hands out of my mouth." I pulled the pill out and held it on my palm. Saliva was on my fingers.

"You're crazy," I said to her. Then I regretted it. I wasn't supposed to say that to her. My mother had taken me aside a few years before and told me that even though my sister and I had lived together all our lives, I might still never understand her. "It's difficult for her to be around all you men," my mother said to me. "You and Lawrence are together somehow, and that's a lot for your sister." Then she told me never to call Darienne crazy. She said this was important, something I should never forget. I was thirteen or fourteen years old. "Whatever you do," she said, tilting her head forward and looking into my eyes, "whatever happens, I want you to remember that."

At the beginning of the summer, before I knew he was leaving, Lawrence said he had something very important to tell me. "But I'm not just going to tell you," he said. "I'll mix it into the conversation. I'll say it some time over the summer." We were working on my motorcycle, which he had given me. "You have to figure out what it is," he said. He had drilled the rusted bolts on the cam covers and we were pulling them out. "It's about time you started doing that anyway."

"Doing what?"

"Thinking about what's important."

We were living in Point Bluff, Iowa, in the two-story, back-porched saltbox my father had bought before he left us. As we took apart the rusting cams I tried to decide what was important in our lives. Nothing had changed since I could remember. Lawrence still lived in the basement, where at night the green light of his computer filled the window. Darienne was using the summer to paint still lifes and practice the Bellini oboe concerto, and I was going to go to baseball day camp in August. My mother sipped vodka cranberries out on the lawn furniture with Mrs. Silver in the evenings, and at night sat on the porch reading the newspaper or sometimes the Bible and watching the *Tonight* show. She was the high school guidance counselor and she believed the Lord had a soft spot for the dropouts and delinquents she had to talk with every day. Mrs. Silver was her best friend. Mrs. Silver was young, maybe ten years younger than my mother, and read the Bible too, although she liked the newspaper more. My mother said she'd led a rough life. She didn't look that way to me though. To me, my mother looked more like the one with the rough life. Sometimes she wore a bathrobe all weekend, for example. I didn't know any other mothers who did that. And except for the two or three times a week when she cooked, Lawrence and Darienne and I made our own dinners. My mother's arms were tan. Mrs. Silver wore three or four bracelets, a gold chain on her ankle, and blouses without sleeves. She came over almost every day. I talked to her sometimes in the backyard when my mother went inside to answer the phone or mix another pitcher of vodka cranberry. Mostly we talked about my future.

"It's not too early to think about college," she told me.

"I know, Mrs. Silver."

"And you ought to be saving money." She put her hands on her hips. "Are you saving money?"

"No."

"Do you know that life can be cruel?" She asked.

"Yes."

"No you don't," she said. She laughed. "You don't really know that."

"Maybe I don't."

"Are you learning, at least?"

"Yes," I answered. "I'm trying to decide what's important." I nodded. "Right now I'm learning about motorcycles."

Lawrence and I were taking apart the Honda CB 360 he had given me. We planned to have it completely rebuilt before base-ball camp. He had given it to me in March, when the weather warmed and the melting snow uncovered it in the ditch by Route 80. It was green. The front fork had been bent double from impact, and when I touched the rusted chain it crumbled in my hands.

The first thing we took apart was the clutch. We loosened the striker panel and let the smooth round plates, bathed in oil, spill one by one into an aluminum turkey-roasting pan. With the oil wiped clean, the plates gleamed like a metal I had never seen before, the way I imagined platinum gleamed. They were polished from their own movement. Lawrence explained that the slotted panels were to dissipate heat from friction. After we took the plates out and examined them, noted how they slipped smoothly over their fellows, we put them back in. "That's how you learn a machine," he said. "You take it apart and then you put it back together."

I thought about this for a moment. "Is that what you were going to tell me?"

"No, Edgar," he said. "That's not important enough."

That spring, before he gave me the motorcycle, he had taught me his theory of machinery. In April he took me out to the back yard, to a patch of softening earth that he had cleared of the elephant grass that grew everywhere else on the lot. He had sunk four poles there and made a shanty with fluted alu-minum, sloping the ground so that snowmelt poured into gul-leys and flowed away from the center, where his machinery lay. His machinery was anything he could get his hand on. He got it from junkyards and road surplus, brought home sump pumps, rifle mechanisms, an airplane engine, hauled them in a borrowed truck and set them underneath the shanty to be taken apart.

"Every machine is the same, Edgar," he told me one evening. "If you can understand two sticks hitting together, you can understand the engine of an airplane." We were standing underneath the shanty with Darienne and Mrs. Silver, who had wandered out to the back yard after dinner. Out there Lawrence kept a boulder and a block of wood and a walking stick to demonstrate the lever. "I can move the boulder with the stick," he said that evening, and then he did it. He wedged the stick between the wood and the rock, and when he leaned on it the boulder rolled over. "Fulcrum-lever-machine," he said. "Now"—and then he took the oilcloth tarp off the drag-racer engine and Cessna propeller— "this is the very same thing."

"Spare me," said Darienne.

"If you don't want to learn," said Lawrence, "don't come out here."

Then my sister walked back across the yard, stopping to pick up a cottonweed pod for one of her still lifes. Lawrence watched her go in through the screen door. "She's crazy," he said.

I turned to him. "It's hard for her to be around all us men."

Mrs. Silver looked at me. "Good, Edgar," she said.

I smiled.

My brother picked up a wrench. He cleared his throat. "That's peckerdust," he said.

"Pardon me," Mrs. Silver said.

"I said that's peckerdust. Darienne can take what I give her. People like it when you're hard on them." He looked at her. "Everybody knows that. And you know what?" He transferred the wrench to his bad hand and pushed back his hair. "They come back for more."

"A lady wouldn't come back for more," said Mrs. Silver. She put her hands together in front of her. "And a gentleman wouldn't say that."

Lawrence laughed. "Well, Dary sure likes it. And she comes back."

"It's a nice night out here," I said.

Mrs. Silver smiled at me. "It is," she said. Then she turned and walked back to the house. The kitchen light went on. I saw Darienne at the sink putting water on her face. I watched her wipe the water from her eyes with a paper towel and then move away from the window.

Sometimes I tried to look at my sister as if she were a stranger. We spent a lot of time in the house together, she and my mother and I, and I had a lot of time to look at her. She was tall, with half-curly, half-straight hair and big shoulders. Sometimes Mrs. Silver sat with us. Mrs. Silver was lonely, my mother said. She had a husband who drank. She was beautiful, though. "I'm your mother's charity case," she would say, sitting in our yard chair while she and my mother waxed each other's legs. "Your mother just feels sorry for me." Sometimes I compared her with my sister. I watched her in the yard or on the other side of the family room as she smiled and laughed, as she brushed her bangs from her forehead or drank a vodka cranberry from a straw. Then I looked at Darienne. While she painted or played oboe, as if I were seeing her for the first time at a dance, I watched her. Her hands moved. She had the potential to be pretty but she wasn't. This is what I decided. Not the way she was now, at least. Her face was friendly, but she wore boy's cotton shirts and slumped her shoulders. In her shirt pocked she kept oboe reeds, which she always sucked.

"You ought to stand up straight," Lawrence told her.

"So I can be prettier for you? I'd rather die."

"No you wouldn't," said my mother.

"And you shouldn't suck those things in public," said Lawrence.

Darienne closed her lips tight. Whenever Lawrence corrected her, she pursed them so tight so that they turned almost white. I thought this had something to do with her epilepsy, which she'd had since childhood, but I wasn't sure. She had been a special needs student in high school. Although we were never allowed to see her report card, I think she flunked most subjects. It wasn't because she was unintelligent, my mother said to Lawrence and me, but because there was a different force driving her. She painted beautifully, for example—"Like a professional," said my mother—and played second oboe in school orchestra. But something about the epilepsy, I guess, made her slow. My mother parceled out her medicine in small plastic bottles that Darienne kept on her dresser. She never had any fits— she only had the petit mal disease—but she slept with cloth animals in her bed at age nineteen and used a Bambi nightlight. It was small and plastic and shaped like a deer.

Although Lawrence never paid much attention to her, Darienne still liked to show him everything she made and everything she found. At the end of most days she went downstairs to the basement with sheets of her sketch paper in her hand. She stayed in his apartment for a few minutes, then came back up.

"Why do you just draw lines?" I said to her one afternoon when she came upstairs.

"I don't. I draw plenty of things."

"I've seen you just drawing lines." I grab her hand. "Let me see."

"Edgar, you don't care what I draw."

"I don't care," I said. "You're right. I just want to see."

Really, though, I did care. I wasn't sure whether I cared about her because she was my sister, or just because there was something wrong with her, but I did care. She didn't think I did, though. For my birthday that year she had given me a diary, and inside, on the flyleaf, she had written in ornate calligraphy: I DON'T THINK YOU CARE ABOUT ANYTHING. And below that in small letters: (BUT IF YOU DO, WRITE IT IN HERE). Underneath that, she had made a sketch of the sculpture *The Thinker*. It was a good sketch, and in parentheses even lower on the page, in even smaller writing, she wrote, AUGUST RODIN.

Darienne was a good artist. In the mornings she did drawing exercises. She sat in the window bay of her bedroom, our yard and the drainages canal curving below her, the hills with their elephant grass and vanilla pines in the distance, and she drew lines. She wouldn't show me, but I saw them anyway when I was in her room. They were curved, straight, varied in thickness, drawn with the flat edge or the sharp point of the pencil.

"That's a nice one Dary," I said one morning as I passed behind her while she was drawing at the window. "Where did you get the idea for that one?"

That afternoon she came out to the yard where Lawrence and I were pulling out tiny screws and springs from the motorcycle carburetor. "You know, Edgar," she said, "all the great artists practice their lines."

"Actors practice their lines," I said.

Lawrence laughed.

She pressed her lips together. "You know what I mean," she said. She walked around until her shadow fell on the carburetor. Then she stood there. "Maybe now," she said, "you two want to go out and show some animals."

"You're weird, Dary," said Lawrence.

"I'm not weird. You guys are weird." She threw a dirt clod in our oil pan.

"Not everyone feels the same forces."

"You going to clean that dirt out?" said Lawrence.

"Why? So you can spend eight more hours taking out a cylinder?"

"We're working on the carburetor," I said.

I loosened a small mixture screw. "If I practiced the oboe as much as you," I said, "I'd be Doc Severinsen."

She worked her lips. "Doc Severinsen plays the trumpet."

"He plays the oboe, too." I looked at Lawrence. I had made this up.

"The oboe is a double reed," Dary said. "It's one of the most difficult instruments."

The truth was, she was right. I had heard that the oboe was a fairly difficult instrument, and Darienne was pretty good on it. She could have played first oboe in school orchestra, but she played second because Mr. MacFarquhar, the director, didn't want her to have the responsibility. I felt bad saying the things I said to her. But she brought them on herself. I would have had conversations with her, but they never worked out.

"I hope the dirt clogs your engine," she said.

Lawrence made up a game that year that Darienne hated and that we played on all our car trips. It was called What Are You Going to Do? Lawrence drove and led the game. "You are driving along the summit pass of a mountain," Lawrence said one evening as he drove, "when under your foot you notice that the accelerator has become jammed in the full open position. You are approaching dangerous curves and the car is accelerating rapidly." He rolled down his window, propped his elbow out, adjusted the mirror to give us time to think. My mother shifted in her seat. "What are you going to do?" he asked.

"Press the breaks," said my mother.

"You'll burn them out." He adjusted his headrest.

"Steer like hell," said Mrs. Silver. Lawrence smiled.

"Open the door and roll out on to the road," said Darienne.

"You'll kill the other drivers and possibly yourself." He put the blinker on and passed another car. "Edgar?"

"Shift the transmission into neutral," I answered.

"Bingo," he said. He leaned back and began whistling.

In high school, Lawrence had been in one piece of trouble after the next. He had broken windows and stolen cars and hit someone, or so one of my teachers later told me, with a baseball bat. I knew about a lot of it because the school faculty told me. "You're Lawrence's brother," the older ones always said to me, more than a decade later, at the start of a new school year. Then they told the story about him stealing all the school's lawnmowers or driving a car into the Mississippi River. I never asked Lawrence about the bat because I couldn't imagine my brother doing that to anyone. I did ask him about some of the other things, though. He had broken into a gas station one night with his friends, poisoned a farmer's milk herd, set fifty acres of woods on fire. One night, racing, he turned too wide and drove his Chevy Malibu into a living room of a house. He had a juvenile record and was headed, my mother said, for the other side of the green grass, when, the day he turned eighteen, like a boiling pot coming off the fire, he just stopped.

It didn't seem that anybody just changed like that, but evidently Lawrence did. This was how my mother told it. "The candle of the wicked shall be put out," she said. I was seven years old then. Lawrence was supposed to move from the house but she let him stay, and some sense just clicked on in his head. He stopped going out and his friends started calling him less, then stopped calling him completely. He cut his hair and bought a set of barbells that he lifted every evening, standing shirtless in the window of his room.

A few years later, when I was in junior high and after he had bought his computer, he began telling me to stay out of trouble. I had never gotten into any, though, I didn't want to steal cars or hit people. "It's not something I want to do," I told him.

"You will, though," he said. He looked at me. "That's for sure—you will. But be careful when you do." Then, to show me that he had said something serious, he put his left hand behind him. My mother had taken tranquilizers when she was pregnant with Lawrence, and now his hand had only two fingers. He always held it behind his back when he said something important. The lame fingers were wide at the knuckles and tapered at the ends, and the skin over them was skink and waxlike. I hardly noticed it anymore. I remember my mother had once told me that Lawrence's hand was my father's legacy. She said this was how my father lived on in our lives.

I didn't understand at the time. "What do you mean?" I asked.

"It's cloven," she said.

One night we drove until dawn. Darienne and my mother and Mrs. Silver slept in the back while I sat in front with

Lawrence. He held the wheel with his knees and put his arms behind his head. Then he glanced behind us. "I slept with Mrs. Silver," he said.

"What?"

He put his hands back on the wheels and whistled the opening of Bellini oboe concerto. I looked behind us.

"You did not."

"I sure did. In the basement."

For some reason, although it had nothing to do with Mrs. Silver, I thought again about whether I really cared about my mother. Then I thought about whether I really cared about anybody. Then I thought about Mrs. Silver. I put my arm across the seatback. "Did you really?"

"Women are afraid of getting old," he said.

"So?"

"So, you play on that."

I tried to look behind us again without turning my neck. Mrs. Silver was asleep with her head leaning back over the seat. Her mouth was open and I saw her throat. She was married to a drunk. I knew that much. I also knew that her husband had been in prison. I paused while we passed some telephone poles. "That's what you were going to tell me, isn't it?"

"Nope."

I couldn't imagine what could be more important than that. Mrs. Silver's throat was white as bath soap, and she was in our house practically every day. When she waxed her legs they shone like my polished clutch plates. I looked at the road and tried to think of what it was like. I imagined waking up one night in my room to find her at the side of my bed, whispering. "Edgar," she would say. Her voice would be low and soft. "Edgar, I can't resist." At a party that year I had felt the breasts of a girl two grades ahead of me.

That afternoon Lawrence and I were in a gas station bathroom. We were drying our hands under the heat fan. "Lawrence," I said. I rubbed my hands together a few times. "Did *she* ask *you?*"

"Did who ask me?"

"You know," I said. The dryer stopped and I put my hands in my pockets. "Did Mrs. Silver ask *you?*"

"In a way."

"In what way?"

"In the way women ask for a thing."

"How do women ask for a thing?"

He walked out to the parking lot and I followed him. We were in the desert. The tar was soft under my shoes, and Darienne and my mother and Mrs. Silver sat on towels on the car hood. Mrs. Silver was wearing a halter top tied high over her abdomen. "They ask for a thing by making you think of it," said Lawrence.

When we got home from our trip that year I started my diary. I hadn't written anything in it before. It was leatherette, with my initials embossed, and it locked. The key was attached by a piece of yellow string. I opened it and reread the inscription. Then I turned to the first page.

June 21st—

I wrote.

LAWRENCE IS LEAVING.

I thought of writing about Mrs. Silver. I closed the diary and locked it, then got a paper clip from the desk. When I tried it, the paper clip opened the lock. I decided not to write about her.

Darienne knocked on the door and came in. "I have to tell you something," she said. She looked at my desk. "You're using that," she said.

"What did you have to tell me?"

"That you can't tell anybody about the cyanide." She stepped behind me.

"And you can't write about it either."

"Why not?"

"It's not even cyanide," she said. "It's a diet pill. You wrote about it, didn't you?"

"Maybe."

"Let me see."

I closed my diary and locked it. She took two oboe reeds from her shirt pocket and put them in her mouth. "You ought to wash those first," I said.

"I knew you'd already written about it."

"I have not. And what do you care if I did?"

"I don't want Lawrence to know. I want him to remember good things about me."

"What if he does know? He knows everything else about you."

"He does not."

"It doesn't matter," I said.

"It does so."

I looked at her. There was always something about her that made me angry. I didn't know what it was. She looked at me as if I were about to hit her. I turned and faced right into her eyes. "It doesn't matter," I said, "because he hates you anyway."

She stepped back and felt for the door handle, and for a moment I thought she was actually going to fall. Then she left, and I didn't see her again until that afternoon, when she came outside to the yard. Lawrence and I were patching the muffler. She stood off to the side of us, humming the Bellini concerto. Even when she hummed, she repeated parts, went over and over bars as if she were practicing. It was a warm afternoon and I didn't want anything to bother me. I was cutting squares of fiber-glass mesh to fit the rust holes in the tailpipe. Lawrence was mixing the hardener. Darienne stopped and repeated a phrase. Then she repeated it again, louder.

"Hi Dary," I said.

"Hi, Edgar. Hi, Lawrence."

"You're crossing railroad tracks," Lawrence said.

"What?" said Darienne.

"You're crossing a set of railroad tracks," he said, "when the car you're driving stalls." He squeezed out a ribbon of fiber-glass putty onto the plastic spatula and mixed it with the hardener.

Darienne had stopped humming. "You look up and see that around the bend the locomotive is coming. You're right in the middle of the track and the engineer won't see you in time to stop." He picked up the mixture with a spreader and pressed it into the dent in the rear of the tailpipe. "What are you going to do?"

"Start the car," said Darienne.

"It won't start."

"Give it gas."

"It still won't start. The train is coming," he said. He looked at me.

I cut four neat corners on a square of mesh. "Get out of the car," I answered.

"Bingo," said Lawrence.

Darienne took a step toward us, reached with her leg, and kicked our parts tray upside down. "You'll never get a job with that hand," she said.

Lawrence laughed. "What did you say?"

"It's a beautiful day out here," I said.

"I said you'll never get a job with that hand of yours."

Lawrence turned around in his crouch. "Damn you," he whispers. He gathered up a couple of bolts that had rolled next to him. Then he picked up a hammer from the tool chest. So quickly that it seemed to be done by someone else, not by any one of us, but by a fourth, by another person, he grabbed Darienne and threw her to the ground. She hit hard on her hip. She was alongside the motorcycle, on her side in the dirt, and he raised the hammer over her face. For a moment its shiny head was above us. My brother's arm was cocked back, stiff with anger. I watched it. I saw the hair and the sweat on his wrist. I saw the hammer's rubber handle and the red steel of its shaft. AMERICAN BEAUTY HARDWARE, it said. The words were printed on aluminum tape wrapped at the neck. There was a rose emblem, black and silver, at the top. At the height of his swing it reflected brilliant light. I didn't say anything. I stood behind them. Darienne screamed. I stepped forward and grabbed Lawrence's hand.

His arm relaxed, and while Darienne scrambled up beside him he let the hammer fall from his grip. Darienne stood. Her skirt was marked with dust and oil. She brushed her cheeks, first one, then the other. Then she turned around and ran into the house.

I turned the parts tray over and began picking up springs and bolts. "Jesus, Lawrence," I said.

"She'll get over it."

In front of me, in the pan, bits of dust floated on the oil. "But you wouldn't have hit her."

"Probably not."

"You can't hit somebody like that." I looked up at him and smiled. "Come on."

He picked up the hammer and put it back in the toolbox. "What the hell would *you* know about anything?" he said.

We brought Lawrence to the bus station the week before baseball camp started. He left Darienne's painting behind because, he said, he would be back for it. After breakfast we hung it in the living room. Lawrence said goodbye to Caramel and we got into my mother's Dodge and drove to the station.

When the bus came I helped him on with his stuff. The driver put his duffel underneath and I carried his small suitcase, which had been our father's, into the coach for him. The bus was blue inside and smelled of smoke. It didn't have a skylight. Lawrence took a seat toward the back, next to a middle-aged woman. The driver got back in. I could see Darienne and my mother waiting at the front door. Lawrence went up the aisle and kissed my mother. I watched Darienne let him kiss her also. I got out.

When the bus started to move my mother held Darienne's arm. "When will he be back?" asked Darienne.

"He walked in all the ways of his father," said my mother.

"Dary, you're not thinking about what's important," I said.

We watched the bus go out to the highway before we got back in our car. On the ride home we stopped for ice cream cones. That evening Mrs. Silver came over and drank vodka cranberries with my mother in the back yard. I drank one too, without ice, and it made me a little drunk. Darienne stayed inside.

I sat on an aluminum chair, my hands tingling from the liquor, and thought of a time when I would barely remember my brother. He would be in California in two days. Then, for as long as I could imagine, I would be living in this house with my mother and sister. I knew I would never finish the motorcycle. It would lie out in the yard and the rust would eventually enter the engine. But that didn't bother me. I looked at my mother. She was stirring the ice in her glass. Darienne was probably upstairs drawing one line and then another, changing the shading, changing the edge. The light was fading. It seemed to me that all of them, she and my mother and Lawrence, had suffered a wound that had somehow skipped over me. I drank more of my vodka cranberry. Life seemed okay to me. It seemed okay even now, the day my brother left. It even seemed pleasant, which was the way, despite everything she said, I thought it probably seemed to Mrs. Silver.

I looked at her. She was leaning back on a lounger, reading the newspaper. She didn't seem upset about Lawrence leaving. But that's what I would have expected. She wasn't like my mother, and she wasn't like Darienne or Lawrence. Life just flowed over her. It melted over her like wax. I wondered if *she* cared about anybody. She looked up at me then, as I sat watching her, and I saw that her mouth was rimmed with cranberry.

I smiled. She smiled back. I stood up and went into the house, and after I looked at our new painting for a while I walked upstairs to see my sister. When I came into her room the lights were off except for the Bambi nightlight. It lit the baseboard. In its small, yellow glow I could see Darienne on the bed. Her white legs were drawn up against her chest and she was crying. I went over and sat next to her.

"Hi Dary."

She didn't say anything. We sat there for a while. She rocked up and back against the wall.

"You shouldn't be so sad," I said. "He was a pecker to you."

We sat for a few minutes. I thought about things. Then I leaned back next to her. "Dary," I said, "you are driving on a very hot day." I could smell the herbal shampoo in her hair. "A day in which it is over one hundred degrees outside, when you notice halfway up a mountain grade that the temperature gauge on the dashboard indicates hot." I got up from the bed, took a couple steps across the room, came back. I picked the dirt from my fingernails. "What are you going to do?"

"Edgar, I'm your older sister."

"Come on."

She pulled her knees up.

"The car is overheating."

"I don't know what to do," she said.

I sat lower on the bed again. The two of us pushed together on the quilt. Then next to her, I started to cry too. I was thinking of Lawrence. Last night I had gone down to his apartment to see him. I almost never went in there. The computer was in a box and his clothes were folded in stacks on the bed. The door was open and the sun was setting, so we went and stood together on the steps. He picked up pebbles from his entranceway and threw them into the yard.

"Have a good time," I said.

"I will."

"When will you visit?"

"I may not be back for a while," he said.

"Not for a while."

"That's right."

"I'll finish the Honda."

"Good."

Then Darienne came down from the house. She walked past Lawrence and stood between us. "I have something to ask you, Edgar," she said.

"What is it?"

"I want to know whether he was going to hit me."

I laughed. I looked at Lawrence's back.

"Tell me," she said.

I laughed again. "Were you going to hit her?" I said to Lawrence.

"I asked *you*," Darienne said.

"You can't ask me that, Dary," I said. "You can't just ask me whether another person was going to do something," I put my hand on her arm.

"Tell me," she said.

"Dary, I can't tell you that. I can tell you what I would have done." I leaned down and picked up a couple of pebbles. "But Dary, you knocked over our parts. They're covered with dirt now. There's gravel in the transmission. I can't tell you what Lawrence would or wouldn't do."

"Would he have hit me?"

"I can't tell you that."

Lawrence tossed a pebble over the hedge. "Tell her what you think," he said.

She looked into my eyes. I wanted to change the subject, but I couldn't think of anything to say. I smiled. I really tried to think about it. "Yes," I said. "I think he would have."

Darienne turned and went back to the house. I stayed behind with Lawrence. Even from the back I thought he was smiling. I threw the pebbles in my palm one by one over the hedge.

"Do you think *you* would have hit her?" he said. He didn't turn around.

"No," I answered.

He chuckled. I thought he was going to say something more, but he didn't. He let the pebbles drop from his hand.

"You know what I'm waiting for?" I asked.

"You're waiting for me to tell you what I was going to tell you."

"That's right."

"Well," he said. "This is it." He turned around and faced me. "You're a bastard, too," he said.

"What?"

"I mean, yes, you would have hit her too. You just don't know it yet." He pointed at me. "But if something ever goes wrong, you're going to turn into a son of a bitch, just like me." He smiled slightly. "Just like every guy in the world. You don't know it yet because everything's all right so far. You think you're a nice guy and that everything hasn't really affected you. But you can't get away from it." He tapped his chest. "It's in your blood."

"That's what you were going to tell me?"

"Bingo," he said.

Then he brushed past me and went into his apartment. I followed and stood behind him in the doorway. A wind had come up and I put my hands into my pockets. He stood with his back to me, placing shirts into a box, not saying anything. He was wearing a jean jacket and chino pants with pleats. We were silent, standing in his darkening apartment, and I tried to imagine what the world was like for him.

John Edgar Wideman

———— ✧ ————

doing time

Robby hugs me, we clasp hands. My arm goes round his body and I hug him back. Our eyes meet. What won't be said, can't be said no matter how long we talk, how much I write, hovers in his eyes and mine. We know where we are, what's happening, how soon this tiny opening allowing us to touch will be slammed shut. All that in our eyes, and I can't take seeing it any longer than he can. The glance we exchange is swift, is full of fire, of unsayable rage and pain. Neither of us can hold it more than a split second. He sees in me what I see in him. The knowledge that this place is bad, worse than bad. That the terms under which we are meeting stink. That living under certain conditions is less than no life at all, and what we have to do, ought to do, is make our stand here, together. That dying with your hands on an enemy's throat is better than living under his boot. Just a flash. The simplest, purest solution asserting itself. I recognize what Rob is thinking. I know he knows what's rushing through my mind. Fight. Forget the games, the death by inches buying time. Fight till they kill us or let us go. If we die fighting, it will be a good day to die. The right day. The right way.

After that first contact, after that instant of threat and consolation and promise flickers out as fast as it came, my eyes drop to the vinyl cushioned couches, rise again to the clutter of other prisoners and visitors. I force myself to pretend the eye conversation never took place, that Robby and I hadn't been talking about first things and last things and hadn't reached a crystal-clear understanding of what we must do. We'd lost the moment. The escape route closed down as he looked away or I looked away. We're going to deal with the visit now. We're going to talk, survive another day. I have to pretend the other didn't happen because if I don't, disappointment and shame will spoil the visit. And visits are all we have. All we're going to have for years and years, unless we choose the other way, the solution burning in Rob's eyes and mine before each visit begins.

The last iron gate, the last barred door. The visit proper doesn't begin until after we meet and touch and decide we'll do it their way one more time. Because the other way, the alternative is always there. I meet it every time. We know it's there and we consciously say, No. And the no lets everything else follow. Says yes to the visit. The words.

Whatever else the visit turns into, it begins as a compromise, an acceptance of defeat. Maybe the rage, the urge to fight back doesn't rise from a truer, better self. Maybe what's denied is not the instinctual core of my being but an easily sidestepped, superficial layer of bravado, a ferocity I'd like to think is real but that winds up being no more than a Jonathan Jackson, George Jackson, Soledad-brother fantasy, a carryover from the old Wild West, shoot-em-up days as a kid. The Lone Ranger, Robin Hood, Zorro. Masked raiders attacking the bad guys' castle, rescuing trusty sidekicks in a swirl of swordplay, gunfire, thundering hooves. Maybe I needed to imagine myself in that role because I knew how far from the truth it was. Kidding myself so I could take the visits seriously, satisfy myself that I was doing all I could, doing better than nothing.

Point is, each visit's rooted in denial, compromise, a sinking feeling of failure, I'm letting Robby down, myself down, the team . . . Always that to get through. The last gate. Sometimes it never swings all the way open on its hinges. A visit can be haunted by a sense of phoniness, hollowness. Who am I? Why am I here? Listening to my brother, answering him, but also fighting the voice that screams that none of this matters, none of this is worth shit. You missed your chance to put your money where your mouth is. A good day to die but you missed it. You let them win again. Humiliate you again. You're on your knees again, scrambling after scraps.

Sometimes we occupy one of the lawyer-client tables, but today a guard chases us away. Robby's had trouble with him before. I commit the guard's name to memory just in case. My personal shit list for the close watching or revenge or whatever use it would serve if something suspicious happens to my brother. I consider making a fuss. After all, I'm a professional writer. Don't I have just as much right as a lawyer or social worker to the convenience of a table where I can set down the tools of my trade, where my brother and I can put a little distance between ourselves and the babble of twenty or thirty simultaneous conversations?

The guard's chest protrudes like there's compressed air instead of flesh inside the gray blouse of his uniform. A square head. Pale skin except on his cheeks, which are bluish and raw from razor burn. His mustache and short curly hair are meticulously groomed, too perfect to be real. The stylized hair of comic-book superheroes. A patch of blue darkness etched with symmetrical accent lines. His eyes avoid mine. He had spoken in a clipped, mechanical tone of voice. Not one man talking to another but a preemptory recital of rules droned at some abstraction in the idle distance where the guard's eyes focus while his lips move. I think, Nazi Gestapo Frankenstein robot motherfucker, but he's something worse. He's what he is and there's no way to get around that or for the moment get around him because he's entrenched in this no-man's land and he is what he is and that's worse than any names I can call him. He's laying down the law and that's it. The law. No matter that all three tables are unoccupied. No matter that I tell him we've sat at them before. No matter that I might have a case, make a case that my profession, my status means something outside the walls. No matter, my pride and dander and barely concealed scorn. I move on. We obey because the guard's in power. Will remain in power when I have to leave and go about my business. Then he'll be free to take out on my brother whatever revenge he couldn't exact from me and my smart mouth. So I talk low. Shake my head but stroll away (just enough nigger in my walk to tell the guard I know what he thinks of me but that I think infinitely less of him) toward the least crowded space in the row of benches against the wall.

Not much news to relate. Robby cares about family business and likes to keep up with who's doing what, when, how, etc., but he also treats the news objectively, cold-bloodedly. Family affairs have everything and nothing to do with him. He's in exile, powerless to influence what goes on outside the walls, so he maintains a studied detachment; he hears what I say and quickly mulls it over, buries the worrisome parts, grins at good news. When he comments on bad news it's usually a grunt, a nod, or a gesture with his hands that says all there is to say and says, A million words wouldn't make any difference, would they? Learning to isolate himself, to build walls within the walls enclosing him is a matter of survival. If he doesn't insulate himself against those things he can't change, if he can't discipline himself to ignore and forget, to narrow the range of his concerns to what he can immediately, practically effect, he'll go crazy. The one exception is freedom. Beneath whatever else Robby says or does or thinks, the dream of freedom pulses. The worst times, the lowest times are when the pulse seems extinguished. Like in the middle of the night, the hour of the wolf when even the joint is quiet and the earth stops spinning on its axis and he bursts from sleep, the deathly sleep that's the closest thing to mercy prison ever grants, starts from sleep and for a moment hears nothing. In the shadow of that absolute silence he can't imagine himself ever leaving prison alive. For hours, days, weeks the mood of that moment can oppress him. He needs every ounce of willpower he possesses to pick up the pieces of his life, to animate them again with the hope that one day the arbitrary, bitter, little routines he manufactures to sustain himself will make sense because one day he'll be free.

I arrange my pens and yellow pad atop the table. But before we begin working on the book I tell Robby my sawing dream.

I am a man, myself but not myself. The man wakes up and can't see the stars. The smell of death surrounds him. Fifteen hundred other men sleep in the honeycomb of steel that is his home forever. The fitful stirrings, clattering bars, groaning, the sudden outcries of fear, rage, madness, and God knows what else are finally over at this hour of the night or morning as he lies in his cell listening to other men sleep. The monotonous saw-ing sounds remind him of the funny papers, the little cloud con-taining saw and log drawn above a character's head so you can see the sound of sleeping. Only the man doesn't see logs float-ing above the prisoner's heads. As he listens and shuts his eyes and gets as close to praying as he ever does anymore, praying for sleep, for blessed oblivion, the cartoon he imagines behind his closed eyes is himself sawing away the parts of his own body. Doggedly, without passion or haste, drawing a dull saw up and back, up and back through his limbs. Slices drop away on the concrete floor. The man is cutting himself to pieces, there is less of him every time he saws a section. He is lopping off his own flesh and blood but works methodically, concentrating on the up-and-back motion of the saw. When there's nothing left, he'll be finished. He seems almost bored, almost asleep, ready to snore like the saw's snoring as it chews through his body.

Robby shakes his head and starts to say something but doesn't, and we both leave the dream alone. Pass on to the book, the tasks still to be accomplished.

Robby had said he liked what he'd seen of the first draft. Liked it fine, but something was missing. Trouble was, he hadn't been able to name the missing ingredient. I couldn't either but I knew I had to try and supply it. By the book's conclusion I wanted a whole, rounded portrait of my brother. I'd envisioned a climactic scene in the final section, an epiphany that would reveal Robby's character in a powerful burst of light and truth. As the first draft evolved, I seemed to settle for much less. One early reader had complained of a "sense of frustration. . . . By the end of the book I want to know more about Robby than I actually know. I know a lot of facts about his life but most of his inner self escapes me." On target or not, the reaction of this early reader, coupled with Robby's feeling that something crucial was lacking, had destroyed any complacency I had about the book's progress. I reread Robby's letters, returned to the books and articles that had informed my research into prisons and prisoners. I realized no apotheosis of Robby's character could occur in the final section because none had transpired in my dealings with my brother. The first draft had failed because it attempted to impose a dramatic shape on a relationship, on events and people too close to me to see in terms of beginning, middle, and end. My brother was in prison. A thousand books would not reduce his sentence one day. And the only denouement that might make sense of his story would be his release from prison. I'd been hoping to be a catalyst for change in the world upon which the book could conceivably have no effect at all. I'd been waiting to record dramatic, external changes in Robby's circumstances when what I should have been attuned to were the inner changes, his slow, internal adjustment day by day to an unbearable situation. The book was no powerful engine being constructed to set my brother free; it was dream, wish, song.

No, I could not create a man whose qualities were self-evident cause for returning him to the world of free people. Prison had changed my brother, not broken him, and therein lay the story. Then changes were subtle, incremental; bit by bit he had been piecing himself together. He had not become a model human being with a cure for cancer at his fingertips if only the parole board would just give him a chance, turn him loose again on the streets of Homewood. The character traits that landed Robby in prison are the same ones that have allowed him to survive with dignity, and pain and sense of himself as infinitely better than the soulless drone prison demands he become. Robby knows his core is intact; his optimism, his intelligence, his capacity for love, his pride, his dream of making it big, becoming somebody special. And though these same qualities helped get him in trouble and could derail him again, I'm happy they are still there. I rejoice with him.

Chris Bohjalian

——— ✺ ———

my brother's a keeper

It has now been over forty years—two full generations—since protestors and police battled in the streets of Chicago at the 1968 Democratic convention and much of America first heard the word *yippie* as a noun instead of a synonym for *hooray*. I was a boy in 1968, a second grader with little interest in politics, the Vietnam War, and the logistics of nominating a presidential candidate. And yet I have memories of that nominating week that are vibrant and vivid, and they seem to begin and end with my brother.

My brother is five years older than I am, which means there has never been much sibling rivalry or competition between us. I figured out early on that he was always going to whip me soundly at everything. In one-on-one football, which we played often in our front yard, he invented a rule where each of us could pass the ball to ourselves, which worked to his advantage since he had as much as a foot on me. In "Denny McLain Real Action Baseball," a baseball board game with a magnetic diamond and a wooden, spring-loaded bat, he was able to pitch the small marble so that it actually curved beyond the reach of the bat and plopped into the game's strike zone. And when he dealt poker, a computer couldn't have kept track of the combinations of cards he'd call wild. I spent my childhood losing to him in every imaginable sport and game we could play.

Actually, I have spent my entire life losing to him in every imaginable sport. For a time, not long after I graduated from college, we both lived in New York City: He was in Manhattan and I was in Brooklyn. In those years we would often play tennis on

Saturday afternoons in a bubble atop the health club to which I belonged. The bubble was heated for the winter, but lacked air conditioning for the summer. After all, who wants to play tennis indoors in July? Well, we did, simply because it was a killing sauna in there and added an element of unpredictability to the proceedings: Even the tennis balls seemed to sweat. And though one would think that my age would have served me well in that cauldron—Wasn't my heart five plus years younger than my brother's?—I still couldn't beat him. Some afternoons I might have him on the ropes, down a set and behind a few games, but I was never able to put him away. He was my older brother and old habits die hard: Invariably, I would wilt first. I took an occasional set from him in what we called the Hell Invitational, but I never won a match.

At middle age, however, I have come to realize something important about our childhood: When we were growing up, my older brother was shouldering a lot of the heavy lifting that is usually reserved for a boy's dad. We had—we have—a loving father, but he worked long hours and his commute from Connecticut to Manhattan was arduous. He was the sort of businessman who once hitchhiked from our house to the train station in a blizzard because the snowplows hadn't reached our street, was virtually alone on the train into the city, and then wondered why he was the only executive that day in the office. He wasn't an invisible presence in my childhood, but he was gone by the time I got up in the morning and he would return home just in time for a late dinner. After supper he usually went right to bed, falling asleep before Merv Griffin had introduced his very first guest.

And so although my brother was finding ways to beat me in board games and sports that ranged from devious to inspired, he was also the one who was teaching me how to throw a football, what an earned run average meant in baseball, and—in the heated swimming pool of a hotel in Atlantic City one long Thanksgiving weekend—how to swim. Later, he was the one explaining to me why the music of the Beatles and Joni Mitchell mattered, and why I should be more circumspect in my affection for the work of Jeannie C. Riley ("Harper Valley PTA"). He would be the one who would gently offer guidance about what sorts of I.D. bracelets were best if, in the sixth grade, you were going to ask a girl to go steady (as I recall, the less expensive the better, and silver-plated was best).

At the time, of course, I was likely to be filled with as much resentment as I was gratitude. This was true partly because he never lost and he was always right—even when, I figured out years later, he was wrong. Let's face it: Older siblings invented the mind game. My older brother did not tell me that Thomas Edison invented the vegetable, as one older sister I know convinced her younger sister. But there was no shortage of misinformation he was happy to share. To wit: When I was in the seventh grade, I came across the word "cunnilingus" in an issue of National Lampoon. (National Lampoon is the periodical teen boys once read between Mad Magazine and Rolling Stone. Now they go straight to Maxim or Internet porn on their cell phones.) I had no idea what the term meant and the context wasn't especially helpful. And so I asked my older and wiser brother.

"It's a Latin word for talking with your mouth full of food," he explained with great earnestness. "The Romans were known for their table manners. Use it at dinner tonight with Mom and Dad. They'll be impressed."

I did and they were. But mostly they were impressed with how clever and funny my brother was. My mother christened him "Perfect Person" around the time he was in the ninth grade and was voted Student Council President. For the rest of her life she would call him that because of the penumbra of success that seemed to follow him. He was popular with everyone: He wasn't a varsity athlete, but the varsity athletes all seemed to be his friends. He wasn't a spectacular drummer, but he was part of a rock band that seemed to have gigs most Saturday nights. And though he wasn't tall or especially handsome, he always had

girlfriends who were smart and beautiful and remarkably interesting dressers. I will never forget one who would wear one of
her father's dress shirts—and little else—to school. It was a bold
fashion statement, somewhere between slutty and haute cou-
ture, but she was gorgeous and no adult seemed especially moti-
vated to send her home for a pair of pants. I never begrudged
my brother the moniker of Perfect Person, because I understand
that our mother said it with equal measures of sarcasm and affection. If I resented anything in my brother's relationship with our
parents, it was that he was given a subscription to *Playboy* when
he turned sixteen, and I got to move from Florida to New York
and change high schools in my junior year.

He was close to finishing college by then and I was morph-
ing into his clone—a "Mini Me" straight from a Mike Myers
movie—who was consciously replicating his C.V. As a high
school senior, I applied to exactly one college, his recent alma
mater, where I followed him onto the school newspaper and
the school radio station, and then chose the very same major.
Professors, I imagine, must have wondered at either the tenac-
ity that was fueling my fraternal demons, or my stunning lack of
originality.

But it honestly wasn't rivalry that was driving me: It
was veneration. My father tended to take slide pictures in the
1960s and the 1970s, and I have wound up with most of the slide
trays because I live in Vermont and have a barn and an attic.
I have lots of room to store the Kodachrome detritus of my
family's life. Occasionally I will grab one of those trays and flip
through the slides as if they were old baseball cards. Inevitably
I find that the vast majority of the images are of my brother and
me together, and they will all share something I find fascinating:
I am more likely to be looking up at my brother than I am at the
camera. There are slides just like that of me watching him—trying to sense his mood, emulate his demeanor—on beaches in
at least six states, on the steps of museums in Manhattan and
Madrid, and atop massive antique cannons at forts in upstate

New York and Portugal. He seemed to endure the reality that we were dressed in an eerily similar fashion—though it wasn't that my mother was dressing us alike, trying to pretend in some twisted way that we were twins separated by a mere sixty-two months. Rather, it was that I was trying to look like him and he was a good egg who was going to tolerate it. I was, thus, the only second grader at Northeast Elementary School to be wearing Nehru shirts and love beads. He wore a peace medallion and so I would wear one, even if the pendant at the end of the chain was the height and width of my second grade head.

And he had long hair and so, of course, I had long hair. These days, alas, we are both balding—though we have approached the fact we are both hairline-challenged in wildly different ways. I spend shameful amounts of money on haircuts with a stylist who manages to shape the little that's there into something that looks closer to receding than receded. He gives himself a home buzz cut every Saturday morning, and—in my opinion—looks like a freakishly wizened five-year-old from the Eisenhower era.

But my sense is that I learned far more from my brother than I did from most of the grownups around me—which, of course, is one of the gifts of being a younger sibling. We have extra people around us to guide and influence and inspire.

And as a teenager, my brother was more than happy to do all of those things. For a time we lived in a house with a large, finished basement, and with the exception of a small closeted corner that housed a washing machine and a dryer, every single square foot of that basement belonged to my brother and me. On summer nights when we were on school break, we would sleep down there on the dismantled bunk beds that served as two couches by day. The basement had a ping-pong and a pool table and the walls—especially the stairway that led down to it—were decorated with black light posters and the massive black and white personality posters that were hip at the time: Images of W.C. Fields, Steve

McQueen, and Ali MacGraw. Late at night when my brother would return home from a date, he would regale me with stories and opinions in a way that I have since learned is rare for a sixteen-year-old: My brother was more storyteller than surly teen, and when we had finally grown tired—he of talking, me of listening—we would fall asleep on those couches, listening to radio raconteur Jean Shepherd. I don't think I ever felt safer and more secure.

Today, nearly forty years later, it only takes an unexpected reference to Fields or Shepherd or MacGraw to remind me of the contentment I would experience those summer evenings.

And in late August 1968, he was the one who would bring up the riots in the streets of Chicago over dinner and, though he was only in middle school, plant himself in front of the news at six o'clock and watch the chaos there both unfold and be explained. By ninth grade he would be attending anti-war coffeehouses at a nearby church and by tenth he would be standing for hours in anti-war candlelight vigils. His moral compass was accurate—and that may explain both why I found myself emulating him, and why so many of my memories of my childhood begin and end with a war that was incomprehensible to me as a second or third grader. Even now, whenever I watch a portion of a presidential convention, at least once or twice I will recall my brother as a middle school student on the floor in the dark paneled living room of our home, staring intently at the TV screen. At the time I didn't understand what was occurring at the convention, but it mattered to my brother and so I knew that it must be important—and, thus, it should matter to me.

Daniel Menaker

headlock

We were ten and seven years old. We cut the heads off wooden matches with an X-Acto knife, then used wire-cutters to cut off the heads of pins. We pushed the blunt ends of the pins into one end of the decapitated matchsticks. At the other end, we used the knife to make tiny perpendicular slits, and then slid small pieces of paper into the slits, to form fins. The result was tiny missiles with pinpoints that we would hurl at each other, with the Geneva Elementary School Convention that we could aim only for the shoulders down. If the velocity and trajectory were good enough, the little darts could go through clothes and sting the target nicely. Where my brother heard about this weapon I don't know. But when my parents found out about it, they were horrified and shut the game down. Or so they thought. It was too much painful fun to forgo immediately. Anyway, all those dire childhood warnings about having one's eyes put out and falling out of trees and tripping over untied shoelaces: None of those things ever really happen, do they?

My brother, Michael Grace Menaker, died more than forty years ago, on December 10, 1967. He was twenty-nine, I was twenty-six. There were just the two of us. He died from a systemic staphylococcus blood infection—septicemia—in a Brooklyn Hospital after routine surgery to repair a torn knee ligament. I remember that the hospital had low, mean ceilings, and that the neighborhood around it was flat, looked flattened. A doctor friend of our family's performed the surgery. Imagine how he must have felt for the rest of his life. Mike had gotten married a couple of years earlier. (Methycillin, which generally cures septicemia, was put into hospital use less than a year after Mike's death.) He had graduated from Dartmouth and the University of Virginia Law School and was an associate at the New York City law firm of Davis Polk. He and his wife lived in Brooklyn. I was teaching English at Collegiate School, a private school in Manhattan that my mother's brother, Theodore Grace, had attended decades earlier. Uncle Ted also died young, during the Second World War. I was going out with a beautiful dark-haired girl from the South who was in New York studying acting at The Neighborhood Playhouse.

When Mike and I were born, our family lived in Greenwich Village. The first stop was 50½ Barrow Street, right around the corner from the famous bar Chumley's—where, when it was a speakeasy, my handsome, feckless, romantically Marxist Jewish father, Robert Owen Menaker,[1] the son of utopian Russian immigrants, had proposed to my fetching, patrician Protestant mother, Mary Randolph Grace, a Bryn Mawr Classics major and a proofreader at *Fortune* magazine. As my mother at least on the surface shared the "progressive" ideas so widespread among educated people in New York during that era, *Fortune* might seem like a strange place for her to have worked. But Time, Inc. was replete with Socialists then—Dwight MacDonald, J. Kenneth Galbraith, James Agee, Joseph Kastner, Walker Evans, to name a few of the more famous

---

1. My father's mother and father, the children of Orthodox Jews, from Odessa and Vilna, respectively, never married. As radicals, they viewed marriage as a bourgeois institution, one of capitalism's many oppressions. They had seven sons, each—except the first, George—named after Marxists, socialists, etc. William Menaker was William Morris Menaker. Peter Menaker was Peter Lvrov Menaker. Nicholas Menaker was Nicholas Cherneshevsky Menaker. Enge Menaker was Frederick Engels Menaker. Leonard Menaker was Leonard Aveling Menaker. Then came my father, Robert Owen Menaker. Actually, no. My father Robert Owen Menaker followed the first Robert Owen Menaker, who died in early childhood, which was the only reason that my unwed grandparents decided to have another, and final, child. Starting with conception itself, happenstance rules the lives of all of us, in case you didn't know.

ones. Mike and I both went to The Little Red Schoolhouse, on Bleecker Street, whose principal, Randolph Smith, was a person of interest to the House Un-American Activities Committee. We moved next to Horatio Street, and then to 290 West 4th Street. The man who eventually sublet the top floor of that house from us was a Welsh poet and children's book writer named Ruthven Todd. His friend Dylan Thomas came to visit him from time to time. I remember answering the door and thinking how ugly he was—"a boily boy," as he called himself.

As small children, we were always fighting, of course—roughhousing, my parents called it. Mike beat me up a lot—I spent a significant part of my younger years in a headlock—but I was a kind of genius teaser, an unremitting and scathing critic of his asthma and flat feet. This rivalry, tempered somewhat by maturity and a recognition of the strong bond between us, remained in force until he died. And, I am convinced, it had something to do with his death. I don't know if the rivalry was unusually intense, but it was *our* rivalry, and I couldn't imagine any other brothers' competition being fiercer. I took pride in its fierceness, as Mike may have, too. It was like a project of ours—an enterprise that for a long time we felt some obligation to sustain and renew. We were, after all, competing in a great contest for the greatest prize in the history of the world—our mother's attention.[2] But from time to time, I saw protectiveness

---

2. She was a brilliant and beautiful woman, with a husband who, as he often said, felt "inadequate" beside her. Her father was Lee Ashley Grace, a New York City business-man. One of her sisters was the mistress of Arthur Brisbane, a newspaperman who was at one point a likely candidate for the vice-presidency of the United States. My mother's mother was Virginia Fitz Randolph Grace—perhaps not as fancy as it sounds, since "Fitz" often indicates illegitimacy. Anyway, an uncle told me that early in their marriage, my father, who, I learned later, was no stranger to infidelities during his travels to Chile and Brazil, stood up angrily at dinner and said, "I am married to a round-heeled woman!" (He once told a hilarious story about trying to explain to a Brazilian named Felix dos Santos diSilva etc. how it could be that "women" was the plural of "woman.") I think she had an affair with Reginald Marsh, the Ashcan artist and another leftie contributor to *Fortune*.

underneath Mike's bullying, as when I was eleven and a friend and I spent a little too much time in the bathroom together and Mike figured out what was going on in there and put a stop to it.

A black woman from South Carolina, Theareatha Dixon, who lived on Perry Street, took care of Mike and me during the day. She later told me stories of eating clay when she herself was a child. "Pica" is the medical name for this eating disorder, often caused by poor nutrition. "*Pica*" is Latin for magpie. It was, I suppose, entirely random that she ended up looking out for us, but, given my mother's alternating unavailabilities and flirtatiousness with us, it seemed like a fated emotional compensation that she did, and so I say thank God she did. Readie died only a couple of years ago, at the age of ninety-seven, and I stayed close to her until the end. She was diagnosed with diabetes in her sixties, and she watched her diet and weight like a Prussian and had many more good years. When her kidneys finally failed, the doctors said it was the diabetes finally taking its toll, but, I wonder, hopefully, having recently been diagnosed with this nasty condition myself, couldn't it have been simply ninety-seven? Here's how unusual

---

I inherited a watercolor by Marsh of my mother daintily lifting her long dress and wading in the ocean in Point Pleasant, New Jersey, where her family went to a "compound" and Irish nursemaids for the five Grace sisters and their brother, Ted. And when she died, I found at the back of the top shelf of her closet in Nyack a cache of love letters to her from someone else—and I think I know who—which were written in the kind of formal, worshipful romantic language that you don't see much anymore. There was a note under the ribbon that bound them—it said "Please discard." I thought I had followed this request until last summer, when I found them where I had put them, many years before, among a big stack of boxes full of my family's memorabilia in the barn in back of the house in Massachusetts that used to be my uncle's and that is now mine.

Within editorial circles in New York my mother became well-known for her expertise in our language. When I was made a copy editor at *The New Yorker*, Lu Burke, a tough "OKer"—final reader—who had been (at first correctly) skeptical of my prospects in this finicky trade, changed her mind when she heard of my pedigree. She came into my office and said, "You're the son of *Mary Grace*?" Once, when I was sixteen, after that onerous bus ride home from the city, my mother came into the house and said to me and Mike, "I saw two Negro boys at the bus stop and one was on a bicycle and he said to the other one 'Get the fuck up on the bicycle!' I wonder what part of speech 'the fuck' is."

it was to have a nursemaid back then in the Village: Readie told me that once when she was wheeling Mike up Bleecker in a baby carriage, an Italian shopkeeper who often saw them pass by came out of his store and asked her, "How come you iss-a so black and you baby iss-a so white?" During the summertimes, she would take Mike and me up to my uncle's house in New Marlborough, Massachusetts, where we would swim and tromp through the woods and shoot cans and birds with .22 rifles. I learned later that these times were sponsored not only by the threat of polio in the city but by my parents' desire to have and go to parties. One September on Barrow Street, when I was three and we had just arrived back in New York, we noticed that there were footprints on the ceiling in the living room. My father told us they were my mother's, and that at certain moments, especially during a party, she could fly.[3]

---

3. When I told an analyst about this earlier memory, as I recall, he asked me, in his thick Spanish accent, "And why do you suppose this memory has estayed in your memory so vividly?"

"I don't know," I said. "It must have been pretty weird for a three-year-old to see footprints on the ceiling and then be told that his mother could fly."

"Who is this three-year-old you espeak of?"

"Me. What do you mean?"

"Oh, I see—you are Richard Nixon now, referring to yourself in the third person."

"Well, I *was* three, you know—hardly the person I am now. I seem like a stranger to myself at that time."

"But not so much a stranger that you do not remember this incident and claim it as your own, before you then disclaim it grammatically."

"What's your point?"

"Well, there is a reason you recall this with such intensity and then disown it."

"What is it?"

"This is for you to discover, but I will give you a clue. Did women wear eslacks back then?"

"How should I know? I guess not."

"Especially not at a party, eh?"

"I guess not."

"You have now run out of guesses. So how did those footprints appear on the ceiling?"

"They held her upside down."

"Yes, and what was she wearing?"

When we were about four and seven, Readie married the white, Polish handyman, Joseph Rogowski, who worked around my uncle's place during the summers. Joe had lost three fingers to a power saw when he was younger, before we knew him. This was grimly fascinating to a small boy. He is the only person who ever spanked me. He had made some cement for my uncle, in a wheelbarrow, and Mike told me to pour more water in it—to "help" Joe—and I did, thus ruining it. Joe, ignoring my protests of innocence, gave me a spanking and a memorable lesson in the kind of unmete punishment the world sometimes hands out to all of us. He spanked me with his five-fingered hand. Eventually, Readie

---

"I don't know. A dress, a skirt."

"Yes, a dress, an eskirt. And what might happen under these circumstances?"

"___"

"Oh, for the good Christ's sake, I will tell you—you were unconsciously fearful and hopeful then, as you are now, that her dress might have fallen down and people could look at her poosy, which is what you wanted to do too. This is why you packed up your grammar and ran away from it."

This analytic episode occurs to me now because in the same session, connecting one minor enduring memory from the distant past to the more recent major one, my analyst told me that Mike's death was threatening to become a "nuclear integrative fantasy" for me. Nuclear because it was installing itself at the center of my life. Integrative because it created a shape, a terrible and beautiful structure, for everything in my life that came before it and happened afterward. And a fantasy because for reasons of unconscious conflict and patterns, I had imposed its occurrence on many parts of my history upon which it had no rational bearing. He said that Holocaust survivors often presented the strongest examples of this kind of centripetal emotional distortion. ("And who can blame them?" he added.) Their experiences during that time shaped everything that happened to them, not only during the ordeal, but before and after it. No transaction would ever be free of its dark power as long as they lived. When he told me about this, it immediately called to mind a girl I'd flirted with at a bar, The Ninth Circle, in the Village the college summer I worked in the Morgue—as Editorial Reference used to be called—at Time, Inc. She was pretty and nice but seemed somehow dissociated. She excused herself for a few minutes just after we started talking, and the bartender said to me, "Be careful with her—her brother died three years ago, and it seems like it made her really crazy. She comes in here all the time and talks to people about it."

And sure enough, when she came back, she sat down and took out a pen and wrote on a napkin, in very small letters, "My brother died" and gave it to me.

told my parents that she felt she should get married "for the sake of the children." When my mother said, "But you don't have children," Readie was offended and replied, "It's for Mike and Danny."

When I was eleven, my parents could no longer afford the tuition at Little Red and its high school, Elisabeth Irwin. My father did not do well in his business, exporting—brokering construction and plumbing supplies for Latin American hotel projects. It appears that he used his job partly as a cover for missions to South America for the Communist Party of the United States. It couldn't have been anything close to entirely a cover, as his financial disappointments were palpable and cast the whole household into gloom. Deal after deal fell through, and he and my mother argued about the practice of offering kickbacks to try to make them work. In any case, we moved to Nyack, New York, eighteen miles north on the western shore of the Hudson River, and my brother and I went to Nyack Junior-Senior High School. The Thruway had not yet been built, and there were few commuter families in the town. The commute, by bus and then subway, was onerous, I came to understand—often more than an hour and a half in each direction. I don't know how my parents did it day after day. Nyack, up on the hill from the river, had commanding views of the Hudson. There was light industry there, a large black population, and there were a lot of Italian-American families as well. The fancy part was North Broadway and Upper Nyack, where Helen Hayes had a house, and where the Nyack Field Club, a sort of sweet, pale shadow of a real country club, was to be found. There was also a sprinkling of writers and artists—Carson McCullers lived near our house in South Nyack. It was democratic, eclectic. The father of my senior-year girlfriend drove the bus my parents took to the George Washington Bridge bus terminal.

Mainly, for me and Mike, there was school and sports and friends and Fifties clothes, like white bucks and Argyle socks and white shirts and khakis and at one point chartreuse shoelaces, and for the girls sack dresses, girdles, crinolines, white blouses, and circle pins, and romances and soccer and baseball practice and loud-muffler cars that broke down all the time and "marriage manuals" left in the bookshelves for adolescents to read—I recall that after a paragraph of anatomically specific description of intercourse, the manual in our bookshelves said "the act is perfectly normal, natural, and right"—and endless pickup basketball games in the freezing cold, when your hands would start out like slabs of ice and magically end up as warm as you would want, and the mesmerizing Army-McCarthy hearings on television sets that still had test patterns in the mornings and summer jobs as park attendants and toll-takers on the Thruway when it was finally built and the blunt truths, for middle-class white kids, of "race music" and then the rest of early rock and roll. (We knew what was there all along, but we hadn't really heard it given voice before, except, in our case, when we were small, in the Village, by Leadbelly.) Mike was "one of the boys"—despite the fact that he had no nickname. His friends all did. Snooky, Big Ghoul, Sonny, Weasel, Gooch, etc. (My friends in high school were Roach, Sleepy, Pappy, Owl, Buffer, Gigi, Goo-Goo, Geetch. I was Schnoz. Guess why. My nose grew so fast that I dreamed once that I was a fish, because their eyes are on either side of their snouts. The girls didn't have nicknames.) And Mike was a cool guy. Six-feet-two, black hair, white teeth, handsome, smart. On the swimming team. Despite his asthma, he worked construction one summer—he was a hod carrier—and at the end of August he was Mediterraneanly tan and had put on twenty pounds of muscle. He had good girl friends—one especially good one thought I was cute and kissed me—and he drank as much as he should have, as much as we all did, with our class rings turned around to look to bartenders like wedding bands, we hoped, hilariously. The drinking age was eighteen, and kids from neighboring New Jersey, where it was twenty-one, would come across the state line to drink and get in fights with us.

I tended to be anxious and timid, especially outside familiar circumstances—I ascribe this (and diabetes) at least partly to having been very sick as an infant and having been taken to the hospital basically given up for dead, thin as a skeleton, according to Readie, and unable to take nutrition for almost a month. Mike took care of that timidity, too, once we got to Nyack. He made me go out for sports by not allowing me in the house after school. He taught me how to drive and he generally saw to it that I "fit in." He still made terrific fun of me. My hair was thick and, to my shame, curly verging on kinky, and I was always trying to make it be straight, with the aid of Brylcreem or Vitalis. Once, I was going with him somewhere in his '49 Plymouth with Duotone mufflers and I asked him to wait because I had to comb my hair. "Your what?" he said. And from then on, to him, my hair was my what. But I often got the better of him in the taunting that went on between us—I was quicker and sharper with words. I set the record for insult devastation when, after he had punched me in the arm, leaving it close to paralyzed, and called me a "blivet" for taking a long time in the shower, I looked at him, with his towel wrapped around his waist and said, "At least I don't have Jewish nipples." He looked down at his chest with concern and went to find our mother to ask her if what I had said was true.

Mike was always telling me, as I trailed three grades behind him, how much harder school would be the next year. He warned me about Miss Nutt [sic], the geometry teacher equal in dryness and severity to her subject. He warned me about Mr. Beninati, the tyrant of trigonometry. He warned me about Dr. Roody, the Senior English teacher who never gave anyone an A—and who when I got into her class pointed out in front of the class how sad it was that I didn't get quickly enough the religious connotation of the word "grace." But I kept on outdoing him. So then he disdained me as an "intellectual," even though I was also a better athlete than he was—which also made him jealous. But I could tell that he was also proud of me as a student and an athlete—again that kernel of love inside the hard shell of rivalry—especially after I got to college, and my striving was not only to compete with him but to please him. His opinion of me meant more than anyone else's. I want to emphasize that even though younger brothers often idealize their older brothers, Mike still seems to me to have been more idealizable than most. He was admired and praised in high school and at Dartmouth, he was rushed by Alpha Delta Phi, the crazy and wonderful fraternity that became the basis for the movie *Animal House*, and was beloved by his other brothers as well. Chris Miller, who wrote the screenplay for *Animal House*, was a Dartmouth freshman the year after Mike graduated. I actually knew some of the real-life people whose nicknames the movie used—Otter and Flounder, for example. In fact there was a room under the attic stairs in Nyack that my mother named Flounder's Room, because Flounder (the late Nick Fate; I wished at the time that that were my name), being far from his home in Oklahoma, often slept off some of his holiday drunks right there. My girlfriends always but always fell in love with Mike. He was smooth, funny, relaxed. Mike did finally achieve a nickname in Dartmouth—Ted, coincidentally enough. I forget how it worked, but it somehow derived from the fact of his being a suave, cool fellow. It might have started with Little Richard's song "Ready Teddy." He was also called Twigs because, for all his stature, his calves were thin. The shower room originates many insults and subsequent nicknames.

As we got older, he and I talked to each other a lot about sex and other basic matters. He told me about resorting one night, in the absence of something more appropriate, to bacon grease. I told him about sleeping with a girl who, once she was interested and involved in what was going on, could have an orgasm from simply being ordered emphatically enough to have one. He told me about a prostitute he had unwittingly picked up in Copenhagen who was obsessed with Buddy Holly and, to his shock, gave him a squirting demonstration of lactation. On long-distance car trips we wouldn't stop to use gas-station bathrooms but piss in the beer cans we had just emptied—and then marvel at how hot piss is. We spoke flatulence as a second language. For all these and other Minor League transgressions and delinquencies, at Dartmouth, where he careened around the northeast on "road trips" to women's colleges, betting his life against alcohol and sleep, Mike became politically and socially more and more conservative. I think this shift was in reaction to our family's radical background and as a result of hanging around with kids far richer than we were. He wanted us to put "estate lights" around the house in Nyack and was embarrassed that the windows in the house didn't have beautiful curtains. In law school and for a little while afterward, he supported the Vietnam War, which made me and my parents both angry and sad. Before he died, however, he had changed his mind, no doubt partly because of his wife's strong views about the issue. He seemed generally to be headed toward the liberal fold—the fold into which most children of the mid-century Socialists and Communists my family knew herded themselves.

And he began to grow up. Law school made him more studious and serious. He got serious about the girlfriend who ended up his wife—and widow—and never told intimate stories about her. Well, maybe a little, at the start, before he knew they were going to get serious. "A really nice rack." He began to criticize my immaturities, which were many, in a more sober way. When he got to Davis Polk, courtesy of a U. Va. law professor who took a liking to him and overlooked his not quite stellar grades, he found the work almost overwhelmingly difficult and told me glumly that he didn't think he would be made a partner there. He started to show the weight of adulthood, in other words, and in doing so once again showed me the way. I didn't like the way and resisted it—I didn't want to have any part of this weightiness. I wanted my summers off (as a teacher), my work hours limited, my personal life "free." And I wanted Mike to be my brother as he always had been, when we were kids and teenagers and undergraduates. I wanted time to stop for us. I was jealous of his relationship with his wife.

I thought I was losing him, and in a way I was. Surely we would have gone on to have a strong revised relationship, but I didn't know that at the time. He may not have thought of it this way, but he was trying to help me end my childhood. He succeeded, ultimately, but in a way so cruel to me and my family that I think the worst villain would not have willed it to happen.

To this day, as I've said, I can't help thinking that our old competitiveness and my resentment of Mike's new life played a part in his death. It was Thanksgiving of 1967, and we were playing touch football before dinner with some Grace cousins from Boston—two sons of the late Ted Grace, as it happened—on the front lawn of the house in Nyack. It was a pure fall day, with the Hudson all blue and white, the tree branches honest-looking in their bareness, and the air clean and clear. Mike's wife and my girlfriend were standing on the sidelines. Before the game started, I tried to tease him about something, and when he didn't respond, I got him around the waist and tried to wrestle him to the ground. He shook me off crossly and said, "Why don't you grow up?" I was embarrassed and angry.

The game began, with us against the Graces. Because he had bad knees and had already had surgery on one of them, Mike played the more static lineman position and I played backfield. Still consciously smarting from his scolding, I finally said, "I'm tired! You play backfield for once." Mike said, "You know I can't— I don't want to hurt my knee." I said, "Your precious knees will be fine." He said OK. On the very first play, he jumped to try to knock down a pass and came down with one of his legs all twisted up. It buckled beneath him and he tore a knee ligament badly. He was not only furious at me but immediately depressed, almost as if he knew that this would have a dire consequence, and his wife glared at me. I was covered with remorse and shame, and I apologized to them. Mike hobbled through the rest of the holiday, had his surgery in the first week of December, and died.

Before the funeral, Mike's friends from Dartmouth came to Nyack to pay their respects. Dave Hiley, Alex Summer, the

Good McCarthy, the Bad McCarthy, Arnie Sigler, Otter, Roger Zissu. Seeing these young men was unbearable. They cast their eyes down, didn't know how to act, what to say—how could they? As was only fitting, they had had no occasion to learn comportment for such a disaster. And they couldn't help it, but they fairly *glowed* with energy and youth. I remember stretching my arm out as Dave Hiley approached me in the backyard and putting my hand on his shoulder, to keep him away, to draw him close, to keep myself from falling to the ground in grief. The funeral, conducted by my sister-in-law's uncle, the Reverend Frank Sayer, Dean of the Washington National Cathedral, took place in an Episcopal church in Manhattan, Mike's Jewish nipples notwithstanding. Everyone there—and there were hundreds and hundreds—looked sick and white, as if some terrible epidemic had struck them.

In my social life, when I tell people about this event in detail—as I've done seldom and do now only when the conversation makes doing so unavoidable—they tend to wince when they hear that I told my brother to take that small, front-yard-touch-football risk. As if they themselves had been hurt and as if they sensed how deeply I had wounded myself. Because look—I know it's true that I didn't take a vial of staph bacteria and pour it into the incision during surgery, and I know that the accident's outcome was violently random and arbitrary, and I know that we all tend to take on responsibility for things we aren't responsible for. But on the other hand, try telling me that there's no chance that my brother would be alive today if I hadn't done what I did. Try not to grimace when you think of the causal chain that led to my brother's organs shutting down one after another way out in Brooklyn, where there weren't even any tall buildings to confer some metropolitan grandeur on his death.

That challenge isn't as bitter as it sounds. I really *was* still just a kid then, I realize. My son, William Michael Grace Menaker (a name I could and probably would now forbear from giving him), is twenty-five, and in our culture, for better or for worse, that is so touchingly young, especially for boys. And after decades of hard psychological work and simply getting on with things, I've forgiven myself. I understand that what all of us have chosen to do, particularly in our youth, is surely what we were going to do. Mature people may have more to answer for, seems to me—at least to ourselves, and if that's the case, then I certainly do. But still, the past is always the definition of inevitability, isn't it? And as the years have gone by and the emotional bones broken in me by Mike's death have knitted, I've come to understand and appreciate not only what I lost in this catastrophe but what I found. I'm good at consoling others, for one thing. And not a small thing, especially recently, in my fifties and sixties, as the casualties of ordinary life have begun to mount among family and friends. Petty reversals, my own or others', remain more or less where they should among my concerns—in the mind's out-of-town self-storage unit. No, I haven't taken the screens down yet, but hey, there's Darfur, and plus my brother died. I think I respond far more deeply to art, music, and literature because of the lesson in life's fragility I unwillingly learned forty years ago. And as my parents' only child, I assumed and carried out a kind of lonely responsibility toward them, especially as they got older.

And there's this: About ten years after Mike died, it began to dawn on me that his death would ultimately leave me in much better financial shape than I probably would have been if he had lived—my parents' modest estate (mainly the house in Nyack) undivided, my uncle's house and land in the country similarly wholly mine. This came as an almost overnight surprise to me, I'm ashamed to be proud to say—it had never once entered my mind before then—and it made me feel good and awful at the same time. Good for obvious reasons of decent character. Bad because it meant I'd won the battle between us. Somewhere in my baleful id, I'd killed him. I had vanquished him from the field, and the spoils were all mine. And the only thing worse on a primal human level than Oedipal defeat is Oedipal victory.

This one, especially in combination with earlier family dynam-ics, has made emotional closeness difficult for me for forty years now. Somewhere in the dark within, I'm afraid I will prove lethal again to someone I love, and this leads me often to turn away at an angle—often an angle with humor or irony at its point—when people try to get close to me.

But then there's this: Literally this. It allowed me to write. It compelled me to write. For five or six months, I was so paralyzed by sorrow and dismay that it was all I could do simply to func-tion. To go back to Collegiate and teach. To try to figure out how to talk to my parents. To learn how to be an unnatural only child. To brush off kind inquiries from colleagues and students, for fear that if I gave into what pressed down on me so hard, I would never get up. And then out of desperation I wrote a story based on what had happened. And then came more writing—because much as I disliked the actual work of writing, it settled me, made me feel as though I might be able to get hold myself, maybe ultimately answer for the damage done, as nothing else could. I suppose this goes in the plus column, too.[4]

---

4. I've written two stories based on this subject. I wrote the first one, "Grief," about a dream I had about Mike coming back to Nyack for a ghostly visit, a few months before I started working at The New Yorker as a fact checker, in January of 1969. It was turned down and I put it aside. I revised it, submitted it again, and this time it was published. After I was made an editor, in 1976, I wrote another, far more developed story, called "Brothers," and it, too, was turned down. My assistant at the time surreptitiously showed me the written "opinions" on the story from my colleagues and from William Shawn, the magazine's editor then. She asked me if I wanted to see them, because she thought an injustice had been done and I should know about it, but I said no. So she slipped them into the pages of a submission she gave me to read, and there they were. "Just another hospital story," said my fellow–fiction editor Veronica Geng, and Shawn agreed, as he almost always did with Veronica. At the time, I interpreted this reaction as competitive jealousy on her part—one of the themes of the story itself. The marvelous quarterly called Grand Street published the piece not much later.

I hope that three proves a grim charm. I intend this essay to be the last napkin I write on about my brother's death.

But finally there's this: Would I give back every sentence, every lesson learned, every bit of wisdom, every gram of sympathy for others, every sensitivity, every penny, every square inch of real estate to be instead whoever the person would have been who would now be watching Mike just after he turned seventy, still trailing three years behind him? Instead of adding year after year to my unnatural seniority over him? Instead of coming around the bend of the year and into the fall with the usual vestigial schoolboy's summer's-end sadness so uniquely sharpened? Instead of living in the shadow of an alternative unlived life? You tell me.

Pete Hamill

a drinking life

My brother Denis was a wonderfully sweet kid, with big liquid brown eyes, broad shoulders, a wild sense of humor, and an original way of looking at the world. Once, when he was seven and struggling with the mysteries of the Catholic catechism, he was walking with my mother and embarked on a heavy theological discussion.

Mom, he said, is God everywhere?

Yes, Denis, she said. God is everywhere.

Is he in the sky?

Yes, he's in the sky.

Is he in the street?

Yes, Denis, he's in the street.

Is he in the park?

Yes, he's in the park.

Mom?

Yes?

Is he up my ass?

My mother burst into laughter.

By the time he was ten, in 1962, Denis had begun to see me as a kind of father, although I was only the big brother who had lived elsewhere for all of his young life. I didn't mind the role; I was probably a better father to Denis than I was to be a husband to Ramona. Around this time, my father had entered a crabbed, unhappy middle age; there was never enough money and always too much drinking. He beat the kids when they annoyed him or when he thought they weren't doing homework or were talking in too heavy a Brooklyn accent. Tommy was now grown up and gone and Kathleen had a group of girlfriends from school. My father didn't bother either of them. But the smaller boys were always in trouble with him, Denis most of all.

It was no surprise that Denis often turned to me for guidance and male kindness. He was an erratic student, and an unruly street kid, but in his school compositions, he showed hilarious gifts for narrative. His spelling was often atrocious. But he could easily tell a story. I started helping him, showing him ways to develop stories, correcting his spelling, giving him books to read. When Ramona and I took our first small apartment near Prospect Park, he dropped by all the time, glad to run errands, to read some of my books, to talk about movies or comics. Ramona said she didn't mind his unannounced arrivals; she thought he was cute. I took him with me a few times to the newspaper or to the Gramercy Gym to see the fighters. One of those fighters was now my brother Brian, who at fifteen weighed about ninety pounds and was boxing in amateur tournaments, watched over by Jose and other professionals. He had a ferocious left hook, a good chin, and a cocky style. Denis would get excited when he saw Brian sparring, upset if Brian got hit, cheering when Brian was punching; he hated to leave the place. My brother John never came to the gym. He was only a year older than Denis, a fine student with a sweet good heart. But he was shy and self-contained where Denis was direct. If Denis wanted to go with me to a gym, he asked. If he wanted to stay at my house, wherever it was at the time, he said so. John never asked.

One summer afternoon, Denis got into a fight outside at the YMCA, his opponent whipped out a knife and stabbed him in the stomach. He was rushed to Methodist Hospital, where he almost died. I arrived at the hospital after he came out of the operation. His voice was weak and his lustrous brown eyes were full of fear.

Am I gonna die, Pete?

No, you're gonna be all right. The doctors said so.

I don't want to die.

You won't.

You won't let me die, will you?

The doctors won't let you die, Denis. You'll have a pretty funny looking scar, maybe, but you won't die.

I don't want you to die either, he said.

Okay, pal.

Be careful, all right, Pete?

Whatever you say, Denis.

I don't want anyone to die, he said, his voice drowsy.

David Sedaris

you can't kill the rooster

When I was young, my father was transferred and our family moved from western New York state to Raleigh, North Carolina. IBM had relocated a great many northerners and, together, we made relentless fun of our neighbors and their poky, backward way of life. Rumors circulated that natives ran stills out of their tool sheds and referred to their house cats as "good eatin'." Our parents coached us to never use the titles "ma'am" or "sir" when speaking to a teacher or shopkeeper. Tobacco was acceptable in the form of a cigarette, but should any of us experiment with plug or snuff, we would be automatically disinherited. Mountain Dew was prohibited and our speech was monitored for the slightest hint of a Raleigh accent. Use the phrase "y'all" and, before you knew it, you'd find yourself in a haystack French-kissing an underage goat. Along with grits and hush puppies, the abbreviated form of "you all" was a dangerous step on an insidious path leading straight to the doors of the Baptist Church.

We might not have been the wealthiest people in town, but at least we weren't one of *them*.

Our family remained free from outside influence until 1968 when my mother gave birth to my brother, Paul, a North Carolina native who has grown to become my father's best ally and worst nightmare. Here was a child who, by the time he had reached second grade, spoke much like the toothless fishermen casting their nets into Albemarle Sound. This is the thirty-year-old son who phones his father to say, "Motherfucker, I ain't seen pussy in so long I'd throw stones at it."

My brother's voice, like my own, is high-pitched and girlish. Telephone solicitors frequently ask to speak to our husbands, and room service operators appease us by saying, "That shouldn't take more than fifteen minutes, Mrs. Sedaris." The Raleigh accent is soft and beautifully cadenced, but my brother's is a more complex hybrid, informed by his professional relationships with marble-mouthed, deep-country laborers and his unabiding love of hard-core rap music. He talks so fast that you find yourself concentrating on the gist of his message rather than trying to decipher the actual words. It's like speaking to a foreigner and understanding only the terms *motherfucker, bitch,* and *hoss,* and the phrase, "You can't kill the Rooster."

"The Rooster" is what Paul calls himself when he's feeling threatened. Asked how he came up with that name, he says only, "Certain motherfuckers think they can fuck with my shit, but you can't kill the Rooster. You might can fuck him up sometimes, but, bitch, nobody kills the motherfucking Rooster. You know what I'm saying?"

It often seems that my brother and I were raised in two completely different households. He's eleven years younger than I am, and by the time he reached high school, the rest of us had all left home. When I was young, we weren't allowed to say "Shut up," but by the time Paul reached his teens, it had become acceptable to shout, "Shut your motherfucking mouth." The drug laws had changed as well. "No pot smoking" became "No pot smoking in the house," before it finally petered out to "Please don't smoke any pot in the living room."

My mother was, for the most part, delighted with my brother and regarded him with the bemused curiosity of a brood hen discovering she has hatched a completely different species. "I think it was very nice of Paul to give me this vase," she once said, arranging a fistful of wildflowers into the skull-shaped bong my brother had left on the dining-room table. "It's nontraditional, but that's the Rooster's way. He's a free spirit, and we're lucky to have him."

Like everyone else in our suburban neighborhood, we were raised to meet a certain standard. My father had dreams of me becoming a great athlete and attending an Ivy League college. While I was happy to bottle and diaper my first football, I had no interest in actually throwing the thing. My grades were average at best, and eventually I learned to live with my father's disappointment. Fortunately, there were six of us children and it was easy to get lost in the crowd. My sisters and I managed to sneak beneath the wire of his expectations, but I worried about my brother, who was seen as the family's last hope.

From the age of ten, Paul was dressed in Brooks Brothers suits and tiny clip-on red ties. He endured soccer camps, church-sponsored basketball tournaments, and after-school sessions with well-meaning tutors who would politely change the subject when asked about the Rooster's chances of getting into Yale or Princeton. Fast and well-coordinated, Paul never minded sports just so long as he was either stoned or winning. School failed to interest him on any level, and he considered it an accomplishment to receive an occasional D-minus. His response to my father's impossible endless demands has, over time, become something of a mantra. Short and sweet, repeated at a fever pitch, it goes simply, "Fuck it," or, on one of his more articulate days, "Fuck it, motherfucker. That shit don't mean fuck to me."

My brother politely ma'ams and sirs all strangers but refers to friends and family, his father included, as either bitch or motherfucker. Friends are appalled at the way he speaks to his only remaining parent. The two of them recently visited my sister Amy and me in New York City, and we celebrated with a dinner party. When my father complained about his aching feet, the Rooster set down his two-liter Mountain Dew and removed a fistful of prime rib from his mouth, saying, "Bitch you need to have them ugly-ass bunions shaved down is what you need to do. But you can't do shit about it tonight, so lighten up, motherfucker."

All eyes went to my father, who chuckled, saying only, "I guess you have a point."

A stranger might reasonably interpret my brother's language as a lack of respect and view my father's response as a kind of shameful surrender. This, though, would be missing the subtle beauty of their relationship.

My father is the type who will recite a bawdy limerick by saying, "'A woman I know who's quite blunt/Had a bear-trap installed in her . . .' oh, you know. It's a base, vernacular term for the female genitalia." He can absolutely kill a joke. When pushed to his limit, this is a man who shouts the word, "Fudge!" and sometimes follows it with a shake of his fist and a hearty, "G.D. you!" I've never heard him curse, yet he and my brother seem to have found a common language that eludes the rest of us.

My father likes to talk about money. Spending it doesn't interest him, especially when it comes to tipping. He prefers money as a concept, something that, if invested with care, will mature at 6.6 percent inoculated rate of fiduciary-based annuity. Something like that. I can drink eighteen cups of coffee and still collapse into sleep at first mention of the word dividend. Still, though, I make an effort to listen to him, if only because it seems like the polite thing to do. When my father talks finance to my brother, Paul says, "Fuck the stock talk, hoss, you're wearing me out." This rarely ends the scheduled lecture, but my brother wins bonus points for boldly voicing his disinterest, just as my father would do were someone to corner him to talk about Buddhism or the return of the clog. The two of them are unapologetically blunt. It's a quality my father admires so much that he's able to ignore the foul language completely. "That Paul," he says, "now *there's* a guy who knows how to get his point across."

When words fail him, the Rooster has been known to communicate with his fists, which, though quick and solid, are no larger than a couple of tangerines. At five feet four, he's shorter than I am, stocky, but not exactly intimidating. I last saw my brother at Christmas, when he arrived at my older sister's house with a black eye. There had been some encounter at a bar, but the details were sketchy.

"Some motherfucker told me to get the fuck out of his motherfucking face, so I said, 'Chill, motherfucker.'"

"Then what?"

"Then he turned away and I reached up and punched him in the back of his motherfucking neck."

"What happened next?"

"What the fuck you think happened, bitch? I ran like hell, and the motherfucker caught up with me in the parking lot. He was all beefy and shit. The motherfucker had a taste for blood, and he just pummeled my ass."

"When did he stop?"

My brother drummed his fingers on the tabletop for a few moments before saying, "I'm guessing he stopped when he was fucking finished."

The physical pain had passed, but it bothered him that his face was "all lopsided and shit for the fucking holidays." That said, he retreated to the bathroom with my sister Amy's makeup kit and returned to the table with *two* black eyes, the second drawn on with mascara. This seemed to please him, and he wore his matching bruises for the rest of the evening.

"Did you get a load of that fake black eye?" my father asked, struggling for a positive spin. "That guy ought to do makeup for the movies. I'm telling you, the kid's a real artist!"

Unlike the rest of us, the Rooster has always enjoyed my father's support and encouragement. With the dreams of Princeton officially dead and buried, he sent my brother to technical school, hoping he might express an interest in computers. Three weeks into the semester, Paul dropped out, and my father, convinced that his lawn-mowing skills bordered on genius, set him up in the landscaping business. "I've seen him in action and what he does is establish a pattern and really tackle it!"

When the landscaping business failed, my father suggested careers in television repair, stand-up comedy, and, eventually, professional tennis. "I taped that Wimbledon match and I think that, once you put a racket in a kid's hands, the guy will go absolutely bananas. He's got the temperament for it, now all he needs are a couple of lessons."

Eventually, my brother fell into the floor-sanding business. It's hard work, but he enjoys the gratification that comes with a well-finished rec room. He thoughtfully named his company Silly P's Hardwood Floors. When my father suggested that the word *silly* might frighten away the upper-tier customers, Paul thought of changing the name to "Silly Fucking P's Hardwood Floors." The work puts him in contact with plumbers and dry-wallers from such towns as Bunn and Clayton, men who offer dating advice such as, "If she's old enough to bleed, she's old enough to breed" and "If there's grass on the field, I say it's time to play ball."

"Oh Paul," my father says. "Those aren't the sort of people you need to be associating with. If you want to better yourself, you need to spend more time with someone who can read or at least get through a single sentence without spitting."

After all these years, our father has never understood that we, his children, tend to gravitate toward the very people he's spent his life warning us about. Most of us have left town, but my brother remains in Raleigh. He was there when my mother died and, six years later, continues to help my father grieve. "The past is gone, hoss. What you need now is some mother-fucking pussy." While my sisters and I offer our sympathy long distance, Paul is the one who arrives at our father's house on Thanksgiving Day, offering to prepare traditional Greek dishes to the best of his ability. It is a fact that he once made a tray of spanakopita using Pam rather than melted butter. Still, though, at least he tries.

When a recent hurricane damaged my father's house, my brother rushed over with a gas grill, three coolers full of beer, and a traditional "Fuck-It Bucket"—a plastic pail filled with jawbreakers and bite-sized candy bars. ("When shit brings you down, you just say 'Fuck it' and eat yourself some motherfucking candy.") There was no electricity for close to a week. The yard was practically cleared of trees, and rain fell through the dozens of holes torn into the roof. "Shitting in the woods gets old pretty fucking fast," Paul said. "We're living like pioneers, all crusty and shit." It was a difficult time, but the two of them stuck it out, my brother placing his small, scarred hand on my father's shoulder to say, "Bitch, I'm here to tell you that it's going to be all right. We'll get through this shit, motherfucker, just you wait."

Geoffrey Wolff

heavy lifting

On the hot, breathless, fragrant afternoon of my graduation from college it seemed that everything good was not merely latent but unavoidable, folded and in the bag. I'd worked like a Turk those past years, and my labors had been rewarded and then some with fancy Latin on my fancy diploma, *summa* it said and summit I believed. Not one but two ex-girlfriends had come to the ceremony in front of lovely tree-shaded Nassau Hall, and so resolutely happy was I that it didn't even stain my pride to sweat through my shirt and gray worsted suit, to be capped like a monkey in tasseled mortarboard.

Each of my exes had brought me the same gift, a suitcase. It almost occurred to me that unarticulated longings were expressed by these mementos, and coming to them for visits wouldn't have answered their prayers. Sending me off solo on a long voyage would have been in the ballpark, adiós was more like it.

And that too was as I wished it! All was a-okay, on the come and coming! Admitted, I had no money, but a job was waiting nigh September, far, far away, teaching in Turkey, which was even farther from my father in California than I was now in the Garden State, and the further the better. The last time I had intersected with him, two years before, he had swept through Princeton in a car sought for repossession, charging clothes and books and jazz records to my accounts. My stepmother, having just left him again and for good, gave me unwelcome word of him a year later; he was in Redondo Beach, in trouble.

For me, that June, what was trouble? A college friend with a different kind of daddy, the kind who owned a 50-foot paid-for ketch, had invited me to spend the summer with him on that boat in New England, sailing that *Sea Witch* from snug harbor to snug harbor, cleaning and polishing and varnishing, making the boat ready for his parents' pleasure if they wanted to come aboard.

Now, a few days after graduation, we were embarked, tugging at anchor off Cuttyhunk, drinking a rum drink to celebrate our third day at sea. There were four of us, two happy couples laughing and watching sun fall, when my father got through on the radio-telephone. Remembering that conversation decades later I feel foggy dread, as though I've sailed on a cloudless day through deep clear water bang onto a reef. It's the nature of a radio-telephone conversation that everyone aboard can hear it, not to mention anyone else aboard any vessel within miles who wants to listen in.

My father stuttered furiously. He did everything flamboyantly, but his stuttering was grandiose. Moreover, he couldn't get the hang of the turn-and-turn-about of a radio conversation, in which one either speaks or listens. Listening was not my dad's thing, so I heard myself shouting at him, and worse I heard myself stammering back, so that it must have seemed I was mocking the poor fellow, when in fact I was falling into the speech defect I had inherited from him—nature or nurture, who cares?

While my friends, helplessly obliged to eavesdrop, pretended to have a conversation in the cockpit, I was below, where it was dark and close. I stretched the mike on its snaky cord as far from my friends as possible, but the loudspeaker stayed put, broadcasting his invitation:

My father wanted me to come to him for the summer, in La Jolla.

I said I wouldn't.

My father said he missed me.

I said nothing.

My father tried to tell me he had a j-j-j-job.

I said, really, how nice. (I thought, what a piquant notion, my dad working for a living.)

My father said congratulations on the degree.

I wondered how he'd guessed I had one.

He said congratulations on the job in Turkey, did I remember he'd lived there once upon a time?

I said I remembered.

He asked did I have a "popsie" aboard with me?

I reddened; it was quiet in the cockpit; I said I had to get off now, this was too complicated.

He said my brother was coming to La Jolla to visit from Washington state. Learned boy that I was, I didn't believe my father. I hadn't seen Toby for seven years.

My father said it again, my only sibling was right now on the road from Concrete, Washington, arriving in a couple of days.

I listened to static while gentle waves slapped the *Sea Witch*.

He said he'd send airfare.

I said sure. I thought fat chance.

I borrowed ticket money from the yachtsman dad and hopped a Trailway in New York. This would be the place to detail the squalor of a cross-country summer bus journey from the noxious flats of Jersey to the uncompromising wasteland of Death Valley— you know the drill, you've ridden a bus. Assume I was sad, hungry and as funky as everyone else aboard our land-yacht. I kept busy asking myself: *How had this happened to me? Why was I here?*

You might think—noticing the books I was conspicuously reading and annotating, and I'm afraid you were meant to notice them—that the question *why was I here?* was a Big Question and that I was questing for a vision from Sophocles, Erich Auerbach, Sartre, George Steiner. Boy oh boy, you think you know your aliens! I felt so apart from my fellow-passengers that I believed I needed a visa to visit Earth. But at some point west of Gila Bend and east of El Centro, with the air conditioning on the blink again, I commenced to reflect on the situation of La Jolla— seaside, wasn't it? Even a martyr might steal time off for a swim.

Hedonism, taking care of fun before taking care of business, was a legacy from my father. For this he had been thrown out of one boarding school after another. For this he had also been thrown out of two colleges, neither of which, despite his testimony to the contrary, were ancient universities. For buying what he could not afford—sports cars and sports coats, Patek-Philippe wristwatches, dinners at Mike Romanoff's and 21, Leicas and Bolexes, Holland & Holland shotguns—he'd been fired from jobs. These jobs as an airplane designer he had conned his way into with faked-up résumés. Getting fired would put him in a bad mood, so he'd buy more stuff; buying stuff intoxicated him, and so did booze. Drunk, he'd turn on his first wife, my mother and Toby's. After fourteen years of this, she told Dad to get lost, and I moved in with him. When I was seventeen, his second wife—her fortune and good mood seriously depressed by my old man—took the first of several hikes on him, and then he took one on me. In the Wolff nuclear family, fission was the rage.

Dad met me at the same bus station where he'd met Toby more than a week earlier. Visiting San Diego years later I was hard-pressed to find any site downtown as melodramatically seedy as my memory of that place, a set dressed with tattoo parlors, bucket-of-blood bars, pawnshops and, under the hard light of noon, my dad looking bewildered and lost. I had for many childhood years loved him recklessly. Spare any father such impulsive love as I showered on that man. Later, disabused, when I imagined that I understood Duke Wolff for what he really was—a deadbeat bullshit artist with a veneer of charm rubbed right through from negligent over-exercise—I hated him, and like the love before it, that hate too was exorbitant.

This June afternoon outside the bus depot, examining my father blinking behind the thick lenses of owlish Goldwater eyeglasses, I was too wary to indulge contempt. The spectacles, out of register with Duke's formerly stylish presentations, were the least of it. Even at his lowest he'd enjoyed flamboyant temperamental resources: spritz and nonchalance. Now he seemed timid, dulled. What I was seeing lumbering toward me was a polyester jacket. This wasn't what I'd have expected: seersucker, maybe, or the soiled white linen suit that Sydney Greenstreet might sport—tits-up in the tropics and all that—but not this rag that needed a cleaning the day it was sold, tarted up with cheapjack brass crested buttons. Halting toward me was a zombie. Duke Wolff looked as though he'd been shot smack in the heart with about 500cc of thorazine. Talk about taking the edge off! He looked like they'd sawed through his brain.

My brother Toby, days shy of sixteen, was with him, hanging back, vigilant. I felt like someone to whom something bad would soon happen; Toby looked like someone to whom it had already happened. This was the more alarming because he looked so wakeful and sharp. He had a strong, bony face, with steady eyes and a jutting chin. He didn't appear vulnerable; he gave an impression of competence, but after all, he was a kid.

Though I hadn't seen Toby during the past seven years, we'd recently been in touch by telephone and letter, and I knew that he'd had a hard time with his awful stepfather. Coming across the country I'd phoned from a roadside diner to tell Duke which bus to meet and I'd reached Toby. He didn't know where our father had disappeared to. No sooner had Toby arrived than Dad had taken off with a woman friend in a fancy Italian car. He had left his son with some canned soup and a vague assurance that he'd return to La Jolla in a few days.

Behind the wheel of the rented Pontiac, driving to La Jolla, Duke was stiff and tentative. I remembered him as a bold driver, fast and cocksure, every little journey to the grocery store a double-clutching adventure in squealing tires. Now Dad held to the slow lane, glancing anxiously in the rear-view. His face had once been imposing, Mussolini-monumental; now his nose was bulbous, stippled with burst blood vessels. The few times he spoke, I saw that his false teeth, what he used to call China clippers, were loose against his gums. I had questions: Where had he gone, leaving Toby alone? How could he take time off from his job? Asking this question, I might have given the impression that I didn't believe he had a job. How soon could he give me cash (I came down hard on *cash*, to distinguish it from a check, or an I.O.U.) to repay my yachtsman classmate's daddy? These questions immediately returned us to our fundamental relationship: I was the hectoring (and mind-dullingly dull) parent; Duke was the irresponsible (and charmingly fun-loving) kid. The exchange didn't leave much for Toby to do, except sit in the back seat and study his fingers.

Duke was miserly with basic information—what exactly he did for a living, where he had gone "in the desert" (as he put it) or why. But as we approached La Jolla he became effusive about his "lady friend." This conversation had the effect of making Toby visibly uncomfortable, inasmuch as it had been my father's ambition, declared explicitly to Toby, to re-up with our mom if everything this summer went swimmingly, as of course it must. This nutty scheme had a certain appeal to my mother, who had a lifelong weakness for nutty schemes. Her marriage to her second husband, like her marriage to Duke before that, was a disaster, and Duke after all did live in southern California, and my mom, freezing up near the Canadian border, had always had, as she put it, "sand between my toes." But even for this quixotic woman it was on hold as far as a re-enrollment in Dad's program was concerned, waiting to get a report card from Toby on Duke's attendance and comportment.

When we rolled up in front of a tiny La Jolla bungalow, my befuddlement increased. The woman who greeted us, as warily as Toby and I greeted her, was nothing like my father's type. He was drawn to pale-faces, to blue eyes, to understated clothes. This woman was sunburnt brown, her leathery skin set off with much jangly jewelry. She wore, for God's sake, cowgirl boots ornamented with horsehair.

We stood beside the car shaking her turquoised ringed hands and listening to her bracelets ring like chimes; we admired her cactus garden; she got to listen to my father—and not, I suspected, for the first time—inflate my achievements at college and Toby's in high school; she didn't invite Toby or me inside. She didn't invite Dad inside either, but it was clear that inside was where he was going, and without his only children. He gave us rudimentary instructions to "my flat near the beach." Toby, as eager as I to escape, assured me he knew the way. Duke said he'd be along soon, he'd bring home a nice supper. I asked how he'd get home from there, and he waved vaguely, mumbled "taxi." His lady friend seemed as unhappy as a person can be without flooding the earth with tears. Duke, by contrast, had abruptly come awake to joy; he was full of beans.

"Don't you two rascals go getting in t-t-t-trouble," he warned. "And if the manager badgers you about the rent, tell her to go f-f-f-f . . ."

"Go f-f-fish," I s-s-s-said.

Driving south through the attractive neighborhoods to our little second-floor studio apartment on Playa del Sur, fifty yards from the beach, I was mostly preoccupied with Toby, glad for the chance to be alone with him. He too relaxed, lit a Lucky Strike expertly with his lighter, inhaled intemperately, remarked that it had been an oddball visit so far. I asked him to steer while I lit a Camel expertly with my lighter, inhaled intemperately, and warned him that smoking was bad for his wind, especially if he planned to make a name for himself playing football at the Hill School back in Pennsylvania, where he was beginning on full scholarship in September.

My avuncular manner surprised me. I prided myself on being a laissez-faire kind of guy, I'll look out for me, you look out for you. Maybe I was practicing to become a teacher. Maybe I was out of my depth.

I unpacked my worldly goods—mostly books, a few jazz LPs (Bessie Smith, Bud Powell, Miles Davis) I carried with me everywhere—and Toby offered to show me the beach. This generosity was all Wolff—sharing the good news, keeping alert to fun. By then it was late afternoon, and I worried that Dad might come home to an empty apartment, but Toby argued soberly that he didn't imagine Duke would be rushing home from his friend's house. I saw the wisdom in this hunch.

And so, dressed in long trousers and boat shoes and a white Lacoste tennis shirt, I accompanied Toby across Vista del Mar and Neptune Place to the Pump House, and down concrete steps to the beach. The first things I noticed were not the bitchin sets of waves breaking way offshore, nor the surfers paddling way out there waiting to ride, nor the surfers with lots of white hair waxing their boards near the water's edge. I noticed, of course, the babes, and so did Toby.

"Hubba hubba," he said with reassuring irony.

So we sat for a long time on a couple of hand towels, talking about the future, with our eyes cocked on the very here and now, avoiding the subject of our father. Toby was witty, resourceful, a hit parade of corny songs, which he was willing to sing out loud: "On the Wings of a Dove" and "Calendar Girl." He could do Chuck Berry's "Sweet Little Sixteen" and Hank Williams—"Hey, hey good lookin', whatcha got cookin', howsabout cookin' something up with me?" He could do a Jimmie Rodgers yodel in caricature of a locomotive whistle, and he knew the gospel classic "The Old Rugged Cross." He did tenor lead, I did baritone. The dynamite chicks stared frankly at us and our noise, with what I misimagined that afternoon was interest.

It didn't get dark till nine or so. We waited. The landlord came asking for rent. He was kind, pretended to believe that we didn't know where our old man could be found. He said it had gone on too long now, that Duke was months behind, that he had no choice. . . .

"Do what you have to do," I said, thinking about a sailboat waiting for me back east.

"Such a shame," he sighed, "a man of his attainments, with his education!"

"Uh-huh," I said.

When the landlord left, Toby said, "Tell me something. Did Dad really go to Yale?"

"What do you think?"

"So that would pretty much rule out his graduate degree from the Sorbonne?"

Toby's always been a quick study.

Sometime after midnight we quit talking, stopped listening to my jazz records and Dad's Django Reinhardt and Joe Venuti. We'd eaten a couple of cans of Dinty Moore stew, knocked back some Canadian Club we'd found on a high shelf of the mostly bare cupboard. We'd each asked aloud where the other thought Duke might be. We'd wondered aloud whether we should look for him, but I was sure he was drunk, and he was a mean drunk, and I didn't want to find him. I didn't trust myself to keep my hands to myself while he sat on the edge of his bed in his boxers, snarling about how ungrateful I was, how grievously I had kicked him in the ass when he was down: *You're a real pisser, aren't you?* I'd heard it; I didn't think I could sit through it again, especially if it came to be Toby's turn.

A couple of hours before dawn his lady friend phoned. She was shouting, said she didn't know what to do, he wouldn't leave, wouldn't move, wouldn't speak. He'd rock back and forth weeping.

"You've got to get him out of here. I can't take this. What if my husband comes snooping around?"

So I phoned the police. By the time Toby and I got there, the police had called for an ambulance. Dad was breathing, but save for the technicality of being alive, he was gone from this world. His lady friend too said, as so many ex-bosses, ex-friends, ex-wives, creditors, teachers, doctors, parole officers before and after had said, *A man with his educational attainments, what a pity!*

They checked him into Scripps Memorial Hospital. The police had investigated his wallet and he had Blue Cross. Now *this* was a shock, because he had Blue Cross owing to the fact that he also had a job! Just as he'd said. He worked for General Dynamics, Astronautics division. By sunup I knew this, and knew as well that he was catatonic, and roughly what catatonia was. He would be removed that afternoon to a "more appropriate facility," and I could guess what that would be. As obdurately as my heart had hardened, I heard myself telling the doctor to tell Dad his sons were behind him all the way. Toby nodded.

"Well," the doctor said, "he has said a few words. He keeps asking for a woman who lives in town. Could you help out with this, maybe let her know he wants to see her?"

"No," I said.

That morning I worked out a deal with the landlord. On principle he wouldn't let us stay in the apartment on which so much rent was due, but he'd let me lease, in my name, an identical unit down the exterior hall, same monthly rent but this time he required an up-front security deposit, first and last month in cash or by cashier's check by the end of business tomorrow.

I borrowed it from a classmate, the roommate of the son of the yachtsman dad from whom I'd borrowed my bus fare. My classmate friend cabled the money from New York that afternoon, and that night Toby and I moved our father's entirely unpaid-for worldly goods to our new residence.

Drunk on resourcefulness, I bought a car and found a job the very next day. The car caught my eye on the lot of Balboa Auto Sales. I'm confident of the name of the dealer because I still have a copy of my stiff reply from Istanbul to a bill collector in San Diego, begging for the final $150 of the $300 purchase price on a '52 Ford convertible, cream, with torn red vinyl upholstery and bald whitewall tires and an appetite for oil that gave my jaunty wreck a range of about three miles between lube-stops, which made the drive to Tijuana, a popular excursion in the coming weeks, a hardship that only the señoritas of the rowdier cantinas could ameliorate. Ask Toby: he was in charge of oil changing.

The job was easier to cop than the automobile. I simply went to Dad's employer, on the theory that they needed
to replace him, and offered my services. A few weeks ago in
Princeton, getting my diploma, I'd suspected life was going to
go smoothly for me, but this . . . *this* was silky! To build rockets
during the age of the putative missile gap the government had
contracted with General Dynamics Astronautics to supply Atlas
ICBMs at cost-plus. Now cost-plus, I don't have to tell you, is
one sweet deal. The greater the cost, the greater the plus, so
personnel basically threw money at me when I walked through
its door with a bachelor's degree in English Literature. Every
time I opened my mouth to mention courses I'd taken—history,
American civilization, Spanish—they tossed in another jackpot,
so that by day's end I was an engineering writer for more than
eight hundred a month with an advance from the credit union
and a complete understanding of how my father had found a job
with these cheerful jokers.

Dad was embalmed in a private asylum down in Chula
Vista, not much of a detour from my weekend line of march
to Tijuana. Toby and I were permitted to visit only on
Saturdays, which suited my schedule fine, and when we visited he behaved like a simulacrum of his old self. He seemed
oblivious to any inconvenience he might have caused his
sons, made no mention of the carnage of Toby's first week
in La Jolla. Quotidian challenges were beneath his notice:
whether he'd lost his job (he had), by what transport we'd
conveyed ourselves to our audience with him (he did fret
about a car "I had to desert in the desert," a play on words
that amused him so exceedingly that he neglected the situation's starker implication, soon enough to weigh heavily on
him). He was busy with workshop therapy, making a leather
portfolio into which he burned my initials. This was a difficult gift to receive, and to recollect.

Not least because it fell into a category of assets—personalized
keepsakes—that opened a painful fissure between Toby and me.

One thing, and it was a *thing*, was uppermost on my father's mind when my brother and I visited his asylum in Chula Vista. This was a silver cigarette lighter inscribed to him in London after the Blitz by friends in the RAF when he was in England on behalf of North American to deliver P-51 Mustangs. He wanted that lighter; jeepers, did he ever *desire* that silver lighter! He decided that we had lost it during our move from one apartment to another. Oh, was he disappointed! Why didn't we just run back to La Jolla and find it, "chop-chop"?

It's amazing what kids—even kids as old as I was then, old enough to buy a car on the installment plan and to sign a lease— will accept as the way of the world. I don't mean merely that kids are subject to arbitrary tyrannies, though they are; I mean that until I had sons I never really understood how emotionally derelict my father was. I judged the cost of his selfishness on an empirical scale, by the measurable havoc he inflicted on me. It wasn't till I had sons that I began to understand that such lunatic solipsism as Duke's shook the rudiments of his sons' worlds.

How else explain us searching together the fifty-foot walkway connecting those two apartments, as well as the shrubs below that walkway, as well as our new apartment? What warped sense of duty provoked us to knock on the door of the new tenants' apartment during the dinner hour to persuade them that we needed to search every inch of their abode for a lost cigarette lighter? And failing to find it, to phone the car rental company, the very company that was seeking payment from our father, to ask if a silver cigarette lighter had been found in one of their Pontiacs?

I think now, considering my own dear sons, beginning at last to fathom how difficult it is to be anyone's son, that our father drove us insane that summer.

My life with Toby seemed on the surface, subtracting weekend visits to the loony bin in Chula Vista and the brothels of Tijuana, workaday. After staring at my pencils and at my colleagues staring at their pencils for six of the eight hours I "worked" in a hangar, the Ford would stumble up the coast to La Jolla, trailing cloud-banks of exhaust, a whole weather system. I drove with the torn top up to shelter myself from the black fog that swirled around me when I was stopped in traffic.

But there I go, getting gothic on you. At day's end there was home, simple but clean. And the beach. Ah, Windansea! Remember my first visit there, my eyes as big as plates, those surfer chicks? Well, I hadn't completed my second walk from the Pump House south toward Big Rock Reef when a teen approached me.

"Hey!" she said. Her toenails were painted vivid red. Her hair was . . . guess what color. She was . . . (Did you guess pretty?)

I cradled my paperback. "Hey, yourself," I came back.

"You from around here?" she asked.

I chuckled. "No. No, not at all, just visiting on my way to Istanbul."

"Is that on the beach?" (No, of course she didn't ask that. There's no call to get snotty here, just because I was about to have my heart broken.) "Huh?" (*That's* what she said.)

"Are you from around here?" was my trenchant rejoinder.

She was, she said, she was. And her business with me was to invite me to a keg party that night down in Pacific Beach. She was glad I could make it. We'd have a lot of fun. Was I sure I had the address written down? She checked what I'd written on the title page of Camus' *The Stranger*.

"Thing is, me and my friends need some cash to front the keg."

Thing was, I didn't have any cash in my bathing suit. Could I bring it when I came? No? Okay, hang on, don't go anywhere, I'll just run home and get it, which I did. She was waiting by a VW van, pretty much holding her pretty hand out.

I don't have to tell you how the party went. What party, eh? What Surf Boulevard in Pacific Beach?

Seven years later, reading Tom Wolfe's title essay in *The Pump House Gang*, I felt a full flush of shame rise from my toes. The keg scam was a chestnut among the surfers and surfer-babes at Windansea. But that was the least of my mortification there. Frank laughter was the worst of it. Back home at the Jersey shore or on the beach at Watch Hill, blinking contemplatively behind my ground-breaking round, silver-framed glasses (so far ahead of the curve that the nickname "granny glasses" hadn't yet been invented), in my navy polo shirt to hide my chubby tits, in my Brooks Brothers madras bathing costume, by George I was a stud muffin! Here, carrying a Great Book past those hep long-boarders in their nut-hugger nylon suits with competition stripes, I was a freaking joke!

So where, during these humiliating hours after work, was Toby? Safe inside, at his books, writing essays I assigned him. It took him a while to forgive me for practicing my apprentice teaching skills on him. To prepare him for the exactions of a classical education at the Hill School, I obliged him to do a day's work while I did a day's work, to read a book a day and write an essay every week: "Blindness and Insight in *King Lear* and the *Oedipus Tyrannus*"; "The Boundaries of Sea and River: Liberty and Bondage in *Moby Dick* and *Huckleberry Finn*." I guess what I knew best came in pairs. It was crazy the hoops I made my beleaguered, injured, perplexed little brother jump through. He wrote them; he was a better reader and writer for them. But I was a tin-pot despot, as arbitrary in my edicts as Duke sending us on a treasure hunt for his fire-stick. No wonder Toby stole from his father and lied to me.

Did you guess he'd had the sacred lighter all along? Used it to spark up that Lucky during our ride in the Pontiac from the leathery, jangly lady's bungalow to Dad's sea-near studio apartment.

He slept on a pull-out sofa-bed in our one-roomer, and mid-August, when the alarm clock woke me for work, I saw the stupid, pretty thing on the floor beneath his blue jeans. In the sullen light of dawn, I made out an inscription engraved on it. My father's initials in elegant Sans Serif. No RAF boys, of course, but another name for sure, a new engraving, *TOBY*. I remembered the hours we'd spent together hunting for that goddamned thing, Toby's helpful suggestions where next to search: the beach, Dad's suit pockets, maybe it had fallen out of Dad's trouser pocket into one of the shoes in his closet?

That morning was awful, and I want to pull a curtain across it. Duke was coming "home" from Chula Vista that afternoon; I was meant to pick him up after work. I didn't know what we'd all do, where we'd live, how we'd sit together in a room, how we'd look at one another, what in the world we were supposed to do now. What I knew for sure: Toby hated us both, his father and his brother. I knew why he hated the one, but not the other. Now I think I know all I'll ever know about that aspect of that summer, and all I want to say to Toby is, Forgive me. Even though he has pardoned me, and himself, just this last time, I'm sorry.

I fetched Duke; he raged at Toby. We sent my brother home to my mother on a bus. As bad as it was between my father and me, after Toby left it got worse. My father wasn't allowed to drink—all that medication—but of course he drank. How many days did the nightmare last? Few, I think. He tried to talk me into staying with him instead of going to Turkey. I managed not to laugh in his face.

Then Duke got himself arrested in San Diego. For a wonder, he wasn't drunk. He was buying breakfast food at a late-hours store and he'd made a U-turn in my Ford. He'd stuttered when the policeman stopped him. They took him downtown. It went hard on him. Before the police turned him loose, they "checked with Sacramento." Back came a complicated story. It went very hard on him, grand theft auto for the Abarth-Allemagne roadster in the desert, burned and sand-blasted by a desert storm. My father wanted me to go bail for him, but he wouldn't promise to show up in court. I didn't go bail; I went to Istanbul.

Then was then. Now, reading this, I feel jumpy again after many years of enjoying a warm embrace of resignation. That's okay. These shifts aren't spurious, I believe. Family stories are always fluid, and to be emotionally exact is to be inconsistent. Toby and I have talked a lot about this. We've talked a lot about a lot. I love listening to Toby talk, which is my way of saying I love my brother.

Tobias Wolff

a brother's story

When men talk about their brothers, the stories are too often regretful, and sometimes bitter; youthful rivalry persisting unabated into later years, with no end in sight; resentments over the treatment of a wife; the exploitation of a parent's unequal affection; a loan gone bad; feuds so old their causes are forgotten, or too painful to speak of. It is a bitter thing to be divided from your brother. All that makes for closeness, when it goes wrong, also makes for suspicion and rancor. I have a brother myself, and I know how easily things can go wrong. We weren't always as careful as we should have been, Geoffrey and I. We tried each other, naturally. So it's in gratitude, not in pride, that I look back and see that between us things did not go wrong, and that the very moments when our brotherhood was most in danger have become our redemption narratives—the grenade that didn't go off, the flood that never quite reached the rooftop, the terrible crash we walked away from.

This is the story of one of those crashes.

When I was fifteen I took a greyhound from Seattle to La Jolla to spend the summer with my father and brother. This was June, 1961. I hadn't seen my father since 1954, and didn't recognize him when he finally showed up, alone, two hours later, to pluck me from the crowd of sailors and grifters and dirty old men cruising the bus station. His face was bloated and jowly. He was driving a green sports car. He'd been drinking and was nervous with me, and as we drove away from the station he said he wanted to stop by his fiancée's. *Fiancée?* I was whipped—it was well after midnight—but he insisted. The house was dark when we arrived, and my father had to lean on the bell before she came to the door in her bathrobe and let us in. The next day they made it up, and the day after that the two of them headed off to Las Vegas.

May I say that I was a little confused? The idea, as I'd understood it from my father's phone calls, was that he and Geoffrey and I would join up and have some fun together until I left for boarding school in the fall. My brother was the big draw. We hadn't laid eyes on each other in seven years, but we'd exchanged letters and stories, and he'd guided me through my applications for a scholarship to prep school. I was sharply disappointed not to find him in La Jolla when I arrived, and now my father was gone too.

He came back from Vegas a week later minus the sports car—which he'd burned up in the desert—on the outs with his fiancée and about to lose his job at Convair Astronautics for missing work. It became clear to me that I didn't know the man and couldn't count on him. He was hitting the sauce. Sober, he was good company. Drunk, he turned ugly and raged against those who'd disappointed him—my God, who hadn't? This went on night after night. And then my brother arrived.

I will never forget the sight of Geoffrey stepping down off that bus. He wore a rumpled seersucker suit. He looked bone-tired and needed a shave. Though I spotted him right off, he was not the boy I'd known, not the boy I thought of when I wrote my letters and when I said, testing the words, not quite believing them, "My brother . . ." He was twenty-three now, a college graduate. He had the aspect of a man on his own in a foreign country, a cultivated detachment that struck me even then as literary, and romantic. But when he came up to me and shook my hand, I saw in his face the plain wish for friendship, and I could have wept with relief.

My father hit bottom that night. He'd gone out to buy us some steaks and never returned. Geoffrey and I were wakened by a call from his fiancée. It turned out he'd been at her place, where he'd suffered a complete breakdown, speechlessness, paralysis, the works. The police got involved and found a number of warrants for his arrest—speeding, bad checks, grand-theft auto. . . . It turned out that one of the bad checks was for the sports car he'd destroyed. They took him "downtown" but he was obviously *non compos mentis*, so justice deferred to compassion and he was forwarded to Buena Vista Sanitarium, where he was to remain for most of the summer.

Mind you, this all happens on the very night Geoffrey pulls into town. Within hours. And I thought *I* was disappointed!

This is Geoffrey's situation. He has just graduated from Princeton, no mean feat considering he's had to come up with the money himself since the end of his first year there, when my father split from his rich wife and she stopped coughing up the tuition. Geoffrey had sweated his way through, with a good boost from his earnings at poker, and still managed to distinguish himself as a young critic and earn the favor of teachers like Richard Blackmur, Walt Litz, George Steiner.

Graduating *summa cum laude*, he's been offered a teaching job at Robert College in Istanbul, and with that prospect he had mapped out a pretty agreeable summer for himself, sailing the New England coast with a buddy (on the buddy's father's yacht) while preparing his lectures for the coming semester. What dreams he must have had—college friends greeting him in every port with foaming magnums of bubbly, girls swooning to his understated tales of life on the deep, then back to the swelling canvas and the heavy, beautiful books.

Then the old man (Geoffrey's name for him, henceforth mine) calls him, just before he sets sail, and issues a summons to La Jolla for the summer. Hah! Fat chance. The last time they were together was when the old man sold a collection of Revere silver he'd stolen from his wife to pay Geoffrey some dough he owed him, so Geoffrey wasn't inclined. Then the old man played his trump. Toby will be here, he said.

Now why that should have been a strong card is almost beyond me. Geoffrey was a young man. I was still a kid. We'd never been very close, not even before our parents took us to opposite ends of the country eleven years back. Lately there'd been some warmth between us through the mail, but come on. The sailboat. The friends. The rolling seas and creak of the stays, the Shakespeare and Marlowe and Auden and Johnson and James. . . .

Toby will be here, the man said. Okay, Geoffrey said, and said good-bye to his shipmate, and rode the hound across the country.

It doesn't make sense. For years I've wondered at his decision, wondered most of all if I'd have done the same thing in his place. He knew the old man well enough to figure that the plan wouldn't hold up; that there'd be a mess to deal with soon enough (though he couldn't have guessed how soon). Aside from the sailing, he had a pile of work to get done before September. There was no profit for him in this move, no benefit that I can imagine save one, the satisfaction of the desire to know and befriend his brother. I can imagine it because I felt it myself. But it didn't cost me anything and it cost him plenty.

Here he is, then, in a strange town with a brother he barely knows. The support he's been promised will not be forthcoming. The landlord has served notice of eviction for non-payment of rent—several months' worth. So what can Geoffrey do? He can send the kid back to Washington State and hop another bus going east. That's the obvious choice. But again, he does it the hard way. First he goes out to Convair Astronautics and gets himself a job turning technical manuals into English, the same job the old man had; maybe that's why there was an opening. Then he buys a car. Then he finds us another apartment and puts me in a serious schedule of reading and writing. In short, he becomes the father in this family.

Why? It wasn't for the pleasure of my company. I was ignorant and lazy, magnificently unprepared for the rigors of the school I'd be going to. I meant well, in a non-committal way, but I had crooked habits, not unlike the old man's, and these soon made themselves evident in ways that challenged Geoffrey's good will and still give me shame to recall. And yet I imagine that he stayed on not in spite of these deficits of mine, but partly because of them, seeing how much help I needed if I was to survive, let alone prosper, in the new life ahead of me.

Every three or four days I had to produce an essay on an assigned text. I liked to read, but these books, his treasures, were new to me. Greek plays, essays by Camus, novels by Fitzgerald and Faulkner. King Lear. The essay topics might sound a little funny now, highly serious, even owlish, and touching in Geoffrey's ambition for me, but they forced me to think about metaphor, and ambiguity, and language as an end in itself. This concern with language extended to the spoken word. He taught me to say "get" instead of "git," and that the final participial "g" is *not* silent. There were questions of style to be addressed: it seemed that where I was going, boys did not wear their hair swept back into DAs; they did not wear blue jeans low on their hips or belt buckles to the side, or roll packs of Kools into the sleeves of their T-shirts. I caught his love of jazz and jokes and—alas for me—unfiltered Camels. In return I taught him the songs of Hank Williams, whose oeuvre I had by heart.

On Sundays we drove all over creation to get to the sanitarium, where the old man had set himself up as lord of the resident ironists who believed themselves to be more sane than their doctors. He always had a circle of them around him in the lounge when we came to visit, nodding agreement as he ridiculed the entire head-shrinking enterprise. It wasn't altogether amusing. I could sense that Geoffrey was more worried they'd let the old man out than that they'd keep him in. He had his hands full with work, and paying bills, and dealing with me, and trying, with discouraging results, to steal enough time and clarity of thought to prepare his classes. The strain told, on both of us.

Those few months changed me. Of course I mean something other than the grooming I got, which indeed proved not just valuable but essential. But until that summer I'd never known anyone who lived for ideas and words; to whom writing, his own and others', was not a diversion from life but an imperative form of life. Ever since I was eleven or twelve I'd written tales of mystery and horror and adventure, and had notions of being an "author," but after that summer I never really wanted to be anything else. Week after week of breathing the incense of respect for sentences and stories helped bring me to the judgment, right or wrong, that there was no better way to spend my life than in making them. Maybe I would have been a writer anyway. Who knows what he'd have done but for this or that experience? I do know that my brother's conviction of the supreme value of writing something good helped give my own attempts the character of a quest rather than a career, which was damned lucky for me, because seen as a career it would've been frustrating beyond my power to endure.

So here was a lasting gift my brother fashioned from the wreckage of that summer. But in the end it wasn't his material support or his intentional lessons that meant most to me, or even his vocational inspiration, but the abiding knowledge that I had a brother who would act against his own immediate interest on my behalf, not just on impulse but day after day.

I've never asked Geoffrey exactly why he came, or why he stayed. At the time it didn't occur to me to ask. He was there; that was enough. Later on I tried to imagine the reasons, as I've done here, but still without asking, because what he did had an unconsidered, instinctual quality that shouldn't have to explain itself, and probably couldn't. It runs counter to reason, as the world reasons. It answers only to the economy of brotherhood, whose accounting practices defy and embarrass the world's.

What a shambles of a summer it was, though, and how we love to remember it—the essay topics . . . the golden girls who snubbed us on Wind and Sea Beach . . . the party the old man took us to when he got out, all of the guests fruitcakes he'd known in Buena Vista. . . .

That's one crash we lived to tell about. There were others. But it's time to yield the floor. The good luck of having a brother is partly the luck of having stories to tell.

documents

Poem by Father (1972)

One Sunday morning when I was a boy, my father came out of his office and handed me a poem. It was about a honeybee counseling a flea to flee a doggy and see the sea. The barbiturates my father took to regulate his emotions made him insomniac, and I understood that he'd been awake most of the night, laboring over these lines, listing all the words he could think of ending in a long "e." This meant using many adverbs and the elevated "thee" as a form of address. My father was a professor of finance who wrote fairly dry textbooks, where the prose marched in soldierly fashion across the page, broken by intricate formulas calculating risk and return, and this poem was a somewhat frilly production for him. The poem was an allegory about his desire to leave our family. Like a lot of people, my father felt that a poem was a bunch of words with a tricky meaning deeply buried away, like treasure, below a surface of rhyming sounds. I was twelve years old, and I understood the sense of the poem instantly, but the strange mixture of childish diction and obvious content silenced me. I was ashamed. That Sunday morning, I was sitting on the living-room floor, on a tundra of white carpet that my father considered elegant. The drapes were closed, because he worried that sun would fade the fabric on the furniture, but a bright bar of light cut through a gap in the curtains, and that's where I sat, since it was warm there, in a house where we were otherwise forbidden to adjust the thermostat above sixty-two degrees.

Letter from Younger Brother (1997)

Not long ago, I was in Seattle, sitting in a café downtown. It was raining. I'd been there for sometime before I realized that someone was staring at me through the window. I turned around and saw worn tennis shoes and dirty gray sweats. The man outside the window was my brother Mike. My father had three sons. I'm the eldest; Danny, the youngest, killed himself sixteen years ago.

In addition to the tennis shoes and sweats, Mike was wearing a white T-shirt that hung to his knees and a black leather jacket he'd bought with V.A. money at a thrift store. His thinning hair was soaked, and his face had the pallor of warm cheese. In a plastic sack he carried a carton of cigarettes he'd bought at the Navy PX. He's schizophrenic, and on some level I'm always aware that he's a stranger. I went outside, and we talked and, in talking, we were brothers again. He did not look good; he was shivering. He was several miles from his halfway house, but when I offered to give him a ride he said, quite happily, that he preferred to walk. He started up the hill, limping a little from a pelvic injury he received, years ago, when he tried to kill himself by jumping off the Aurora Bridge, in Seattle. Very soon he was gone.

Only a few years ago, Mike was doing much better, and he wrote letters regularly, often two or three a month. Here is one:

Dear Char,

Mike Here, Who Is There? I Am Fine as a Blade of Grass. How About You?

As I was leaving church the other day there was an opportunity to be part of a poor person's Kriss Kringle. I decided to buy an AIDS patient some high-quality gloves. The situation reminded me of Danny—I don't know why. The gift will be given to him although I believe I will never actually see the recipient. I will give him a card that says, "To a friend I don't know."

I don't think of Danny a lot. I don't feel pain about his death a
lot either. Jesus has stepped into his boots and has replaced him.
It caused me to heal and be born again. It is really quite beautiful. My heart is still with that kid like you cannot believe—or
I suppose you could. Love can play a trick on you. It can cause
you pain like you were suffering in hell, but it is still love and
still beautiful like heaven and the heaven and the hell of it are
woven into one fabric, which is love. It's a mindblower to think
like that but that is what Danny has done to me.

Call or write please.

I don't own a cat or dog—but I do the same by looking at squirrels and crows. I plan to buy some peanuts to feed the squirrels
and bread for the birds. It is so much cheaper and I enjoy it the
same as having my own animal.

When I pray I can see my life flash before my eyes. It is very
beautiful. My life flashes before my eyes about twenty times a
year. Other stuff like that happens to me also.

I've been through so much since becoming mentally ill—most
of it, believe it or not, was good. Because of that I became sort of
an indestructible man.

Love, Mike

Letter from Youngest Brother (November 26, 1986)

My brother Danny wrote his suicide note in my bedroom, and
then, after a caesura that I know exists because he had to put
down the pen in order to pick up the gun, he shot himself: For
some reason, I've always been concerned about the length of the
lapse, whether he reread what he'd written or stared dumbly at
his signature, his name the final piece in a puzzling life he was
about to end, before he pressed the gun to his head and pulled

the trigger. Most suicides go about the last phase of their business in silence and don't leave notes. Death itself is the summary statement, and they step into its embrace hours or days before the barrel is finally raised to the roof of the mouth or the finger-tips last feel the rough metal of the bridge rail. They are dead and then they die. But Danny wrote a note, or not so much a note as an essay, a long document full of self-hatred and sorrow, love and despair, and now I'm glad that I have it, because, this way, we're still engaged in a dialogue. His words are there and so is his hand, a hand I'd held, but, more important, one that left words that, like an artifact, are as real and physical to me as the boy who, at twenty-one, in a November long ago, wrote them.

I read the pages he wrote two or three times a month, often enough so that the words ring like the lines of poems I know well. All the struggle is still there in the headlong sentences that tum-ble toward his signature, in the misspelled words and syntactical errors, in the self-conscious language of a boy starved for love and trying, instead, to live a moment more of pride. The note has the back-and-forth of a debate, of words equally weighed and in bal-ance, of a slightly agonized civility. He says, "I stopped making dreams." He says, "I don't know why I am doing this. I don't want to. I have dreams." He says that there is no God and that God is looking over his shoulder as he writes, making editorial remarks. He says, "I am glorifying myself now I am afraid to stop writing though. I want to keep talking." He says, "I don't know what to say except I am sorry and I love. I love the whole family quite a bit and the terrible . . ." He clearly wants to find a way back, but he can't. He asks that we keep "the way" he died a secret and, as though he were done, signs his name. But on the next page, the last, he again asks that we keep "the way" he died secret, and again he signs his name. Much of the note is printed, and those letters stand upright, but in the end Danny slips permanently into a slop-ing cursive as despair and self-hatred accelerate beyond return, as if he were being pulled down by the dark undercurrent of his life, his last words looping quickly across the page, continuous as breath.

Letters from Eldest Brother (2001)

Two years ago, I moved to Philipsburg, Montana. In the fall, I went for walks and brought home bones. The best bones weren't on trails—deer and moose don't die conveniently—and soon I was wandering so far into the woods that I needed a map and compass to find my way home. When winter came and snow blew into the mountains, burying the bones, I continued to spend my days and often my nights in the woods. I vaguely understood that I was doing this because I could no longer think; I found relief in walking up hills. When the night temperatures dropped below zero, I felt visited by necessity, a baseline purpose, and I walked for miles, my only objective to remain upright, keep moving, preserve warmth. When I was lost, I told myself stories, recounting my survival, implying that I would live and be able to look back at it all. At some point, I realized that I was telling my father these stories.

I decided that I would try corresponding with him. I had built a lean-to at seven thousand feet, and I routinely slept there. In the morning, I warmed myself by a fire and then walked home and began writing. I worked for days, even weeks, on the letters. The last time I'd seen him he made a point of showing me the stains in his bed, on the sheets. He pulled away the blankets, revealing bright-yellow splotches of mustard, red patches of spaghetti sauce, something urinous that had spilled from a carton of take-out Chinese. I'm not sure what he meant to show me, and I'm not sure what saddened me more, this man eating alone in bed, who could not clean up after himself, or this man who needed to share with his son a grotesque failure. My father and I had survived the same wounds. His lost sons were my brothers. I believed we might have something to talk about. I was drawn to the antique idea of a correspondence because it seemed restrained and formal, even ritualized. In Philipsburg, there is no home delivery, and people go to town to pick up mail. I always walked to the post office with my dog, and even that little effort, that mile of dirt road, blowing with dust or running with mud or silent under new snow, made the mail that much more meaningful.

I delayed sending my first letter for several months. My father replied with a long, bulleted outline. I read it bullet by bullet, feeling disoriented, despite the orderly indents and the nesting of what, in outlines, are called "children." After four or five readings, I was able to breathe normally. I reread his outline until I lost its meaning, then got out my colored pens and began highlighting. The bullets and dashes and indentations were like the sleeves and straps and buckles of a straitjacket. I've often thought that the unit of measure that best suits prose is the human breath, but there was no air in my father's sentences; he seemed to be suffocating inside them.

I had made an effort to discuss the events of our past, but he regarded this as a trespass. "When did God empower you," he asked me, "with such omniscient abilities?" His position was truth; mine was not. My letter, he wrote, "is incorrect throughout, is a fictional (Having no foundation in fact, *OED*) version of reality (Reality: The quality of being real or having an actual existence, *OED*)." He was defensive, which I should have anticipated: "After nine years of sixty hour weeks of intensive research, not reading and study, but research, I know I was a terrific dad and terrific husband."

I wrote more letters. His replies were long—seven, eight, nine pages. There were words he couldn't get past. He became obsessed with "boundaries." Boundaries were bad. "Those who set them up," he wrote, "protect the dysfunctionality they see in themselves and seek to foist that malady on others through their boundaries." Boundaries, he wrote, "are the antithesis of meaningful honest relations." Boundaries have no place between a father and his children. Instead, he insisted that the proper word was "relation": "Relation is a mathematical notion which means one-to-one correspondence."

Another time, it was the word "gag." He had used the word, saying that I was prevented from speaking honestly;

I objected; he objected to my objection. "Emphasis on the word, gag, denies the act!!! The gag is the aggressive act. The word gag fits, is proportional to, the act. The gag is the loaded act; the word gag fits the denigrative power of the act. The act, not the word, is aggressive and odious. Place the focus where it belongs, properly, on the aggressive and repugnant act, and not on the word."

Some nights, I dug into the lee of a snowdrift and hollowed a shelter for myself: Snow contains air and insulates, holding the body's warmth so that, at a certain point, the temperature remains constant, blood and ice in equilibrium. In deep snow, I dragged supplies with a pulka I'd made from a child's sled and plastic conduit. I was afraid of avalanches and checked a slope meter before traversing open, treeless hillsides. What I feared was suffocation, particularly the inability to make my chest expand. I really knew nothing about winter, nothing about surviving the season beyond the blunt lesson in fatality I'd learned from picking up bones. Sometimes I slept in the open mouths of mine shafts, their crumbled headframes like broken teeth, where twice I found clusters of bats, hanging by their feet, their wings folded in, like the strange fruits of darkness itself.

I wrote, asking him about our home movies. For years I'd kept alive the fantasy that he burned the movies, only because I was haunted by the image of them orphaned in a Salvation Army thrift shop, reels and reels of birthdays, Christmases, and Easters, all reduced to an ironic treasure for strangers. In the past, I had wanted to believe my father was a liar rather than a man who could destroy something so valuable to his children. The movies were old Super 8s, poorly lit and without sound, but the only place left where I could see my brother's face.

I wrote, "You intentionally destroyed something inside your children, a place of warmth and fondness, a cherished dream, a continuity that connects us in time to our history and across space to one another."

His response was icy: "Of what sense of warmth and fondness are you speaking? It is an interesting sentiment, laced with some romanticism, but devoid of reality." And he wanted to know, "What did I destroy in you that was not already destroyed?"

In my father's last letter, the grammar carries the summary tone of a narrative closing down. It is framed by the forms of family affection. He opens with "Dear Char" and parts with "Love," followed by his signature. In between, the language suggests closure, termination. My previous letter, he says, continued an "unacceptable tenor and dead-end focus." It smacked of "recidivism"; it followed a "desolate and vacuous path." None of my letters "added a repairment," he says. "So be it."

I sometimes wonder if by "repairment" he meant "repayment," and I always pause at the caesura created by the simple sentence "So be it," which Catholic kids were once taught is the meaning of "Amen." Was this the phrase that ran through my brother's mind as he paused between his two signatures? So be it: with these, my father's last words, I know I will never hear from him again. But I save his letters, as I save Danny's, as I save Mike's, neatly bound and held between the Army-surplus boots that my brother died in, and which I keep, filled with rocks, on my desk.

~~~~~~

get away from me

The British Wave hit America in January of 1964, and it funneled ashore, at least on the East Coast, principally through two New York AM radio stations: WMCA, the Good Guys—Joe O'Brien, Harry Harrison, Jack Spector, Gary Stevens, and Dandy Dan Daniels—and WABC with Bruce Morrow, or as he called himself, Cousin Brucie. My brother listened to every one of them. The Beatles' first American single—"I Want to Hold Your Hand," with "I Saw Her Standing There" on the B side—traveled from outside our consciousness to Number 1 in the country in about thirty minutes that month, and my brother had the 45 and was playing it in his room about thirty-five minutes after that. At that point he was twelve, and I was seven. He was not yet entirely withdrawn from socializing—he had one or two good friends who occasionally came over and listened to music with him, or much more rarely, tossed around a baseball or football in the yard—but for the most part I experienced him as a shut door from behind which issued all sorts of excited radio chatter, and music. Certainly the most common conversation I had with my parents in those years involved one of them asking, with an understated and anticipatory dismay, "Where's your brother?" and my having to answer, "In his room."

My brother as a mystery; my brother as a shut door: those are some of the first and primary ways I experienced him, and it always seemed, in that sibling way, that he had a right to erect barriers, and that it was my job to get over them. Whenever I opened his door and wandered in—something I'd do periodically, intrigued by the music or just wanting more access to him—he'd go on with what he was doing for a few minutes as a way of suffering my presence and allowing me what I wanted, before finally asking, "Can I help you?"

Sometimes I'd say no and head back out. At other times I'd sit on his bed and he'd say, "Don't you have something you're supposed to be doing?"

To extend the conversation I'd usually ask a question to which I knew he knew the answer. We'd have exchanges like this:

"What time's Daddy going out?"

"I don't know."

"I thought you said he was going out at ten."

"If you knew that, why're you bothering me?"

That February he turned thirteen. He'd prohibited birthday parties in his honor since he'd been a toddler, but he took his birthday money—probably at that point, twenty or twenty-five dollars from our parents, and another ten from our grandparents—and converted it all into English rock and roll: at 79 cents a pop, probably some forty 45's. That summer I remember he went through a dark period in which he was pretty much *only* in his room listening to music, and I'd come back from the beach or wherever and peer at his door. I made Top Ten lists at my desk of my favorites of his new records and changed them daily. Sometimes I poked his door open because I had to identify a new song, or to ask him how to spell a band like Manfred Mann, but mostly I left him alone. I had my own things going on. But one day I didn't. I missed him. I went up to his door and between songs asked him if he wanted something to eat. He said he didn't. I asked if he wanted something to drink. He said no again.

I listened to a few more songs and then opened his door and wandered in, anyway. In the best of times, these weren't visits he welcomed, and these weren't the best of times, though I wasn't sure why. I stood there, concerned and committed to trying to brazen it out, and he sat with his back to me for as long as he could stand it and then he finally turned around. He looked unhappier than even I would have expected a thirteen-year-old could look.

And while he watched, I started bouncing on one leg, and drawing the other knee up high to my chest, and then bouncing on the other, and doing the same thing.

"What're you doing?" he asked.

"Is this how you do The Pony?" I finally asked back.

He kept looking at me until I stopped. "Get away from me," he said.

As part of their attempt to do as much as they could for him, my parents had taken him out of the local public school and enrolled him in a parochial school—Blessed Sacrament, in Bridgeport—and the latter was one of those nightmares that inner-city parochial schools could be in those days. The nicer nuns hit you with an open hand instead of a fist or an object. Any kind of nonconformity or questioning was evidence that you were a wise guy and looking for some correction. Any kind of levity was evidence of the same thing. It was the kind of place in which detention consisted not of staying after school but coming *back* to the school at 7 AM Saturday morning, to spend the day doing janitorial work: bleaching the sinks, mopping the floors, washing the windows.

To say my brother detested it there really didn't capture the desperation, the extremity, of his misery. My parents had already paid what they thought was a lot of money for this education and were also of the generation that thought you didn't take a kid out of a school just because he said he didn't like it. Who liked anything they were doing?

He made no real friends at Blessed Sacrament and even if he had, he wouldn't have been able to play with them; most of them lived all the way across town. He withdrew more and more. When he finally graduated he was allowed to enroll in our local pit of a public high school—my parents having conceded that maybe parochial school wasn't the thing for him—but arrived at Stratford High just as its administration had decided to draw its line in the sand when it came to the culture wars. My brother by that point had what was called long hair—and by that I mean he looked like Ringo Starr in *A Hard Day's Night,* with bangs that dared to obscure part of his forehead and hair over the tops of his ears—and there was a rule about that at Stratford High. My brother would be told to get his hair cut and would head off to the barbers and instruct them to give him the most infinitesimal of trims. He'd arrive back at school and the principal would say, "I thought I told you to get your hair cut," and my brother would tell him he did. And the principal in retaliation would do things like make my brother stand up in the middle of assembly—this is in a group of three thousand—and show the assembled multitudes his hair. Or, when that didn't work, he would send my brother home in the middle of the day: a five-mile walk.

Eventually my brother dropped out. He refused to get a job, or, rather, he got all sorts of jobs and then quit them. By then he had a supernaturally heightened sense of humiliation, and any kind of remark, however well-meaning—a coworker's question, for example, along the lines of "What's somebody like you doing working here?" would ensure that he never came back.

By this point his frustration level was so high that he had periodic explosions. I knew enough to keep away from him at such times but he was good at baiting me and I was good at baiting him—anyone gets tired of always being the good boy—so I didn't always try. At one point he threw me over a sofa with enough brio that my back impacted the wall. Another time he pitched me down the stairs.

My parents tried group therapy. They tried individual sessions with psychiatrists. They finally enrolled him in what they hoped was an innovative experimental program, but as far as he was concerned, he'd been institutionalized at sixteen. He wasn't released until eight months later. The hospital was Yale-New Haven, a teaching hospital, and they either didn't have much of an idea of what to do with him, or they were totally at a loss, depending on which doctor you talked to. We visited him every week and every week he wept and pleaded with us to take him home. And every week we said no, because the doctors told us he needed to stay. Even as they also were telling us that he was remarkably resistant to any sort of treatment.

Since it *was* a teaching hospital, and nothing was working, and this was the dawn of time, when it came to psychopharmaceuticals, they also tried all sorts of new products on him. Some had humiliating side effects. None of them worked.

He was by then eighteen or nineteen and had, as he liked to put it, his whole fucking life ahead of him.

He moved back home. He still had his music, but he also had his rage with it. He sat up in his room most of the day like an unexploded bomb.

As a family it consumed us, and at the same time we became expert at not talking about it. My parents couldn't bring him up without lashing out at each other—since they'd always had diametrically opposed ideas of what would help, and they each thought that time was wasting—and his still-undiagnosed condition seemed both so ineffable and intractable that none of us knew how to articulate it to anyone outside the family. He always came off sounding either shiftless or oblique.

I traded on stories about him sometimes—sometimes for sympathy, sometimes just for color or the memorable anecdote—but mostly I didn't. In college every so often a casual friend might say, a few months into our acquaintance, that he hadn't realized I had a brother. I'd give him some details and then get to that point of having to decide whether or not to open the whole can of worms. Usually I'd opt for the shorter version.

When I first started seriously writing fiction, he never came up. My first novel, which was directly autobiographical, featured everybody important to my life *except* him. (Though I did give my protagonist a younger sister—instead of an older brother—who displayed some of the same worrisome issues. I liked the notion of putting my protagonist in the position of *greater* potential responsibility, in terms of the need to offer help.) As varied as my fiction got during that period that followed, though, for the next eleven years the one thing that was most consistent about it was its refusal to engage, except in the most oblique ways, the single most fraught aspect of my family's history.

I tried to think of it as an admirable restraint. Some of that restraint, after all, had to do with my desire to protect their privacy. More of it had to do with my fear that I couldn't handle the material. And some had to do with my impatience with certain kinds of autobiographical fiction in general: the way such fiction seemed designed to exonerate, confessing to what we suspected was the lesser crime in order to divert attention from even more massive failures, and offering with a kind of a wheedle a pathetic determinism in the form of past injustices that explained present character flaws.

But I also knew that eventually I would deal with that subject. How could I not? And that the attempt to work through that kind of suffering, on all of our parts, depending on the emotional honesty with which it was approached, could proceed from the exploitative to the redemptive.

And I finally found myself doing so the way my family did everything: through the back door.

My whole life, I've had an obsession with tidal waves. Tidal waves at one point cruised through my dreams on the average of once a month. Tidal waves were a subject I could never turn away from, in books, magazines, or movies. Tidal waves turned out to be, I discovered, a difficult thing to work into serious fiction. I gave it a shot at the end of my third novel, if only in my protagonist's imagination.

But I wanted to write about a real tidal wave. And those of us who *are* obsessive tsunami fanatics prick up our ears at almost any mention of Krakatoa, the volcanic island in Indonesia that annihilated itself so spectacularly in 1883. I mean, come on: three hundred foot waves storming in out of the ash-choked darkness with such appalling majesty that survivors from high ground first registered them as far-off mountain ranges that seemed to be moving towards them? I could see them when

I closed my eyes. I could see them wherever I went. Over the years I read everything I could about what they were like, what they might have been like, what happened on Krakatoa.

And of course I wanted to write fiction about it. Maybe something historical? But I wasn't so far gone that I aspired to a cheesy literary version of *Krakatoa, East of Java*. So I had to ask myself what I asked my students: what about the subject was in any way fraught for me? What about it transcended what would otherwise just be your typical small boy's mesmerized fascination with a particular kind of catastrophe?

It wasn't a question easily answered. But I began to feel as though my brother were somehow involved in the project. Thoughts about one led me to thoughts about the other. Though the metaphoric connections that suggested themselves at first seemed reductive and simplistic.

Then it occurred to me that the link that I was seeking had something to do with that very urge to reduce and simplify causality, when it came to dealing with catastrophe. It occurred to me that looking back over the bombed-out ruins of familial dysfunction might well be analogous to retroactively exploring the causes of the great volcanic eruptions in that almost always, when we're trying to understand human behavior, we're not considering single motives but a constellation of interlocking constellations, in terms of braided event: a situation in which each system conditioned others and was conditioned by them.

The jaw-dropping tsunamis that fanned out from Krakatoa in 1883 turned out to not have been generated by any single geologic factor alone, but a massive interlocking system of events: one that could be picked apart with care and appalled fascination, but also one that would never offer up all of its mysteries.

With that understanding, and with that, then, as a shadowy thematic premise, I had my parallel narrative tracks. My protagonist was a vulcanologist studying the eruption at Krakatoa. His brother was the eruptive event in his own history that so complicated the nature of his curiosity. It only remained for me to make sure that the analogy was an analogy that broke down nearly as often as it proved useful; that it continually complicated itself, and enlarged its implications.

And I was liberated in dramatic and aesthetic terms by reminding myself that fiction didn't necessarily become autobiography because some of its elements—even some of its most crucial elements—were autobiographical. I wasn't engaged in replication but in new construction. William Gass had once suggested in an essay I'd come across that memories were balloons into which the past has been breathed, and that fiction was then the twisting that created balloon animals, of pleasing, or silly, or moving shapes.

And writing as directly as I could about just how searingly agonized my brother had been, and how much I'd felt like I'd let him down, led me to other kinds of solace as well, as one kind of unshelled memory unsheathed another. Examination led me to continual revision of my impressions, the same way walking through this account has allowed me to peep around other corners, and to continue to reeducate myself.

Because it's *not* fair to say, as I did earlier, that my initial experiences of my brother were primarily as enigma or closed door. My earliest memory of him, in fact, is of the way, when I was very small and utterly committed to thumb sucking, he'd catch sight of me doing so, and, unsure of what to do with his excess of some sort of tenderness, he'd rush over to me and cup his hands around my fist, the one connected to the thumb in my mouth, so that we'd be nose to nose. I'd always shake him off with a kind of faux irritation, but I knew how loving a gesture it was, and I cherished it for just that reason.

And when I made those Top Ten lists, and when he wasn't in his dark periods, we'd sit in his room and he'd tease me about how I could possibly have elevated the Dave Clark Five to a spot above the Kinks, or what I was thinking of, putting Herman's Hermits on the list at all. "Hey, it's your record," I would tease him back, and he'd shake his head ruefully in agreement, as if to wonder, the same way I wondered: who knows why he did certain things sometimes.

That first short story that dealt with my brother formed the anchor story for my first collection, and then reappeared in a volume of new and selected stories, and then inspired a third collection which turned out to be about all sorts of brother issues, both wide-ranging and close to home. Has my brother read any of those stories? It's hard to say. I don't ask, and he doesn't volunteer the information. He's now living in my parents' condominium in Florida. I do, though, find copies of my books thumbed-through when I visit him down there. As he's gotten older he seems to have shed those rage issues—as if he'd found a kind of peace with his situation—even if he hasn't gotten any more outgoing in social terms. We talk on the phone, not nearly as often as we should, but often enough to retain the intensities of our bond.

Delmore Schwartz has an understandably famous short story called "In Dreams Begin Responsibilities," which features a young narrator who finds himself in a movie theater watching a silent film of his parents' courtship. The narrator in the act of watching is awakened to himself and to his own unhappiness, as he puts it. He stands, at the moment his father proposes marriage to his mother, and shouts at the screen: "Don't do it! It's not too late to change your minds, both of you. Nothing good will come of it, only remorse, hatred, scandal, and two children whose characters are monstrous." But what's wonderful about Schwartz' story is how clear-eyed it is about its *protagonist's* shortcomings. It *is*, after all, called "In Dreams Begin *Responsibilities*." Those responsibilities we have to those in our lives that we love: if we're lucky we rehearse them on paper. There's so much to overcome, both on the page and off. It's easy to think: where to begin? But I take heart from an analogy of E. L. Doctorow's about the act of faith involved in writing fiction. He once remarked that writing a novel was like driving alone at night: you could only see as far as your headlights. But you could go the whole way like that.

James Hurst

the scarlet ibis

Summer was dead, but autumn had not yet been born when the ibis came to the bleeding tree. It's strange that all this is so clear to me, now that time has had its way. But sometimes (like right now) I sit in the cool green parlor, and I remember Doodle.

Doodle was about the craziest brother a boy ever had. Doodle was born when I was seven and was, from the start, a disappointment. He seemed all head, with a tiny body that was red and shriveled like an old man's. Everybody thought he was going to die.

Daddy had the carpenter build a little coffin, and when he was three months old, Mama and Daddy named him William Armstrong. Such a name sounds good only on a tombstone.

When he crawled on the rug, he crawled backward, as if he were in reverse and couldn't change gears. This made him look like a doodlebug, so I began calling him "Doodle." Renaming my brother was probably the kindest thing I ever did for him, because nobody expects much from someone called Doodle.

Daddy built him a cart and I had to pull him around. If I so much as picked up my hat, he'd start crying to go with me; and Mama would call from wherever she was, "Take Doodle with you."

So I dragged him across the cotton field to share the beauty of Old Woman Swamp. I lifted him out and sat him down in the soft grass. He began to cry.

"What's the matter?"

"It's so pretty, Brother, so pretty."

After that, Doodle and I often went down to Old Woman Swamp.

There is inside me (and with sadness I have seen it in others) a knot of cruelty borne by the stream of love. And at times I was mean to Doodle. One time I showed him his casket, telling him how we all believed he would die. When I made him touch the casket, he screamed. And even when we were outside in the bright sunshine he clung to me, crying, "Don't leave me, Brother! Don't leave me!"

Doodle was five years old when I turned 13. I was embarrassed at having a brother of that age who couldn't walk, so I set out to teach him. We were down in Old Woman Swamp. "I'm going to teach you to walk, Doodle," I said.

"Why?"

"So I won't have to haul you around all the time."

"I can't walk, Brother."

"Who says so?"

"Mama, the doctor—everybody."

"Oh, you can walk." I took him by the arms and stood him up. He collapsed on to the grass like a half-empty flour sack. It was as if his little legs had no bones.

"Don't hurt me, Brother."

"Shut up. I'm not going to hurt you. I'm going to teach you to walk." I heaved him up again, and he collapsed.

"I just can't do it."

"Oh, yes, you can, Doodle. All you got to do is try. Now come on," and I hauled him up once more.

It seemed so hopeless that it's a miracle I didn't give up. But all of us must have something to be proud of, and Doodle had become my something.

Finally one day he stood alone for a few seconds. When he fell, I grabbed him in my arms and hugged him, our laughter ringing through the swamp like a bell. Now we knew it could be done.

We decided not to tell anyone until he was actually walking. At breakfast on our chosen day I brought Doodle to the door in the cart. I helped Doodle up; and when he was standing alone, I let them look. There wasn't a sound as Doodle walked slowly across the room and sat down at the table. Then Mama began to cry and ran over to him, hugging him and kissing him. Daddy hugged him, too. Doodle told them it was I who had taught him to walk, so they wanted to hug me, and I began to cry.

"What are you crying for?" asked Daddy, but I couldn't answer. They didn't know that I did it just for myself, that Doodle walked only because I was ashamed of having a crippled brother.

Within a few months, Doodle had learned to walk well. Since I had succeeded in teaching Doodle to walk, I began to believe in my own infallibility. I decided to teach him to run, to row, to swim, to climb trees, and to fight. Now he, too, believed in me; so, we set a deadline when Doodle could start school.

But Doodle couldn't keep up with the plan. Once, he collapsed on the ground and began to cry.

"Aw, come on, Doodle. You can do it. Do you want to be different from everybody else when you start school?"

"Does that make any difference?"

"It certainly does. Now, come on."

And so we came to those days when summer was dead but autumn had not yet been born. It was Saturday noon, just a few days before the start of school. Daddy, Mama, Doodle, and I were seated at the dining room table, having lunch. Suddenly from out in the yard came a strange croaking noise. Doodle stopped eating. "What's that?" He slipped out into the yard, and looked up into the bleeding tree. "It's a big red bird!"

Mama and Daddy came out. On the topmost branch perched a bird the size of a chicken, with scarlet feathers and long legs.

At that moment, the bird began to flutter. It tumbled down through the bleeding tree and landed at our feet with a thud. Its graceful neck jerked twice and then straightened out, and the bird was still. It lay on the earth like a broken vase of red flowers, and even death could not mar its beauty.

"What is it?" Doodle asked.

"It's a scarlet ibis," Daddy said.

Sadly, we all looked at the bird. How many miles had it traveled to die like this, in our yard, beneath the bleeding tree?

Doodle knelt beside the ibis. "I'm going to bury him."

As soon as I had finished eating, Doodle and I hurried off to Horsehead Landing. It was time for a swimming lesson, but Doodle said he was too tired. When we reached Horsehead landing, lightning was flashing across half the sky, and thunder was drowning out the sound of the sea.

Doodle was both tired and frightened. He slipped on the mud and fell. I helped him up, and he smiled at me ashamedly. He had failed and we both knew it. He would never be like the other boys at school.

We started home, trying to beat the storm. The lightning was near now. The faster I walked, the faster he walked, so I began to run.

The rain came, roaring through the pines. And then, like a bursting Roman candle, a gum tree ahead of us was shattered by a bolt of lightning. When the deafening thunder had died, I heard Doodle cry out, "Brother, Brother, don't leave me! Don't leave me!"

The knowledge that our plans had come to nothing was bitter, and that streak of cruelty within me awakened. I ran as fast as I could, leaving him far behind with a wall of rain dividing us. Soon I could hear his voice no more.

I stopped and waited for Doodle. The sound of rain was everywhere, but the wind had died and it fell straight down like ropes hanging from the sky.

I peered through the downpour, but no one came. Finally I went back and found him huddled beneath a red nightshade bush beside the road. He was sitting on the ground, his face buried in his arms, which were resting on drawn-up knees. "Let's go, Doodle."

He didn't answer so I gently lifted his head. He toppled backward onto the earth. He had been bleeding from the mouth, and his neck and the front of his shirt were stained a brilliant red.

"Doodle, Doodle." There was no answer but the ropy rain. I began to weep, and the tear-blurred vision in red before me looked very familiar. "Doodle!" I screamed above the pounding storm and threw my body to the earth above his. For a long time, it seemed forever, I lay there crying, sheltering my fallen scarlet ibis.

the roberts boys

My mother didn't know she was having twins and went into labor a month early. My father was working in New York as a fledgling publisher of children's books, and when he got the word, he rushed back to our hometown of Bayonne, N.J., just across the Hudson River. Told it would be a while, he went out and stocked up on magazines and pipe tobacco and arrived back at the hospital, ready for a lengthy siege in the waiting room. When he walked through the door—it was February 11, 1943—the doctor delivered the unsettling news. He was already a father. Of two boys. Here's how Mom described the scene in our baby book: "The new Daddy didn't believe it was twins and when Dr. Lipschutz finally convinced him, he went over in a corner and had a good laugh at his own expense (and we do mean 'expense')." As for Mom, when she recovered from the anesthesia enough to hear the news, she murmured, "What a lot of baby," and went back to sleep. My grandmother Miriam dubbed us "the twinnies." I was named for my late grandmother Sadie, my brother Marc for a great uncle, Marcus Rogowsky, a newspaper editor back in Russia who had been liquidated by the Bolsheviks. America was in the middle of a war, we had two uncles in uniform, and our middle names were Victor and Jeffrey, which stood for victory and peace (a rough translation of Jeffrey is "God Peace").

Being a twin is a strange and special way to grow up. You are seldom alone. Most of our baby pictures show us together in a carriage, in a sand box, dumping blocks on the floor. Looking back I think it was a good thing. A twin never labors under the illusion that he or she is the sole center of the universe. In my entire life, I've had my own living quarters for exactly one year. And to this day I can't stand celebrating my birthday alone. I have two nephews with similar birthdays and for years we've had a "three cake" party, where we all join together. And my oldest grandchild, Regan, got herself born on February 11 as well. Obviously a clever child. So even when my twin is not around, I'll always have a birthday buddy.

Sure, there were times when Marc and I hated each other—he split my head open at least twice, once with a dried corncob, once with a board that had a rusty nail protruding from it—but we always had a companion and a playmate. (Although my mother does recall the time we appeared at her feet and proclaimed, "We don't have anybody to play with.") We quickly learned, as all twins do, that acts of mischief that seem impossible for one child can easily be accomplished with some twin teamwork. Since this was during the war, rationing made many foodstuffs hard to get, and Mom had been hoarding packets of Jell-O for a special occasion. She woke up one morning to find that her darling boys had stacked enough chairs or boxes on top of each other to reach the food cabinets, where the Jell-O was stored. Then we had proceeded to empty every single precious packet, dissolve the brightly colored powder in water, and wash it down the drain.

There's another story Mom tells that now holds new meaning for me. We lived on the second floor of a two-family house, but one morning we managed to go down the stairs, open the front door, and toddle up the block. Mom was startled by a call from a neighbor saying, "Dotty, do you know the boys are out on the street?" The new meaning comes from my own twin grandsons, Cal and Jack, who at age two and a half decided they would go looking for Sir Toppenhat, a character who runs a railroad in their favorite series of stories. If they found him, they were convinced, he would give them each a new train. So they went to the front door, put on the only shoes they could manage on their own—red rubber boots—and marched out on their mission. (Cal neglected to put on pants but he remembered the boots.) When my daughter realized what they were up to, she did the only sensible thing—grabbed the movie camera and followed them. Twins will be twins. Watching Cal and Jack grow up has been like watching home movies of my own childhood.

When we were six, something happened that would permanently change our lives. In my memory, I was playing with Marc on the floor of a small cottage we owned in the New Jersey countryside, and he couldn't stand up. In his memory he awoke in the middle of the night with terrible pains in his legs. My folks rushed him to the doctor and the diagnosis was crushing. Polio. He was placed in the isolation ward of a hospital and kept away from us for weeks. Mom came back to the car after leaving Marc and said to Dad, "You give them a child and they give you his clothes." There was only one way we could see him: Nurses held him up to the window, as we stood in the street, and we waved to each other. Marc felt "very lonely and frightened," particularly the day his mattress kept slipping. He rang the call button but no one came. When he tried to fix the problem, he fell out of bed: "I lay there on the floor for a long while screaming."

The illness left Marc with a damaged leg, and Dad with a damaged conscience. He convinced himself that he was at fault, and over the years offered several different explanations for how Marc had contracted the virus: He was playing with a stray kitten, he drank from a public water fountain, he used a public urinal. The day before Marc's symptoms surfaced, we were playing with our neighbors in the country, jumping over a series of low fences they used to train beagles. Dad always wondered whether that vigorous exercise somehow made Marc's case worse. There was little scientific or medical basis for any of his theories, but that didn't matter. He couldn't forgive himself. I didn't know it at the time, but he started drinking and taking antidepressants, an unhealthy combination. Finally his father, my Grandpa Abe, sat him down and shook him up. When we came to America, the father told the son, we had no family here, no friends, no one to turn to. You are blessed, you are surrounded by people who care about you. And be grateful your child is alive.

Dad pulled out of his tailspin, but for both of my parents, the pain of Marc's illness never really went away. A permanent cloud seemed to hover over our country house, which was sold a few years later. "Could you put yourself in that position?" Mom asked me. "Could you imagine how you'd react? It was devastating. We had a beautiful, healthy child—I've never liked to use the word—who turned out to be crippled. It's hard to take, and at his age, the child was defenseless." All true, and understandable. But Marc and I agree that Dad's reaction flowed from an even deeper well of feeling. Dad had always been awkward and unsure around women, he married the only one he ever dated, and now he saw a male child scarred and scared. His own anxieties, long suppressed, stormed to the surface. Dad looked at his son and wondered: Would he ever find a woman who could love him? Would Marc's psyche be stunted along with his leg? Years later, as a teenager, in a great display of courage, Marc ignored his disability and danced on the TV show American Bandstand. Dad could not watch the show, or even talk about it, without weeping.

Once Marc recovered, my parents faced a hard decision: How to treat him. And having a healthy twin brother, living in the same room, made matters more difficult. "I tried to be as rational as I could under the circumstances," Mom recalls. "I felt that if we treated Marc differently, if we indulged him or catered to him in any way, that would make him feel different. It would not be doing him a favor. So I decided that I would try to treat him as normally as possible under the circumstances, and for what it's worth, I think it had a beneficial effect." I agree. Marc emerged a strong, confident personality, a gifted teacher who's spent his whole career at Harvard, and now flies around the world to help developing nations organize their health delivery systems. But the process of instilling normalcy—of creating equality between the twins—was not always smooth.

At times, our parents wanted Marc to be like me. So they forced him to walk to school instead of driving him. At other times, they wanted me to be like Marc, and the symbol of that was a bicycle. Since Marc couldn't ride one safely, I couldn't have one either. I felt aggrieved at the time, but in truth the lack of a bicycle didn't mean much in Bayonne. You could walk many places and take the bus to the others. In my entire life, I've never owned a bicycle, and I confess to having a phobia about them. They always seem unsafe and unsteady, and I never feel comfortable riding one. Ironically, Marc came to like that form of transportation, taking his daughter to day care and commuting to work by bike, until two serious accidents dimmed his enthusiasm for the activity.

Even if our parents treated us the same, we were clearly different. I played sports incessantly and Marc only joined our games occasionally. (He did throw a forward pass one day during a game of street football that I caught in the end zone. Unfortunately a large Buick was playing defensive back for the other team and I broke my leg on its bumper.) He spent a lot of time by himself, reading books and making model airplanes in an attic hideaway. Psychologist Nancy Segal, who examined our relationship in her study of twins, *Intertwined Lives*, wrote: "Marc was a university scholar when he was eight. Will Roberts watched his son 'delivering lectures' on the state of the world to anyone who would listen." Occasionally Marc's professorial manner got to me, and in a spasm of resentment, I smashed one of the models he had spent so much time constructing. Dad came up with an ingenious punishment: I was forced to make a model myself, so I could understand the damage I'd inflicted. It worked. I never touched his models again.

While Marc defied the doctors and recovered his ability to walk, he was left with a severe limp. In a curious way, however, his illness led to us joining the Cub Scouts. He loved the uniform, and he harbored a fantasy that if he joined the Scouts, he could somehow manage to march. The pack at the Jewish Community Center was in shambles, but our parents came to the rescue. Dad became the pack leader and Mom a den mother, and that experience symbolized much of my childhood. My folks were always there to lend a hand, and Marc was always there to give me a push. To the outside world we were always "the twins" or "the Roberts boys." We were always being compared to each other, and while that sense of competition made me frustrated and angry at times, it also drove me to match Marc's accomplishments. After Cub Scouts we joined the Boy Scouts, and Marc points out with glee that he made Eagle Scout six months before I did. But I never would have made it at all without him there, egging me on, and one moment symbolizes that for me. Bayonne had a Boy Scout camp in rural Jersey, not far from our country cottage. Marc and I spent parts of three summers there, and one of the merit badges I coveted was hiking, a badge that Marc could never attain. One day a senior leader assembled a group of us for a twenty-mile hike. One by one the others dropped out, until I was the only one left. But I was on another planet. I was going to keep going, no matter what. It was after nightfall when we returned to camp, and I knew I had proven something important to myself.

Boy Scouts really worked for us. We learned self-sufficiency and responsibility. We wanted to win the clean bunk award, and worked hard at it. We battled fiercely against our rival campsites in weekly swimming races and scavenger hunts. On one notable occasion, when a hurricane blew through camp, Marc and I decided to stay in our tent all night, while virtually every other camper fled to the safety of the mess hall. We drove our tent stakes deep into the ground, plugged a small leak with a sock, and stuck it out. When we emerged the next morning, safe and relatively dry, we had survived some rite of passage as meaningful as any Bar Mitzvah, just without the presents.

Even after my hiking triumph, my relationship with Marc did not change much. His dominating personality over-shadowed me all through high school, and I was determined to attend a different college. But sometimes, a five-minute conversation can change your entire life, and I had one of those during my senior year. One night at the Jewish Community Center, I was approached by a fellow named Barney Frank (now a senior member of Congress from Massachusetts). He was a few years older, but I knew his younger sister, Doris, and his uncle was the sports editor of the local paper, where I worked after school. Barney's older sister Ann (as Ann Lewis she's long been one of Hillary Clinton's closest advisors) had gone to Radcliffe. He had followed her to Cambridge and was now at Harvard, and he suggested that Marc and I should apply. I was not quite sure where Harvard was but he made it sound like a neat place; so on a lark, we both filed applications. Marc also visited Princeton, but had an off-putting experience. The student guide told him flatly that Princeton still had a strict Jewish quota, and he shouldn't get his hopes up. So he lost interest.

I had never flown in a plane, and this was not the time to start. I had barely been out of New Jersey before, and going all the way to Massachusetts for a college interview was more than enough stress. So Marc and I took a train from Newark to Boston for our first visit to Harvard. When we got to Boston, we followed Barney's instructions and made our way to the MTA, the local underground transit system. Next thing I knew, this odd-looking vehicle rolled into the station. I was used to New York City subways, and I had never seen anything like it. I thought a bus had made a wrong turn and wound up in the subway tunnel. We got on anyway, and made our way to the Harvard Square stop.

Emerging on an island in the middle of that busy intersection, I walked over to a man running a newsstand and asked timidly, "Where's Harvard?" He looked at me kindly and replied: "It's all around you, son." We were feeling pretty lost when we spied, walking across the street, none other than Barney Frank. What a relief! We stayed in Barney's room in Kirkland House, but were disappointed at the lack of a real, intellectual college bull session. When I mentioned this, Barney pointed to his two roommates and laughed: "We've been roommates for three years. Whatever there is to be said about politics has been said." (Not quite, given the way Barney's career turned out. He's still talking politics almost 50 years later.) We were interviewed the next day by an admissions officer who had spent the war at the Bayonne Navy base, and the fact that he knew my hometown relaxed me a lot. We had something to talk about. And that spring Marc and I both got letters accepting us into the class of 1964.

I was never quite sure why we got in, but during our freshman year, we learned that a Harvard teaching hospital was doing a study of twins, so perhaps they wanted us as subjects. In fact, the hospital did invite us to participate, and I was intrigued by the idea except for one thing: They wanted us to save all of our urine in large plastic bottles. I had enough trouble getting a date, I didn't need to worry about a fluid-filled container that might leak at any moment. We took the bottles home, but never joined the study, and throughout my college years, those damn things gathered dust under my bed, a mute reminder of my social insecurity.

When we got our letters from Harvard, Marc announced immediately that he was going. So I announced that I was not. Since birth, we had always been thrown together—in the same bedroom, the same classes, the same organizations. Sure, my athletics and journalism set me apart in some ways, but to most people we were still the "twinnies" and I was tired of it. The competition between us certainly had a beneficial effect, forcing me to work hard and get good grades. Without his example, I would have shot a lot more baskets and cracked a lot fewer books. But I didn't want to be "Marc Roberts's brother" anymore, and one incident summed up my feelings. Marc was chosen to represent Bayonne High at Boys State, a prestigious gathering of politically minded high school students from across New Jersey. I was not selected, which was bad enough. Then he got elected governor, an honor that entitled him to attend Boys Nation, a meeting in Washington of all the governors from other states. That sealed it for me. No Harvard.

I realize now that we both had issues with each other, that we both felt overshadowed by our twin brother. I envied his titles and achievements. He envied my friendships with girls. For all my awkwardness, I had it a lot easier than he did, and when I started hanging out (dating would be putting it too strongly) with the cutest, smartest girl in our class, he lusted after her from afar. So perhaps we both would have preferred separate schools. My parents played it cool, letting me simmer for a few days. They had no family ties to Harvard, of course. (They had both commuted to NYU in the 30s, subsisting on ketchup sandwiches in the school cafeteria and returning home every night by bus to Bayonne.) But they did have a friend who had gone to Harvard, and she told them strongly: Don't let Steve miss this chance, he'll always regret it. Finally Dad came to me and said, "Look, the place is big enough for both of you." I was still reluctant, but Harvard was the best college that had accepted me, so I grudgingly gave in. Very grudgingly. But a new world was about to open for me. As soon as I arrived on campus, I tried out for The Harvard Crimson, the university daily, and it wasn't long before I started getting bylines and getting noticed. One day when we were still freshmen someone greeted Marc by saying, "Oh, you're Steve Roberts's brother." At that point, I knew Dad had been right, Harvard was big enough for both of us.

Since graduation, the wider world has always been big enough for both of us. Our lives have been like two parallel lines, headed in the same direction, animated by the same interests and values, but not always touching each other. We both went to work for large, established institutions: Marc has taught at Harvard his whole career, I worked for the *New York Times* for 25 years. His field was economics, mine was politics. We haven't lived in the same city for more than 40 years and at times, our emotional connections have frayed and fractured.

But in recent years we've grown close again. He's edged into my field, writing four books; I've moved into his by becoming a professor. Now in our mid-sixties we look more like each other than ever. I'm occasionally stopped in airports by someone who says, "I took your course at Harvard," and I have to answer, "No you didn't, but I know who you're talking about." He often starts his classes by saying, "I'm not the guy you see on television." And our family patterns have been similar: We both married young, and had kids young, and today we each have six grandchildren. When I was writing my last book, *My Fathers' Houses,* I wanted to interview Marc at some length about our childhood. His daughter, who lives in Baltimore, had just had her second child and needed baby-sitting help, so Marc moved in for a week. One sunny day I drove north from Washington to see him. We sat on his daughter's porch, with his granddaughter asleep in the next room, and exchanged reactions and reflections for hours. At the end of the session "the Roberts boys" embraced. The lines of our lives were touching again.

a death in the family

My brother the writer John Gregory Dunne, with whom I have had a complicated relationship over the years, as Irish Catholic brothers of our era often did, died unexpectedly on the night of December 30. I was at my house in Connecticut that night, sitting in front of the fire, reading John's provocative review in *The New York Review of Books* of Gavin Lambert's new biography, *Natalie Wood: A Life*. My brother and I both knew Natalie Wood, and our wives were among her friends. We were also both friends of Gavin Lambert's. I have always enjoyed my brother's writing, even when we weren't speaking. He knew his turf. He understood about getting at the essence of things. His first major work on Hollywood, *The Studio*, was an insider's unsparing, yearlong look at how Twentieth Century Fox was run. His bestselling novel *True Confessions*, about two Irish Catholic brothers, one a priest and the other a police lieutenant, was made into a film starring Robert De Niro and Robert Duvall. In his review of Lambert's fascinating book, John wrote about Natalie, "She was a movie star out of a post–Joan Crawford, pre–Julia Roberts age—promiscuous, insecure, talented, irrational, funny, generous, shrewd, occasionally unstable, and untrusting of anyone who would get too close to her—except for a Praetorian Guard of gay men." I was thinking to myself as I read it, He got her—that was Natalie.

Then the telephone rang, and I looked at the clock. It was 10 minutes before 11, late for a country call, especially the night before New Year's Eve. When I said hello, I heard, "Nick, it's Joan." Joan is Joan Didion, the writer, my brother's wife. It was rare for her to call. John was always the one who made the calls. I knew by the tone of her voice that something terrible had happened. In our immediate family there have been a murder, a suicide, and a fatal private-plane crash.

My brother and sister-in-law's daughter, Quintana Roo Dunne Michael, a recent bride, had been since Christmas night in an induced coma in the intensive-care unit of Beth Israel hospital, because of a case of flu that had turned into a virulent strain of pneumonia. There were tubes down her throat, and her hands were restrained so that she could not pull the tubes out. The night before, my brother had called me after a hospital visit and sobbed about his daughter. I had never heard him cry. He adored Quintana and she adored him, in that special father-daughter way. I don't think I have ever seen a prouder father than when he walked her to the altar at her wedding last summer. "It was like watching Dominique on life support," he told me on the phone. He was referring to my daughter, who had been strangled and then kept on life support for several days on police orders back in 1982. Hearing Joan's voice, I thought at first that she was calling to tell me of a setback in Quintana's condition, or worse. Instead she said, in her simple, direct manner, "John's dead." There were long seconds of silence as what she had said sank in. John's and my journey had been bumpy, sometimes extremely so, but in recent years we had experienced the joys of reconciliation. After the closeness we had managed to rebuild, the thought of his not being there anymore was incomprehensible.

Since Quintana's hospitalization, it had become their habit, that week between Christmas and New Year's, to visit her each evening and then have dinner in a restaurant before returning to their apartment on the Upper East Side. That night, after leaving the hospital, they didn't feel like going to a restaurant, so they went directly back to the apartment. Once inside, John sat down, had a massive heart attack, fell over, and died. "The minute I got to him, I knew he was dead," Joan said. She was crying. "The ambulance arrived. The medics worked on him for 15 minutes, but it was over." Joan went in the ambulance to the hospital, where he was pronounced dead. In recent years he had had a history of heart problems.

Joan Didion and John Dunne, or the Didion-Dunnes, as their friends referred to them, had a superb marriage that lasted 40 years. They were ideally matched. Once, years ago, they thought briefly about getting a divorce. They actually wrote about it in a weekly column they were then contributing to the *Saturday Evening Post*. But they didn't get a divorce. Instead they went to Hawaii, a favorite getaway place of theirs, and began a life of total togetherness that was nearly unparalleled in modern marriage. They were almost never out of each other's sight. They finished each other's sentences. They started each day with a walk in Central Park. They had breakfast at the Three Guys Restaurant on weekdays and at the Carlyle hotel on Sundays. Their offices were in adjoining rooms of their sprawling apartment. John always answered the telephone. When it was someone like me calling with an interesting bit of news, he could always be heard to say, "Joan, pick up," so that she could hear the same bit of news at the same time. They were one of those couples who did everything together, and they were always in accord on their opinions, whatever subject was under discussion.

They were very much a part of the New York literary scene. Major American writers such as David Halberstam, Calvin Trillin, and Elizabeth Hardwick, whom they called Lizzie, were their close friends. In John's obituary in *The New York Times* on January 1, Richard Severo wrote, "Mr. Dunne and Ms. Didion were probably America's best known writing couple, and were anointed as the First Family of Angst by *The Saturday Review* in 1982 for their unflinching explorations of the national soul, or often, the glaring lack of one." They dined out regularly, primarily at Elio's, a celebrity-oriented Italian restaurant on Second Avenue at 84th Street, where they always had the same table, next to framed jackets of two of their books. They wrote their books and their magazine articles separately, but they collaborated on their screenplays for movies.

I was the second and John was the fifth of six children in a well-to-do Irish Catholic family in West Hartford, Connecticut. Our father was an extremely successful heart surgeon and the president of a hospital. In Irish Catholic circles, my mother was considered a bit of an heiress. We lived in a big, gray stone house in the best part of town, and our parents belonged to the country club. We went to private schools and to Mrs. Godfrey's dancing classes. We were the big-deal Irish Catholic family in a Wasp city, but we were still outsiders in the swanky life our parents created for us. John once wrote that we'd gone from steerage to the suburbs in three generations. We were so Catholic that priests came to dinner. John was named after Archbishop John Gregory Murray of St. Paul, Minnesota, who had married my parents.

Our grandfather Dominick Burns was a potato-famine immigrant who came to this country at 14 and made good. He started in the grocery business and ended up a bank president. When we were kids, we stressed the bank-president part of his life rather than the grocery part. He was made a Knight of St. Gregory by Pope Pius XII for his philanthropic work for the poor of Hartford. A public school in a section of the city known as Frog Hollow—the old Irish section—is named after him. John kept a large photograph of him in the living room of his apartment. Papa, as we called him, was an extraordinary man, and he had an enormous influence on my brother and me. It was as if he spotted us for the writers we would one day be. He didn't go to school past the age of 14, but literature was an obsession with him. He was never without a book, and he read voraciously. Early on, he taught John and me the excitement of reading. On Friday nights we would often stay over at his house, and he would read the classics or poetry to us and give us each a 50-cent piece for listening—a lot of money to a kid back then. John and I had another thing in common: we both stuttered. We went to an elocution teacher named Alice J. Buckley, who must have been good, because we both stopped stuttering years ago.

In 1943, at the age of 18, I was drafted out of my senior year at the Canterbury School and sent overseas after six weeks of basic training. I was in combat and received a Bronze Star Medal for saving a wounded soldier's life in Felsberg, Germany, on December 20, 1944. John was always fascinated by that period of my life. Several times in magazine articles he mentioned my wartime experience at such a young age. Just this past Christmas, a few days before he died, he gave me a book by Paul Fussell called *The Boys' Crusade: The American Infantry in Northwestern Europe, 1944–1945*. When it came time for college, my father was adamant that we go to the best schools in the East. My older brother, Richard, went to Harvard. I went to Williams, John went to Princeton, and my youngest brother, Stephen, went to Georgetown and Yale graduate school. After college, I went into television in 1950 and married Ellen Griffin, a ranching heiress known as Lenny, in 1954. Three years later we moved to Hollywood with our two sons, Griffin and Alex. I had known all my life that I was going to live in Hollywood one day, and Lenny and I were instant successes— knew everybody, went everywhere, gave parties, went to parties.

John graduated from Princeton in 1954, worked for *Time* magazine for five years, traveled to fascinating places, did an army stint, and married Joan Didion, who was not yet famous, in Pebble Beach, California. I photographed their wedding. In 1967, when they left New York and moved to California, Joan wrote her beautiful piece "Farewell to the Enchanted City" for the *Saturday Evening Post*. It later became the final essay, renamed "Goodbye to All That," in her widely heralded best-selling book *Slouching Towards Bethlehem*. While my wife and I were strictly Beverly Hills people, John and Joan lived in "interesting" places. Joan put an ad in the paper saying that a writing couple was looking for a house to rent. A woman replied, offering an attractive gatehouse on an estate on the sea at Palos Verdes and explaining that the main house had never been built, because the rich people who had commissioned it went bust. The lady wanted $800 a month. Joan said they were prepared to pay only $400. They settled at $500. As they got to know the movie and literary crowds, they started to move closer to town, at first renting a big, falling-apart mansion on Franklin Avenue in old Hollywood. Janis Joplin went to one of their parties in that house, as did other fabled figures of the 60s. Then they bought a wonderful house on the beach in Trancas and rebuilt it. They contracted Harrison Ford, who was not yet a movie star, to do the work. When Quintana was old enough to go to school, they moved to their last California house, in Brentwood.

Our worlds grew closer and closer. In the early 70s, John, Joan, and I formed a film company called Dunne-Didion-Dunne. They wrote, and I produced. Our first picture was *The Panic in Needle Park*, for Twentieth Century Fox, based on a *Life*-magazine article by James Mills about heroin junkies. I remember sitting in the projection room and watching the dailies for the first time. In the darkness, John and I looked at each other as if we couldn't believe that two Hartford boys were making a big Hollywood-studio movie on location in New York City. It was Al Pacino's first starring role, and he was mesmerizing as the doomed Bobby. It was a marvelous period. We were in total harmony. The picture was picked as an American entry to the Cannes Film Festival, and we all went over and had our first red-carpet experience. The film won the best-actress award for a young beginner named Kitty Winn. There were cheers and huzzahs and popping flashbulbs. It was a thrilling experience for all three of us. The following year John and Joan wrote the screenplay for *Play It As It Lays*, which was based on Joan's best-selling novel of the same name. I produced it with Frank Perry, who also directed. The picture, made by

Universal, starred Tuesday Weld and Anthony Perkins. It was an American entry at the Venice Film Festival, where Tuesday Weld won the award for best actress. That was our last film together. John and I came away from that picture not liking each other as much as we had after the first. Then Joan and John made a mint on the movie *A Star Is Born*, starring Barbra Streisand, which was an enormous success, and in which they had a share of the profits. I remember being at the star-studded premiere in Westwood, when Streisand made one of the great movie entrances. And there were John and Joan, up there, having arrived, being photographed, getting celebrity treatment. Was I jealous? Yes.

I had begun to fall apart. Drink and drugs. Lenny divorced me. I was arrested getting off a plane from Acapulco carrying grass and was put in jail. John and Joan bailed me out. As I was falling and failing, they were soaring and gaining renown. When I went broke, they lent me $10,000. A terrible resentment builds when you've borrowed money and can't pay it back, although they never once reminded me of my obligation. That was the first of the many estrangements that followed. Finally, in despair, I left Hollywood early one morning and lived for six months in a cabin in Camp Sherman, Oregon, with neither telephone nor television. I stopped drinking. I stopped doping. I started to write. At about three o'clock one morning, John contacted me through the telephone of the couple from whom I rented the cabin to tell me that our brother Stephen, who was particularly close to John, had committed suicide. We all gathered in New Canaan, Connecticut, a few days later to attend Stephen's funeral. There were misunderstandings and the kinds of complications that so often occur in large families. Stephen was the youngest of the six of us, but he was the first to go. After his funeral, I began to rethink my life. In 1980, I left Hollywood for good and moved to New York. Even when John and I weren't speaking, we would meet up at family funerals. Our sisters, Harriet and Virginia, both died of breast cancer. Our nephew Richard Dunne Jr. was killed when his plane crashed in the airport at Hyannis, Massachusetts. His two daughters survived.

The major experience of my life has been the murder of my daughter. I never truly understood the meaning of the word "devastation" until I lost her. Since I was still a failed figure at the time, an unforgivable sin in Hollywood, where the murder took place, I was deeply sensitive to the slights I met with when I returned there. In "Justice," an article about the trial of the man who killed my daughter, the first article I ever wrote for *Vanity Fair*, in the March 1984 issue, I said:

> At the time of the murder Dominique was consistently identified in the press as the niece of my brother and sister-in-law, John Gregory Dunne and Joan Didion, rather than as the daughter of Lenny and me. At first I was too stunned by the killing for this to matter, but as the days passed, it bothered me. I spoke to Lenny about it one morning in her bedroom. She said, "Oh, what difference does it make?" with such despair in her voice that I felt ashamed to be concerned with such a trivial matter at such a crucial time.
>
> In the room with us was my former mother-in-law, Beatriz Sandoval Griffin Goodwin, the widow of Lenny's father, Thomas Griffin, an Arizona cattle rancher, and of Lenny's step-father, Ewart Goodwin, an insurance tycoon and rancher. She is a strong, uncompromising woman who has never not stated exactly what was on her mind in any given situation, a trait that has made her respected if not always endearing.
>
> "Listen to what he's saying to you," she said emphatically. "It sounds like Dominique was an orphan raised by her aunt and uncle. . . . And," [she] added, to underscore the point, "she had two brothers as well."

When the trial of John Sweeney, my daughter's killer, was due to start, there were serious conflicts between my brother and me. John, who knew his way around the Santa Monica courthouse, thought that we should accept a plea bargain, and emissaries from the defense were sent to us to effect one. Lenny, Griffin, Alex, and I felt pushed, as if we didn't matter. The district attorney wanted a trial, and so did we. So we went to trial. John and Joan went to Paris. The trial was a disaster. I hated the defense attorney. I hated the judge. The killer got out of prison in two and a half years. The experience changed me as a person and changed the course of my life. Out of that disaster I began, at the age of 50, to write in earnest, developing a passion for it I had never felt before.

More problems arose between John and me when I changed careers. I was, after all, moving in on turf that had been his for 25 years. I was the upstart. He and Joan were the stars. But I wrote four best-sellers in a row, all of which were made into mini-series, and I wrote regular features for *Vanity Fair*. Was John jealous? Yes. Our books came and went, but we never mentioned them to each other, acting as if they did not exist. There was no resemblance between our writing styles. His novels were tough and dealt with low-life criminals. My novels were more socially rarefied and dealt with high-life criminals. There were difficult periods. Sometimes we maintained civility, despite bad feelings on both sides. Sometimes we didn't. We were always competitive. If I called him with a hot piece of gossip I'd heard, rather than reacting to it, he'd top it with a story he'd heard.

The final break came over the defense attorney Leslie Abramson, who defended Erik Menendez, one of two rich Beverly Hills brothers who shot their parents to death in 1989. Abramson gained national attention during the Menendez trial, which I covered. My brother and I both wrote about her. She was a character in his novel *Red, White, and Blue*. John admired her, and she doted on him. I despised her, and she despised me right back. It got ugly. The crux of our difficulties came when John dedicated one of his books to her at the very time she and

I were in public conflict. After that my brother and I did not speak for more than six years. But our fight really wasn't about Leslie Abramson. She played no part in my life. I never once saw her outside of the courtroom. An eruption had long been building between John and me, and Abramson just lit the match. When a magazine wanted to photograph us together for an article it was doing on brothers, each of us declined without checking with the other.

Because we had overlapping friends on both coasts, our estrangement made for social difficulties from time to time. If we were at the same party, Joan and I always spoke and then moved away from each other. John and I never spoke and stayed in different rooms. Our brother Richard, a successful insurance broker in Hartford, managed to remain neutral, but he was troubled over the schism. The situation was particularly hard on my son Griffin. He had always been very close to John and Joan, and now he had to do a balancing act between his father and his uncle. I'm sure that, as the years passed, John grew as eager to end the conflict between us as I was. It had become too public. Everyone in the worlds in which we traveled knew that the Dunne brothers did not speak.

Then, three years ago, I was diagnosed with prostate cancer. It's a scary thing when they call to tell you that you have cancer. Mine has subsequently been licked, by the way. I told Griffin. He told John. Then, by happenstance, I ran into my brother at eight o'clock in the morning in the hematology department of New York-Presbyterian Hospital, where we were both giving blood samples, he for his heart, I for my P.S.A. number. We spoke. And then John called me on the phone to wish me well. It was such a nice call, so heartfelt. All the hostility that had built up simply vanished. Griffin has reminded me that John then called him and said, "Let's all go to Elio's and laugh our asses off." We did. The thing that made our reconciliation so successful was that we never tried to clear up what had gone so wrong. We just let it go. There was too much about each other to enjoy. During this time John was having problems with his heart. He had several overnight stays at New York-Presbyterian for what he always referred to as "procedures." He was dismissive about their seriousness, but Griffin has told me, "He always thought he was going to keel over in Central Park."

Let me tell you about reconciliation. It's a glorious thing. I hadn't realized how much I missed John's humor. I'm pretty good in that department myself. We called it our Mick humor. We quickly fell back into the habit of calling each other at least twice a day to pass on the latest news. We have always both been message centers. It was good to speak about family again. We talked about our grandfather, the great reader, and about our mother and father, our two dead sisters, and our dead brother. We talked about Dominique, who had been close to John and Joan and Quintana. We kept in touch with our brother Richard, who had retired and moved from Hartford to Harwich Port, on Cape Cod. We had our picture taken together by Annie Leibovitz for the April 2002 issue of *Vanity Fair*—something that would have been unheard of two years earlier. We even began to talk to each other about what we were writing. Last December he FedExed me an early edition of *The New York Review of Books* with his review of Gavin Lambert's book in it, which I was reading when Joan called to tell me he was dead. Last year, when I was sued for slander by former congressman Gary Condit, I was loath to go out in public, but John insisted we have a family meal at their regular table at Elio's. "Be seen," he said. "Don't hide." I took his advice.

It's hard to assess your own family, but I had the opportunity to watch my brother and sister-in-law quite closely last summer when Quintana, 38, was married to Jerry Michael, a widower in his 50s, at the Cathedral of St. John the Divine, on Amsterdam Avenue at 112th Street. It was the middle of July, desperately hot in New York, but their friends, mostly literary, came to the city from whatever watering holes they were vacationing in to watch John and Joan, in parental pride, beam with approval on their daughter and her choice. Joan, wearing a mother-of-the-bride flowered hat and her ever present dark glasses, was escorted up the aisle of the cathedral on the arm of Griffin. She gave little waves to her friends in the pews as she passed them. I had become used to Joan over the last 40 years, but that day I realized again what a truly significant person she is. She had, after all, helped define a generation.

Joan may be tiny. She may weigh less than 80 pounds. She may speak in such a soft voice that you have to lean forward to hear her. But this lady is a dominant presence. As a brand-new widow with a daughter in an induced coma who didn't yet know her father was dead, she made decisions and went back and forth to the hospital. She stood in her living room and received the friends who came to call. Joan is not a Catholic, and John was a lapsed Catholic. She said to me, "Do you know a priest who can handle all this?" I said I did.

Joan decided that there was to be no funeral until Quintana recovered. My nephew Anthony Dunne and his wife, Rosemary Breslin, the daughter of the writer Jimmy Breslin, went with Joan and me to identify John's body at the Frank E. Campbell funeral home, on Madison Avenue and 81st Street, before he was cremated. We walked silently into the chapel. He was in a plain wooden box with no satin lining. He was dressed in the uniform of our lives: a blue blazer, gray flannel trousers, a shirt with a button-down collar, a striped tie, and loafers. Tony, Rosemary, and I stood back while Joan went to look at him. She leaned over and kissed him. She put her hands over his. We could see her body shaking as she cried quietly. After she turned away, I stepped up and said good-bye, followed by Tony and Rosemary. Then we left.

Floyd Skloot

jambon dreams

It was a winter night in 1952. My brother Philip was thirteen and famished, though we'd finished dinner only an hour earlier. He tip-toed into the kitchen and approached a pan of leftover stuffed cabbage cooling on the counter. I followed, wearing black Hopalong Cassidy pajamas and an empty holster on my hip, toy six-gun cocked in my hand. I was five and learning how to be a food thief.

It was vital to know the whereabouts of the authorities: my mother sat at her desk in the foyer, talking on the phone, and my father slept, hoping to get eight hours in before waking at four to open his poultry market. *Don't make a sound*, Philip whispered.

The kitchen window was steamed over, but I could still see lights from apartments that faced ours in the east Flatbush neighborhood. I could hear traffic below on Lenox Road. The room smelled of tomato, ground beef, onion, and the rank biology of cabbage wrappings cooked so long that the outer leaves flopped into the sauce. My parents called this concoction *galooptchy*, and loved to eat it for days as leftovers. Those loosed leaves were Philip's target. If he could be delicate enough in his touch so that nothing looked out of place afterwards, and careful not to drip sauce once he'd liberated the goods, he could pilfer a few and eat them without getting caught.

He didn't particularly like cabbage leaves. But he liked foiling our parents' plans, he liked taking forbidden food, and he needed the practice. I was there to appreciate the moves.

The week before, I'd witnessed his failed Velveeta Caper. My mother had brought home the smallest available block of the cheese, Philip's favorite, and placed it on the refrigerator shelf with a warning: *this has to last the whole week*. When she'd gone downstairs to visit her friend Ann, Philip opened the box, unfolded the foil packaging, and cut chunk after chunk, devouring each one plain—without crackers or bread, without offering any to me, and without pause—until just a thin slice was left. Then he crumpled up wax paper and shaped the mass into a rectangle, stuffed it against the remaining slice, refolded the packaging, and slipped the box top back into place.

"Don't touch that," he said. "I'll finish the last piece in a week."

Of course, it had been a trap. Food provision, like food thievery, was a highly nuanced business in our family. As soon as she came home, my mother checked the refrigerator. She touched the Velveeta box, which yielded to her finger's pressure, and screamed. She demanded our presence before her. *I hope you two enjoyed your feast!* Philip ate no dinner that night. Neither did I, his ravenous sidekick.

But he got away—we both got away—with his cabbage operation. I remember that near the end of it, rapt in his work, Philip did drip a freckle of sauce onto the linoleum. Like our mother, I raced to grab a paper towel, gasping instead of screaming. After I'd cleaned the floor, he winked at me. Then we tip-toed back to our room.

One Sunday morning in 1956, my father woke me and Philip by slapping our feet with a spatula. He wore his chef's apron, and stood between our beds with his right index finger pressed to his lips. *Shhhhh. Don't wake her.*

I'd never seen my father cook, and didn't know he could. He sold the stuff that other people cooked, he ate stuff that other people cooked, and I figured he had nothing to do with what happened in between. The apron, I thought, was only for when he served drinks before a dinner party.

Usually, we had Sunday breakfast at Toomey's Diner on Empire Boulevard, then went to Prospect Park or Coney Island or the cemetery where my father's father was buried. But this morning it was raining, and he'd heard that Toomey's was closed all week because of a death in the family, and since we'd all be driving up to Connecticut later that morning to visit my mother's cousins, we couldn't do our usual Sunday outing.

"Breakfast in ten minutes," he whispered. "Get yourselves ready."

Soon there was an alarming smell from the kitchen. I looked at Philip and he smiled, raised his eyebrows, and rubbed his hands together. "Baloney and eggs!"

This was another revelation for me. I hadn't known it was possible to cook baloney, or to eat baloney with eggs, and survive. Besides, such a combination might be against the rules.

We weren't exactly Kosher in the house, though our father's was a Kosher market, its poultry slaughtered according to the rules. We routinely mixed meat and dairy at the same meal, and didn't keep separate meat and dairy dishes, or buy specially blessed foods, so I figured Kosher only applied when people visited other people's homes. I knew it didn't apply to meals eaten in restaurants, unless we were in a restaurant with family or friends who kept their homes Kosher. I knew about the restaurant exception to Kosher rules because we could have pork in restaurants. The truth is, I lived for ham: ham steak, country ham, Virginia ham, fried ham, sliced ham, ham with eggs, ham in baked beans. We could sometimes have pork at home, but only when our father brought fresh pork sausage from the Italian butcher next door to his market. Probably keeping Kosher, when it came to pork in the home, only applied when people got their food from strangers. At home, we ate only beef hot dogs or cold cuts, except when at Ebbets Field or when the grocery store had a special on bratwurst or braunschweiger, so the rules about pork also had something to do with sports and economics. Similarly, we ate shrimp and lobster in Chinese restaurants, but not at home, so I figured that the Chinese had special access to Kosher shellfish. To poultry as well, since their restaurants were my father's best wholesale customers, in which case it was all right to ignore the fact that their kitchens were contaminated, or *trayf*, as my parents called anything non-Kosher when we weren't eating it. Clams we ate only at restaurants located near the ocean, which led me to believe that clams were Kosher if consumed within sight of their homes. The rules were sometimes a little hard to follow.

But my shock over baloney and eggs wasn't about violations of rules. It was about the strangeness of eating baloney and eggs together, even if the combination was technically permissible. The smell, and the way the meat curled away from the eggs no matter how I tried to flatten it, certainly suggested they didn't belong on the same plate.

I was learning that most of my assumptions about food were false. Every time I thought I understood what we did and didn't do, something strange would occur. There seemed to be few guiding principles other than stealth and the violation of all rules. Eat what you want, especially what you're not supposed to, whenever the opportunity presents itself.

When my father sold his poultry market in 1957, we celebrated with a series of dinners. One for his employees and best customers at a restaurant in Red Hook. Another for his fellow butchers, bakers, and produce men on Union Street, where almost every guest had provided one of the menu's fresh items, from the mussels posillipo and garlic bread to the roasted meats and desserts. There was a dinner for the Skloot uncles and aunts and cousins, held at our grandmother's home because she was the one who had gotten the family started in the poultry business originally. We had dinner at the home of the Italian family who bought the market. And dinner for just the four of us, a final feast shortly before we moved away from Brooklyn, featuring poultry my father had killed and cleaned with his own hands. My mother, who had been urging him to sell his market for the last three years, burst into tears when she set the heaped platter down. She left the room for a minute or two, then as we were about to begin eating that last dinner, my father took off his glasses and wept. It was the only time I ever saw him cry, and it made me cry. My brother laughed, but then his laughter converted to crying too. We sat there, all four in tears, watching the pullet give off steam and sag into its bed of fennel.

Like so many families, we celebrated holidays, events, and achievements by eating. For us, though, as with the rules of keeping Kosher, these celebrations had fine calibrations governed by complex regulations. If I brought home an especially good report card from school, we would go out to eat, but not at an Italian or seafood restaurant, the most expensive cuisines we liked. Grades might be worth dinner at a diner, or a sit-down deli feast, but not fancy chicken cacciatore or fresh lobster. After the first week of my brother's new job at a clothing factory, we ate at a restaurant in the west end of town famous for its spare ribs, but we weren't allowed to order appetizers and skipped dessert. The end of a week of continual rain was worth a Chinese dinner, but only combination plates, not separate main dishes, which were proper for adult birthdays and certain holidays. When my mother got a singing role in a community theater production, we had steaks all around. Some visitors merited better meals than others when we went out together. My mother's brother and his wife, so successful in the garment industry, got the full Italian restaurant treatment. My father's eldest sister, a distinguished interior decorator, and her well-to-do husband, got to eat at Meyer & Kronke, which my mother called a four-star Manhattan restaurant stranded in Oceanside. But my father's middle sister and her traveling salesman husband, on the rare occasions we ate with them, got the small café with its burgers and sandwiches.

If we celebrated by eating, and entertained by eating, we also grieved by eating. Four years after my father sold his market, when we'd left Brooklyn and settled in a rented home on the south shore of Long Island, he died suddenly at the age of fifty-three. Only Philip and I were home when the phone call came, and our first act was to open the refrigerator and slap together roast beef sandwiches. A day later, family and friends returned home with us from the cemetery and shared a catered feast. Kosher, from the restaurant on Park Street, because my father's mother and eldest brother would be with us. Wearing a black dress and demure white apron, Hannah—the woman who helped my mother cook and clean—took me into a corner and whispered, "You Skloots is the eatin'est people I ever saw." Then she continued rushing through the living room, dodging mourners, carrying heavy trays.

She was right, and I've remembered her observation for forty-four years. We ate a lot, we ate meaningfully, and we ate recklessly. A family given to heart disease, strokes, and diabetes, we gorged on fatty foods, salty foods, sweets. We often ate with abandon, especially Philip and I down at our corner of the table, grabbing for dishes if they weren't passed quickly enough, snaring morsels from one another's plates, licking our fingers to lift a few final crumbs of bread.

Meals could be a time of peace, if the food satisfied in quality and amount, if everyone's mood was stable, if the stars were aligned. But meals could also be a battleground, every member of the family looking out for himself only, seizing what they wanted, hunching over the plate to guard their food like animals. Tempers could flare, the day's misdemeanors and insults and losses tossed into the mix as forks shoved food into mouths between accusations and recriminations.

Food mattered to us, to me, in ways that evolution may not have intended. It sure seemed to be the center of all attention.

"Don't get any on the seat," Philip said.

I leaned further outside the car and said, "Don't worry, I know what I'm doing."

"And don't get any on the door, either."

As usual, Philip and I were trading *don'ts* as we ate. We were hunkered back-to-back in his new, white 1961 Plymouth Valiant, eating ham sandwiches on loaves of crusty bread. The car's front doors were wide open, oil and vinegar dressing dripped down our chins to land between our feet on the asphalt, and bread crumbs exploded all around us. We didn't look around when we talked, and we didn't stop chewing, but none of that mattered because we didn't have to hear each other to conduct this conversation.

"Don't talk when you eat," I said. "You spray food all over the place."

"Don't be a wise guy. And don't forget, last week, there was mustard all over the floor on your side."

I leaned further out the door, held the sandwich at arm's length, stretched my neck like a goose in flight, and took another bite. "Don't distract me."

That sunny Saturday afternoon still lingers in memory because it was the one time my brother broke with his routine. Instead of the usual hero sandwich, he'd ordered what I'd ordered, ham and Swiss with extra lettuce and dressing.

"Don't kid yourself," he said as we neared the end of our meals. "This isn't a real sandwich, it's an *hors d'oeuvre*."

Lacking the proper variety of meats, containing only one kind of cheese, missing the pickles and tomatoes and onions and peppers, my regular Saturday lunch seemed like diet food to Philip. A semi-sandwich. But it was the kind I loved, the kind I'd even begun to dream about.

Halfway through lunch, he began the ritual quiz: "Okay, what's a hero sandwich called in Philadelphia?"

"A hoagie."

"In Boston?"

"Grinder."

"What about Chicago?"

"A sub."

"And why do they call it a sub?"

"Because it's shaped like a submarine."

He nodded. I could hear sea gulls bugling as they circled above us, coming in off the bay just beyond the playground where we were parked. If one landed near us, hoping for a scrap of bread, Philip would roar like a walrus till the gull fled. We had just finished playing a doubleheader in a men's summer softball league. The rest of the team had gone home for showers, but we'd headed straight to the deli, as always. He'd ordered a ham sandwich, I believe, to reward me for having hit my first home run of the season. Even though, as he pointed out immediately after I'd reached the dugout, it was an inside-the-park homer and therefore not a REAL homer, like the kind he hit.

"Yonkers?"

"Wedge." I didn't know if his information was correct, but Philip had taught me the regional names for hero sandwiches and my job was to learn them as he instructed, not to challenge his data.

Names, I'd come to understand, mattered when discussing food. It was essential to know what you were talking about, even if correct names were as fluid as the rules that governed my family's diet. Maybe that's why our chatter was as packed with *don'ts* as a hero/hoagie/grinder/sub/wedge was with fillings.

"Very good. Don't put the napkin on the seat." *How did he know I'd wiped my lips?* "I'm done with my cream soda," he said, "let me have a sip of yours."

I was, thanks in large part to Philip, a serious student of food information. Not a scholar, not in my brother's league at all, but no slouch either. Even after our father's market was sold and he went to work for his brother-in-law in the garment district, even after he died, we felt it was our business to recognize fine culinary distinctions, particularly among meats and fish. To carry on the tradition. By the age of fifteen, as Philip left home to marry, I could differentiate between littleneck and cherrystone clams by taste alone, and knew that soft-shell clams really had hard shells and were best for steaming. I knew that head cheese was not cheese, but jellied meat from a cow's head, and that the baloney with pearly white chunks of fat scattered throughout was called Mortadella, which—since I'd taken Latin in school—sounded to me like Death Meat. I knew, of course, that the difference between a capon and a pullet had more to do with tenderness than gender. I knew that gefilte fish was made from pike or carp, which was like a Jewish version of scrapple, which was a Pennsylvania Dutch concoction made of boiled pig scraps and cornmeal. The connection, Philip had explained, was that both were garbage foods given fancy names to make them sound better.

Our teacher-student relationship regarding food was like our coach-rookie relationship regarding softball, where Philip was the team's founder, captain, and slugger, and I was the fourteen year old shortstop among men in their twenties, a slick fielder and a speedy singles hitter, learning the game. But as I sat there beside him, chewing and acing his quiz, I knew in my rebellious adolescent soul that the secret to a hero sandwich was the bread. Had to be crusty outside and chewy-soft inside. Philip said I was a fool, it was all about the proper mass and balance of ingredients. Which was why the plain ham sandwich we were eating did not hold up to a hero's standards.

As a high school football and baseball player, I somehow remained lean despite my family's eating habits. Maybe it was all the exercise I got, or youthful metabolism, or the fact that I had distractions that sometimes made me rush away from the table. Maybe, as I often hoped, not being fat meant I was not really my parents' child. My mother, barely five feet tall, weighed a hundred eighty pounds. My father, in the years shortly before his death, was all belly and jowl, a man only three inches taller than his very short wife and at least as heavy. My brother, the only one of us to grow taller than five-four, eventually topped out at five-nine and three hundred fifty pounds. Through college and into the early years of my first marriage, I held my weight at a hundred fifty. But then, at the age of twenty-five, I lost control. At my peak, I carried two hundred pounds spread over my sixty-four inch frame. I still tried to play ball with my friends, but my knees and back hurt from carrying all those pounds. I wore polka dotted polyester suits to work that had belonged to my Uncle Saul, wore soft wide shoes to cushion the load, and spent my weekends in a vast ochre jumpsuit. I met people who hadn't seen me in a couple of years and barely recognized me. At a Skloot family picnic during the summer of 1974, a cousin joked that I was finally starting to look like a member of my family. One evening, dressed in undershorts and walking past a mirror in my den, I glanced sideways and saw that I was already shaped like my father in his final years. All I needed to complete the look was a fat Havana cigar.

Late that fall, I invented a diet that I thought I could manage. First, I focused on breakfasts, changing my morning habits but not worrying about lunches or dinners yet. No more breakfasts in restaurants. No sausage and gravy, ham and eggs with an extra order of ham, hash browns, buttered toast, side of pancakes. I ate a bowl of cereal at home, with my infant daughter beside me in her high chair sharing the same meal, both of us playing with our Cheerios and jabbering at each other. At work, when colleagues went out for mid-morning coffee and snacks, I forced myself to stay at my desk. For a month, that was all I did about dieting. Then, when I felt in control of my morning eating, I worked on lunch. No more lunches in restaurants, I told myself, till I weighed 150 pounds again. No ham. I brought to work baggies filled with sliced carrot sticks and celery stalks, red pepper strips, rounds of cucumber, cherry tomatoes, apple slices. For protein, I brought a small chunk of low-fat cheese or a few almonds. At lunch time, I retreated to a disused vault in the state capitol building where I worked, and ate as I read the daily newspaper. Before long, and without saying anything about it, two friends began to join me. I hadn't realized they'd noticed what I was doing. Craig and Ruby said they wanted to lose weight too, but I believe they were actually trying to support me. Instead of going to the news stand at mid-afternoon and buying a candy bar from the blind vendor there, I went for a quick walk with Craig and Ruby up the capitol's five flights of stairs. By early February, with my morning and afternoon eating mastered, I worked on dinner and evening snacks. Small portions of chicken or fish. Salad, green vegetables, no ham.

There is a photograph of me, taken just before my diet began, wearing a white tee shirt and bulging with fat all around my daughter's small form as she sleeps in my arms. A companion photograph, taken during our trip to Disney World in March, 1975, shows me in a pair of new shorts and a vertically striped polo shirt, fifty-two pounds lighter, seated beside her in a toy car in which I'd never have been able to fit five months earlier. Nearby, oddly enough, was a Disney World staffer dressed as Porky Pig. Ham incarnate.

It was late-September, 1984, the night before my second marathon, and I was carbo-loading with a group of fellow runners at an Italian restaurant in Portland. The atmosphere was businesslike, a half dozen skinny men and women too busy fueling themselves to joke around, argue, or brag about their best times. In lieu of chatter, silverware clanked. Huge bowls of pasta circled the table, followed by bread and a small plate of skinless, boneless, grilled chicken breast. We all ate at least two helpings. But if I weren't eating to fuel a twenty-six mile run, I'd have had less than half a serving.

Once I began running, in 1982, I also began evaluating my weight by the ounce. Childhood's dietary rules may have been complex, the parsing of minute distinctions among poultry or types of baloney fanatical, my history with food bizarre, but my mid-life weight management techniques verged on the pathological. I kept records of miles run and food consumed. Though I normally ran close to fifty miles a week, I would add more miles to compensate for the occasional large meals that accompanied social occasions. Though I weighed less at age thirty-seven than I'd weighed in junior high school, I talked and worried about my weight all the time. Diagnosed with high cholesterol despite the good diet and exercise, I took medication and became even more rigorous about what I ate. If I liked it, I avoided it, or found substitutes that would have made my brother weep, buying ham made out of soy, yolkless egg substance in milk cartons, sugar-free taste-free cereals and cookies.

I thought I had my diet under control. I thought I had broken all my childhood food habits and escaped the family's culinary grip. But the truth was that food was still the center of attention.

Then neurological illness, caused by a viral attack, disabled me in 1988. Once it became clear that I would survive, what terrified me most was that I might get fat again. Because I couldn't run, couldn't exercise, because I was largely bedbound for a year and walked with a cane for another fourteen years, I dreaded adding weight. For a few years after getting sick, I was as crazy in my restricted eating as I'd been when running. If the first half of my life was about obsessive excess around food, the second half threatened to be about obsessive diligence.

Gradually, I came to understand that I needed to ease my grip, that the stress I felt over diet and weight was making my other health problems worse. I needed to integrate everything I did into an overall strategy of consistent health management. I had to rest for several hours daily, lower my expectations about what I could accomplish, structure a life that was stable, balanced. Illness, it turned out, nudged eating from the center of my attention. It was, after all, acceptable to eat what I wanted. I had even grown to like such things as soy baloney and soy cheese, cereals sweetened with fruit juice, cooked vegetables, raw nuts. I no longer wanted the food of my childhood, so it was no longer necessary to untangle the rules that governed it.

Except for ham. I still have dreams about ham sand-wiches. In last night's, for instance, I was wandering through an unknown city feeling hopelessly lost and disoriented. Then I noticed a pushcart in the distance, where a man was selling baguettes so stuffed with ham that they seemed impossible to eat. Sandwiches were stacked behind the cart's glassed front and drooped from its edges. More sandwiches dangled from the cart's roof like skewered fowl in a butcher shop while others peeped like flowers from wicker baskets on the ground. I approached the cart and realized that suddenly I felt at home, though I still didn't know where I was. I reached out, the vendor said *don't get any on the seat*, and I awoke just before touching the proffered sandwich.

I knew right away what the dream reflected. Earlier this sum-mer, my wife, Beverly, and I had spent eighteen days in France. We were in Paris for the final week, where I taught at the Paris Writers Workshop, and it was there that feelings of dislocation surged. I was tired from the heat and the travel and the seven flights of stairs I had to climb to reach our apartment; I couldn't speak the language; I was homesick for our isolated, tranquil, country way of life back home; I got lost as I tried to walk from our apartment to the place where I taught. But one afternoon near the end of our stay, walking back from class to the apart-ment, I stopped at a boulangerie to buy a sandwich. The counter display was like the pushcart's in my dream: baguettes every-where, stuffed with meats that stained their wax paper wrapping, and though I couldn't read the signs I had no trouble decipher-ing the choices. It felt as though Philip were over my shoulder, urging me to buy one that had the greatest variety of meats. But I chose the plain ham sandwich with lots of lettuce, *jambon et salade*, then walked happily—even jauntily—down the Rue de Sévres, eating amidst a shower of crumbs, feeling almost purely at home.

Surely this feeling wasn't associated with ham alone, with satisfying my hunger in a way that was so deeply rooted. I think it was associated with freedom, with a sense of Home as the place where I could enact my deepest desires because they were truly mine, not my brother's or mother's or father's. They were right for me, trustworthy. I could allow myself to eat and enjoy, guilt-free, a *jambon et salade* sandwich knowing it was something I could do in moderation. Besides, after so many years of slow neurological recovery, I was now capable of walking off the calories. The feeling of being at home was present, too, because Philip was there, alive within me eight years after he had died from complications of diabetes brought on by morbid obesity. He was yakking as usual about my choices. I listened to him, but I could make my own decision. And the bread in my dream, like the baguette in Paris, was perfect, crusty on the outside but chewy-soft inside.

Jay Neugeboren

imagining robert

At 3:00 AM, on a cool summer night—a few hours after my youngest son has graduated from high school—I find myself cruising the deserted streets of Northampton, Massachusetts, searching for the fifty-year-old man who is my brother. I have considered calling the police, but I know that if a policeman actually finds my brother and approaches him, Robert might, as in the past, panic and become violent.

My brother Robert has spent most of his life, since the age of nineteen, in mental hospitals and psychiatric wards in and around New York City. The list is long: Hillside, Creedmoor, Elmhurst, Gracie Square, Bellevue, Kings County, Rikers Island, Mid-Hudson Psychiatric Center, South Beach Psychiatric Center, and others.

Until the time of his first breakdown in 1962, Robert had been a delightful, popular, and gifted boy and young man—talented at dancing, acting, and singing, invariably winning the lead in school and camp plays and skits. He'd had a love and talent for many things, including tennis, writing, art (painting, drawing), and chess. (He was in a chess club with Bobby Fischer at Erasmus Hall High School in Brooklyn, but Fischer refused to play with him; "'With you, Neugeboren, I don't play,' he always said to me," Robert says. Why not? "Because," Robert says, smiling, "I played crazy.") He was a good if erratic student in high school, won a New York State Regents Scholarship to college, and successfully completed his freshman year at the City College of New York.

He was, in short, a bright and idiosyncratic young man with a sense of life and humor all his own, a person who showed no signs, until his first breakdown (except for those that, looking back, any of us might find in ourselves), that such a breakdown was at all likely, much less inevitable.

Robert's diagnosis has changed frequently in the past thirty years, depending largely upon which drugs have been successful in keeping him calm, stable, and/or compliant. He was schizophrenic when enormous doses of Thorazine and Stelazine calmed him; he was manic-depressive (bipolar) when lithium worked; he was manic-depressive-with-psychotic-symptoms, or hypomanic, when Tegretol or Depakote (anticonvulsants), or some new antipsychotic or antidepressant—Trilafon, Adapin, Mellaril, Haldol, Klonopin, risperidone—showed promise of making him cooperative; and he was schizophrenic (again) when various doctors promised cures through insulin-coma therapy or mega-dose-vitamin therapy or Marxist therapy or gas therapy. At the same time, often in an attempt to minimize side effects, other drugs were poured into him: Artane, Benadryl, Cogentin, Kemadrin, Symmetrel, Prolixin, Pamelor, Navane. . . .

During these years, Robert also participated in a long menu of psychotherapies: group therapy, family therapy, multifamily group therapy, Gestalt therapy, psychoanalytically oriented psychotherapy, goal-oriented therapy, art therapy, behavioral therapy, vocational rehabilitation therapy, milieu therapy, et al. Most often, though—the more chronic his condition, the truer this became—he was treated solely with drugs, and received no therapy at all.

It is as if, I often think, the very history of the ways in which our century has dealt with those it calls mentally ill has, for more than thirty years now, been passing through my brother's mind and body.

Robert and I talk with each other almost every day, and see each other often, sometimes in New York and sometimes in Massachusetts, and though our visits are not without their difficulties (why should we be different from other brothers?), visits in my home, with my children, have invariably been without incident.

I've never seen Uncle Robert this way, each of my three children said to me in the hours before and after my son Eli's graduation. Is he going to be all right? Can I help? And then: And what about you, Pop—are you going to be all right?

Robert spent the day and evening of Eli's graduation in and out of the house, withdrawing hundreds of dollars, ten dollars at a time, from automated teller machines; buying secondhand clothes at local thrift shops; leaving trails of clothing, coins, cigarette butts, small paper bags, and crumpled snot-filled tissues in virtually all the rooms of my (eleven-room) house; going from room to room and turning lights on and off; showing me pieces of paper upon which he had written indecipherable messages while demanding that I understand what they meant; and, whenever my children and their friends arrived home, hurrying from sight and hiding.

Eli returned home from his all-night (supervised) graduation party at the local county fairgrounds at about 6:00 AM, and Robert, whom I had not seen since we had left for Eli's graduation ceremonies at about 6:00 PM the night before, arrived not long after that, and ordered me to put him on a bus for New York immediately. He looked ghastly (he had—inexpertly—given himself a haircut, and had shaved off his mustache), and seemed totally disoriented: his hands and arms were flapping uncontrollably, his body was hunched over, his eyeglasses were covered with a milk-white sticky substance ("Scum!" he declared, when I asked), his movements were jagged, and he kept turning on me, ordering me around, screaming things that made no obvious sense.

Whether I did or did not reply, he became more and more enraged, telling me again and again that I wasn't listening to him, that I never listened to him, and that if I didn't do what he said he didn't know what he might do. "I want letters!" he kept shouting. "I want letters!"

At the bus stop he scurried around wildly, virtually on all fours, picking up cigarette butts and searching for money. He wore a wide-brimmed straw hat, a tuxedo vest over a T-shirt, tight white extra-short pants, bright knee-high red socks. He went to each of a half-dozen sidewalk newspaper kiosks and began putting quarters in them, taking out papers, and either stacking them on top of the kiosk or putting them in a mailbox. He went back and forth to a pay phone, dialing for information about people on Staten Island and yelling at the operator; he walked across the street to a parking lot and shouted questions at me; he wept and he screamed, and I found myself hoping that the bus would come on time (or ahead of time), that he would be allowed to board it, and that he would somehow get back to his halfway house (located on the grounds of South Beach Psychiatric Center) safely.

I had been in situations like this with Robert before—dozens of times through the past four decades—and though, as I said to my children, seeing Robert like this was not new for me, each time it happened it did still take me by surprise, and each time it happened, it seemed unutterably sad and heartbreaking.

How could it be that somebody who was so warm and loving, so charming, happy, and seemingly normal one moment—one day, one hour—could become so angry, wild, and lost moments later? And how could it be that each time it happened—no matter the years gone by—it felt as if it were happening for the first time?

Though, with the years, I've learned to cope with these situations—to be able to help me and Robert get through—and though, with the years, Robert has actually reversed the path his life had been on (despite dreadful prognostications, he had come, in the eight or nine years preceding Eli's graduation, to be able to spend more time out of hospitals than in them, and had made more of a life for himself than most people had dreamed possible), I still found myself going through litanies of familiar questions and doubts: Should I call the local police and have them take him to a hospital and deal with getting him back to New York City? Should I ask Robert where he was all night, and if he had been drinking and/or doing drugs, and if he thought he could get back to the city by himself? Should I leave my children and try to drive Robert the two hundred miles back to Staten Island? Should I call the hospital on Staten Island? Should I call some local psychiatrists and social workers I knew? Should I stay with Robert, or leave him alone? And how should I respond to his outbursts of anger, his bizarre behavior, his accusations, his questions, his tears?

Robert had stayed away from my children most of the time during his three days with us, and—his innate kindness, as ever, at work—had kept both his anger and his confusion hidden, for the most part, when in their presence. Still, each of my children noticed what a hard time he was having, and each came to me and offered sympathy, and help.

When, while changing from cap and gown into casual clothes, for his graduation party, Eli asked if he could do anything to help, and I told him the best thing he could do was to go off and enjoy the party, that Robert was my responsibility and not his, Eli had replied, "But he's mine too, Pop."

I smiled. "Maybe," I said. "But today is your day. This one's on me, okay?"

So I did what I usually do when things get bad for Robert. I tried, gently and firmly, to be as patient and direct with him as I could (telling him, for example, that I would call ahead to his halfway house to let them know he was on his way; asking him, again, if he did, in fact, want me to drive him back to Staten Island), and, when he came near to me—and when he walked off and seemed especially lost—I put my arms around him, and told him I loved him, and talked with him about whatever came to mind—his meals (I'd packed him a lunch), the bus, the trip back, the weather.

While people waiting for the bus stared, or tried not to stare, or moved away, Robert stayed close to me and seemed to be listening: I was glad he'd been able to visit, I said, and I wished he wasn't having such a hard time again, and we'd talk on the phone that evening after he was back at his halfway house, and I was very glad he'd been able to be here for Eli's graduation and had seen Miriam and Aaron, and we would see one another again soon.

Robert navigated the eight-hour trip home—bus, subway, ferry, and bus—successfully. We spoke that night—he cried a lot, complained about the hospital and the medications, and then he was off on flights of words that, because I knew the reference points (events and people from our childhood, jokes we loved, experiences we'd been through together), seemed more poignant than strange. "I didn't embarrass you, did I?" he asked at one point. "I didn't embarrass the children, I hope. . . ."

The following morning, for the first time in a year, and for at least the fiftieth time in his life, he was hospitalized. When I called the doctor in charge of Robert's ward and he asked what I thought had precipitated Robert's break, I said that there were some immediate causes that seemed obvious, but that the real precipitant, it seemed to me, was simply the fact of Robert's life—of the last thirty-one years of his life. If you'd been where Robert had been, and suffered all the drugs, abuse, incompetence, and pain he'd suffered, the wonder, it seemed to me, wasn't why he'd broken again, but why he hadn't, like so many others he'd known, died or killed himself or deteriorated completely.

But after I said this, I did name some of the things that had been going on in Robert's life that might have precipitated this break. There was the graduation itself, and being with family (but Robert had been in this situation dozens of times before and had had no difficulties). There were his desires and fantasies about living in my home with me in Massachusetts, now intensified because Eli would be going off to college and I would soon be living alone (but I'd been the single full-time parent of my three children for nearly a decade, and though Robert often asked about moving in with me, I'd never encouraged him, and he himself had begun saying he didn't think it was a good idea). There was the fact that, a few weeks before, Robert's best friend had been moved out of the home in which he and Robert had lived together for two years and into which Robert had been hoping to return (so where would he live now?). There was the fact that he had been out of the hospital for eleven months, and the better he became—the more alert, the more himself—the less the make-work activities of the hospital's day center interested him, and the more bored he became. There were all the feelings (of failure, envy, love, resentment) aroused by being with me and my children—seeing Eli graduate (and at the age Robert was when he had his first breakdown), and seeing us move ahead with our lives while his life seemed, still, to be going nowhere.

Though I could, as ever, talk about what I thought had caused Robert's condition, long-term and short-term, the more important question, it seemed to me (or was I thinking this way in order to give myself heart, in order to find something good in a situation that was god-awful?), wasn't what had caused this breakdown, or any of the others, but what, given his life, had enabled him to survive, and to do more than survive—to retain his generosity, his warmth, his intelligence, his pride, humor, and his sense of self. This, it seemed to me, was, as ever, the true miracle and mystery.

I had, not long before, asked Robert the same questions the doctor asked me. Did he ever have any sense of what made him go off the way he did sometimes—of what the difference was, of what made things change for him, or in him? He had been silent for a long time, and then had said, "No answer."

These were, I said at once, afraid my questions might have hurt him, questions nobody seemed to know the answers to.

"So why should I know?" Robert said then. "Am I different from anybody else?"

The doctor at South Beach Hospital concluded that Robert's breakdown had been precipitated by alcohol and substance abuse. Robert had admitted that on the way up to visit me he had had a few beers and had inhaled amyl nitrite. The amyl nitrite ("poppers") was "part of the gay lifestyle," the doctor said, and was taken by homosexuals to increase sexual pleasure. The alcohol and substance abuse, he concluded, had clearly "destabilized" and "unhinged" the parts of Robert's brain that his medications—lithium and Depakote—had stabilized. The problem, therefore, was "noncompliance."

I had heard this from doctors before, and I responded with an obvious, if rhetorical question: Okay, but what was it that had caused the noncompliance? If mental illness was as debilitating and awful a condition as it seemed to be (as surely it had been for Robert), and if the medications alleviated that condition, why would anyone ever stop taking the medications, or do anything to interfere with their beneficial effects?

As my father had once put it, to a doctor who refused to continue treating Robert because Robert had stopped taking his pills, "So where, Doctor, is the pill to make him want to take the pills?"

When I visited Robert after his breakdown—on a locked unit at South Beach Psychiatric Center (a New York State facility where he has been hospitalized, on and off, for the past twenty years, and which is located on Staten Island, a half-mile or so from Staten Island Hospital), he was, as before, on isolation: living, day after day, twenty-four hours a day, in a bare room in which there was nothing but a sheetless bed and an empty dresser. This was called, by the staff psychologist, Henry Grossman, "reduced stimulation."

When I had, previously, questioned, as gently as I could, whether being on isolation, and on heavy doses of Thorazine (the medication Robert hated above all others), and not being permitted to make or receive calls, or to have visitors, might not feel to Robert like punishment instead of therapy, Henry Grossman had replied that this might temporarily be the case. "But our experience," he said, "is that in retrospect patients come to appreciate the reduction of stimulation—the limits and boundaries that have been set for them."

He had also assured me that Robert was not just locked away in a room—that every hour on the half hour, for five minutes, Robert was taken to the bathroom and for a walk down the hallway. When I asked if Robert had had or would be receiving any therapy—if he was talking with anybody in any regular way about what he was going through—Henry's reply was abrupt: "Robert cannot tolerate therapy."

This seemed to me an absurd statement—Robert couldn't tolerate therapy? You mean you can't tolerate trying to work with him, I wanted to scream. Why are you a therapist if you don't want to work with patients, to listen to them? And when will Robert be able to "tolerate" therapy—when he's well?

But it was the same old story, and I was in the same old quandary: if I complained too much, or confronted Robert's health care workers with their inadequacies, or sent off the long letters I often composed in my head (to *The New York Times,* to hospital and state officials, to doctors, etc.), I feared they would only take out their resentments of me upon Robert—that they would (as had happened before) simply talk with me less, care for Robert less, and/or ship him off to a ward where he would receive even less attention (and more drugs) than he was now receiving.

Robert had been here, in this ward and ones like it, and in worse places, before. (One time at Mid-Hudson, a forensic facility, when they had him in a straitjacket for a long period of time, I remembered him telling me, he asked for a smoke, so he could let the ashes fall on the jacket and set himself on fire. He succeeded. After the aides got him out of the straitjacket, one of them took him to the basement, where he beat him up and warned him never to do what he had done again.)

Now, on a warm summer day in July of 1993, because of my visit, Robert has been granted courtyard privileges, and we sit at a picnic table by ourselves. He opens the bag of food I've brought him for lunch, but his hands are shaking so badly that when he tries to eat an egg salad sandwich, the egg salad sprays everywhere. He is frustrated, apologetic, embarrassed. I talk with him easily, we joke back and forth, and after a short while I scoop up pieces of egg, tomato, lettuce, and bread, he takes his false teeth out, and I feed him with my fingers, placing the food directly into his mouth.

When he cannot tolerate his tremblings any longer, he walks away. He calls to me, and I go and sit next to him on a different bench, and we talk about the ward, and the doctors, and my trip down, about Eli's graduation, and the floods in the Midwest, and our cousins. We have more than three dozen first cousins (both our parents came from large, extended families), and I fill Robert in on who is where and doing what—our cousins, and the children of our cousins, and the children of our cousins' children—and which relatives I've seen or heard from. Suddenly Robert turns, leans down, and, with great gentleness, kisses the back of my hand several times, after which he begins weeping.

"Oh, Jay, Jay," he cries softly. "They're barbarians here. Barbarians, barbarians! Pavlovians . . ."

He presses his mouth to the back of my hand, and I take him to me, hold him close. A few minutes later, we walk around the courtyard, and then he tells me that he likes to walk back and forth, in a diagonal, between two trees—they are about ten yards apart—and count the number of times he can do this. So we walk back and forth together, and I sing to him, and then he joins in—putting his arm around my waist, leaning on my shoulder—and we go back and forth again and again, loudly singing old camp songs, in English and Hebrew, that we remember from our childhood.

He eats some more, and then we walk again, side by side, our hands clasped behind us, mimicking two diplomats, trading stories and news. He clutches his dentures in one hand, a piece of bread locked in their bite, and when he puts the top bridge back in his mouth, I say something about his being on uppers.

He starts giggling, inserts the lower bridge.

"And now you're on lowers," I say, and add that I don't understand why, since he's on uppers and lowers, which probably balance each other, the hospital has to give him any other medications.

"It's how they make their profit," he says.

When I call Robert from Massachusetts after our visit, he is flying—repeating everything he says twice, rambling on about people living and dead as if they were there with him on the ward, thanking me for visiting him and for the things I brought him, giving me lists of all the foods he has eaten and all the things he wants me to send him, mixing these lists with references to scenes in movies and to scenes from our child-hood, talking about Adlai Stevenson and Bill Clinton (who is, he says, his son) and how the whole country is in a very big depression—and every few seconds he tells me that he has to hang up, he has to hang up (though he never does). And then, when he finally takes a breath, and I tell him I love him, his voice suddenly drops and slows down, and he talks to me in a way that is totally natural.

"Oh, Jay," he says, "don't you see? There's nothing better in my life than what's happening! You don't know. You don't know, Jay. You don't want to know. . . ." He weeps freely, keeps talking. "This life of working here and there in hospitals, or as a volunteer, and being here now, and doing nothing—isn't there ever going to be anything better for me? Please get me out of here, Jay. Please, please . . ."

When, later in our conversation, I tell him that I called him the day before but nobody could find him, he asks me what I called him, and when I say, "I called you my brother," he laughs, says, "That's an old one, Jay. That's an old one—but listen, I'm going to switch the phone to my good ear, all right?"

"There," he says, a few seconds later. "Now can you hear me better?"

Moved as I am by Robert's situation and his life—and his plea for a life different from the one he has—I find, after our visit and our talk, that I am feeling relieved, and, even, mildly exhilarated. (I am also feeling exasperated, yet again, with the treatment, and lack of treatment, he receives from the staff; when I talk with his new prescribing psychiatrist, his fourth since his hospitalization, I discover, for example, that this man—"So why are you calling me?" are his first words to me after I identify myself as Robert's brother—has been prescribing and changing Robert's medications for a full week without having spoken with or examined Robert. When I complain about this to a part-time staff psychiatrist who has previously treated Robert, she is appalled, though not surprised.)

But I am feeling better about Robert and his situation because the truth (I shrug when I realize this, as if to say to myself: What can I do? That's the way it is) is that when Robert and I are together, whether in my home or on his ward, whether on the West Side of Manhattan (where we lived next door to each other in the mid-sixties, during his first year out of Creedmoor), or in Atlantic City (where, six weeks before Eli's graduation, Robert and I went together for two days, at his request, to celebrate his fiftieth birthday), we're happy. Not always, and not without a pervasive sense of loss and sadness, but happy to be with each other, no matter the context, because it seems good, simply, in an often frightening and miserable life, to be known—and to be able to be near the person who knows you and is known by you.

Herbert Gold

king of the cleveland beatniks

I believed from childhood on, that part of my job in life was to be a proper big brother to Sid. We escaped the neighbor boy in Lakewood together, but there were demons that Sid never found a way to evade.

He is years gone now and the novel he spent nearly fifty years writing, never finished, sits in four sagging boxes in my bedroom. I try and keep trying to read it. I carry a crate out into a sunny room, take out a handful of paper, admire some of the sentences and paragraphs, and can't go on. I follow a story until it stops without coming to an end and then start another story. There is a search going on here, a sadness, explosions of wrath and fantasy, and then an abrupt halt, sometimes in the middle of a sentence. I put the paper back in the box and carry it to my bedroom.

"Sid passed." For a moment I thought our brother Bob in Cleveland was calling me in San Francisco to tell me Sid had taken a driving test.

"What?"

He repeated the words and I was irritated by the language. Bob had telephoned Sid for three days, he didn't answer the phone, and finally Bob went to his apartment. His car was in the parking lot; he had to be there. The custodian wouldn't open the door until they called the police. They found him sitting in the bathroom and Bob said, "Why don't you answer the phone?" The cop took his arm, held it, and said, "Because he's dead."

He was the kid brother I bullied, nagged, and loved, the one who remembered the childhood we shared. He was the one I took long confiding walks with. We became restless boys again in our hometown, or sometimes in San Francisco, and even in Paris the one time I managed to persuade him to use his passport.

When he died, he had been writing his novel for fifty years. I keep watch over the four cardboard boxes filled with it. He was gonna finish it and let the world know where on earth he had been.

"Let me see some of it," I would ask on my visits to Cleveland or when he visited me in San Francisco.

"Next time," he would say. "Next time, I promise. I've just got to pull some things together."

"Let me see a few pages. Sometimes a reader helps."

"It's going good. I want to get it organized first, Herb."

"When?"

"I'll send it to you. I've got the mailing envelopes already. It just needs a little more work."

He worked as a cabdriver, as caretaker of a laundromat, and in a Ford factory. As a cabdriver, didn't like the scams of hookers, johns, and pimps; as a laundromat operator, got bored with the smell of detergent, left the place in a buddy's charge, went off to drink coffee and make notes; as an auto worker, left his paychecks in his pants until they expired (in the meantime, had no money). For awhile, he ran a poker game. That worked okay; he took his share of the pot, gave advice, bought sandwiches and made instant coffee. During the years traveling through the south in a carnival, he wanted no contact at all with anyone back home, wherever home was for him. Later he said he planned to write or call, but it just got away from him. He postponed. He was just gonna do it, maybe tomorrow.

When I married, I put that advertisement in Billboard, in the Traveling Show issue, asking in capital letters for MY BROTHER SID GOLD to come meet my wife. Maybe he hunkered down in a boarding house near Tuscaloosa,

Alabama, for some relaxing reading of classified ads; maybe someone said, "Hey Sid, that you?" It must have been the right time for him to leave his silence, this perturbed abstention. Along with the Pendleton shirts and the Indian blanket, he brought stories about sheriffs, gypsies, addicts, a down-home American foreign legion. We talked about the midway, about carnie life and language, the interrogatory that went: "Are you with it? . . . With it and for it." I was sure he was planning to write about it. "Naw," he said. "You do it, Herb. I got something else in mind."

I wrote a novel, "The Man Who Was Not With It," which I dedicated to him. I thought the book was fantasy, my own dream of wandering and escape, built out of the carnival of my adolescent dreams, but a review in Billboard accused me of giving away the secrets of the midway and words I made up appeared in glossaries of carnie argot.

Sid explained that this was because carnie folks didn't know what was real and what was their dream. "Their world is made of sawdust and smoke, Herb. The same for me. Like it is for me, Herb."

That's why he was writing something else, he said, something that wasn't sawdust and smoke. It would be ready soon.

"What is it?"

He blinked behind his glasses. He drew on his pipe—he'd given up cigarettes because any fool knew they were bad for the health, but he inhaled deeply from his pipe. He could tell me this much about his novel; I shouldn't crowd him: He was writing about the radical splinter movements of the Thirties. He was interested in the Schachtmanites and the Lovestoneites (Trotsky was too mainstream for him). He was writing about the dark poor of the Depression. There was a Croatian coal miner in Appalachia, a man who had run away from a city slum. He and his friends lived without women in rural boarding houses and sent money home.

"It's complicated, Herb, but I'm putting it together."

In the late Fifties, when he was broke as usual, just fired from one of his jobs, I wrestled a story away from him, a tale about a stubborn thief in jail at Christmastime, and it was printed in one of the *Playboy* imitations of the time. There was a dreamy longing for love in it, and the editor of *Nugget* (or was it *Dude* or *Gent?*) had a sentimental streak. It appeared in the December issue with a collection of nude girls-next-door under mistletoe or wrapped in red ribbon. Opposite his story, a cutie, naked except for roller skates and some discreet Fifties airbrushing, was pursued by a panting Santa. By the time Sid was holding court at Arabica for the beatniks of Cleveland, the roller-skater was probably a grandmother. The story of the lonely thief during the season of celebration is his only published work.

I told him it was a good story. It had his devotion to adventure, and in the pain of a soul behind bars in a small-town jail (was it in Georgia or Alabama?) at that holiday season which haunts everyone for different reasons, it gave a sense of the general isolation. He wondered what those who bought the magazine for the roller-skating cuties would make of his story and I delivered a little lecture about the ways of commerce, the need of men's magazines to avoid trouble with their mailing privileges, and assured him that the editor of *Nugget* (or *Dude* or *Gent*) really valued literature above everything except his job and staying clear of federal, state, or local obscenity experts.

"That's not what writing is about," he said.

Agreed, and he shouldn't have to think about it. So I told him I could help him find an agent.

"Naw," he said. "That's not what I want to write. As soon as I get the novel together, you'd like to read it, wouldn't you?"

"Let me see what you've got."

"Good idea. Right, right. Pretty soon, Herb."

Over the years I expressed my exasperation with his floating, postponing, late-sleeping life by criticizing his language, as if better explanation would resolve matters. When I telephoned, he would say, "I was just gonna write to you, Herb," or, "I was just gonna send you part of my novel," or, "I was just gonna call you." I told him he had invented a new grammatical form, the Future Conditional Imperative Subjunctive, the I-was-just-gonna.

As children, we slept in twin beds in the same room. We took turns telling stories to each other at night, the usual ones—flying over houses to escape monsters, swimming under seas to find lost continents, battling in jungles for justice or for our lives. When we were told by our mother to be quiet, tomorrow was a school day, we continued in whispers. I frightened him or he frightened me and then we faded into the miracle of sleep, continuing our adventures without companionship because that's the way the world often was.

This busy dreaming may have set us permanently into the storytelling mode. Although the stories go on and on, some find ways to end them and he never did. His dreams wandered the skies and swam the seas and gazed at monsters and never reached a state of mere meditation upon the partial wholeness of the world. That acceptance of shapely incompleteness is the paradox of finishing. For him, nothing ever finished.

I remembered something of the spirit of our sleepy adventures when it came time to tell stories for my children. They also liked to walk with him and listen to his ramble, his explorations, his far-fetched dartings into anecdote and fabulous inventions, sometimes ending in bursts of unexpected laughter. They made links where he made none, or perhaps they didn't need links, since the adventures were exotic and his grin was reassuring. "Did that really happen to you, Uncle Sid?"

"What do you think?"

"Well, maybe . . ."

"So that's why I'm telling you." And they preferred that it did happen, the sea lion must really have carried him under the ice, it was much better to think so.

Among his papers were photographs, faded brown, of the two of us in short pants, probably three and four years old, sitting proud in a cart pulled by a goat. In our hearts we were fighter pilots, or perhaps fighter goat riders. I am holding the reins. Surely both our mother and the proprietor of the goat and the cart are standing nearby, begging these solemn boys to smile. But we have our own intentions, we don't smile. This is our serious business, too important for us to waste energy listening to a mother and a gypsy with a goat. I'm sure Sid wants to hold the reins. I'm not sure if I let him.

When our mother caught us fighting (translation: I was beating Sid up), she reached for the telephone and asked for the police department. "Hello, Officer Cecil? I have a very bad boy here." Next I would be going to jail and it would serve me right. I folded my arms and looked my best hardened criminal, waiting for the swift chariot of justice to carry me away, but Sid begged piteously, "Don't, don't, we were only playing."

"Playing? Playing? You call that playing?"

"Herb was showing me how to wrestle."

"*Boxing*," I muttered. "Didn't grab him by the neck."

"Just a second, Officer Cecil." She paused, the telephone in her hand. "Promise you'll stop with the funny business?"

While I stood there, arms still folded in defiant miscreant mode, Sid said, tears streaming, "Yes, we promise—please?"

"Officer Cecil? I think we may be able to deal with this." Reluctantly she replaced the receiver.

Years later, when I fled to Sid for comfort, and I did, it was because of trouble in a marriage. When family shipwrecks, a welcome from family is salvation for a drowning man. He listened to me as I repeated the helpful nonsense of a surgeon friend who said, "Cut off a leg and it's gone forever. But psychological pain doesn't last." He knew better than most that this is helpful and untrue. It lasts. He walked with me; he listened to my troubles until they repeated themselves into post marital whining, as repeated pain does; we went to all-night movies together; I slept on his couch, my head buried in a tufted mohair Goodwill pillow.

"It's okay, Herb," he said, "it's okay." Since we were brothers, I understood him. It was not okay, we both know it was not okay, but Sid and Herb would always be brothers and that could be counted on. For awhile, I gave up judgment of him—all the judgment I had in stock was turned against myself. I told him thanks and his lips moved, murmuring like a soothing parent. I wrapped myself in an overcoat and sank into the dusty couch.

In Cleveland, at the memorial ceremony, I found that this man who lived alone, seemed so lonely, had a life filled with companionship. The king of the Cleveland beatniks had held court daily at his table in Arabica. A chess player, a genial loafer, a pronouncer of verdicts, a man with ambitions, he hung with those who were like him. Single mothers and rock band roadies, crazed stock market and racetrack fanatics, guys with surefire systems and those who knew how to work other people's systems to get various kinds of public assistance, genial easers who pretended to be psychologically disabled but really were, they were his colleagues through the vicissitudes. Sid counseled them on how to trade their food stamps for necessities, if cigarettes happened to be a necessity; how to avoid the fines for overdue books or tapes at the public library; how to duck the hassles.

My kid brother, the closest to me. That older brother–kid brother unequal tug of war altered as we traveled through boyhood, youth, middle age, on the road to our shared inevitable destination; the rules of the play were also set down. For years I nagged him and finally resolved to stop asking to see The Novel. I managed to carry out my resolution. It ate at both of us when I brought it up; anger rose in me, hurt rose in him, when I would say, "Okay, just a piece of it, feedback helps. Okay, just a few pages. It doesn't have to be retyped."

"Pretty soon, Herb. Next time I see you. Right now my allergies are bothering me."

So finally I stopped. He seemed to miss my asking; I wasn't playing by the rules, so he brought it up himself, he would tell me anyway. "I'm having trouble organizing. The story keeps changing. I got a good story going, but . . . I've got it in geological layers."

"Geological layers?"

In the months after he died, his friends from Arabica sent me drawings they had made of him, photographs, even a tape recording of one of his political rants. In the comic strip drawn by R. Crumb, Sid's name was unchanged, the beatnik beard a little less gray than it became, but still looking as if it had been trimmed with toenail scissors. Crumb, working as an artist for American Greetings in Cleveland, had been part of the radical bohemia in the Paris of Northeastern Ohio until he moved first to San Francisco and then to the south of France. An outpost of Arabica philosophers kept the faith in the North Coast, the Great Lake Erie country.

I carried his ashes back to San Francisco. I shipped his manuscript in four large boxes which stand in a corner of my bedroom. Sometimes I carry one of the boxes into the sunny front room and excavate one geological layer or another. Stuck among the haphazard piles of paper, file folders, and notebooks are old letters from me, some dating back to my Army days during the War. I reread my letters, remembering myself as an eighteen-year-old stranger; I read a geological layer of the novel. The story abruptly shifts from Appalachia to Pittsburgh to Columbus. The plan is not revealed; the people, sometimes vividly evoked, just disappear and give way to new characters.

There are also journals in which he records his daydreams, his disputes with our mother and father, his ambitions. He writes about not sleeping, about sleeping too much, about passing time and not knowing how it has passed. As a freshman at Ohio State University, he describes riding a motorcycle—whose?—into the farm country outside Columbus instead of going to classes. He makes resolutions. He complains about not being able to keep his resolutions. He discusses Dostoevsky, Kafka, and Faulkner with himself. He promises to get organized. "Weather permitting," he writes, with an echo of our father's lugubrious humor.

The manuscript ("The Novel") was stealing his life, his dreams taking over his world; at the same time, The Novel gave him a life, his hope that somehow, someday, he would carve out of this accumulating mass of paper his being in the world. As time went by, it diminished him, the rivulets of fantasy draining down the slope of years. The young man became an old man and remained a boy. He was afflicted with an impatient lyricism which never stopped to say: this much and no more; here's the beginning and here comes the need for an end; and now, wait, there *is* a way to stop.

After awhile, I load the paper back into its box and think to myself: I've got to go at this systematically, try to figure out where something begins and where it ends. When he writes about the weather in Cleveland, I remember our hikes through the snow and our destination to hot chocolate at Clark's on Detroit Avenue; the snow is always new-fallen and white when I remember it. He was the guardian of childhood, the only person who still remembered our lives together in family. Now no one keeps me company in these memories, though his presence keeps flooding back in avalanches of geological layers, a lava flow of discovery, eagerness, hope, pain. I excavate in the California sun and find only more headlines from the *Plain Dealer*, more geological layers.

Sometimes I talk about him. I tell my children, his nieces and nephews, that he wasn't unhappy and they tilt their heads and try to figure out why their dad is telling them something they know not to be the case. Okay, so he was unhappy, yes, but within the depression, kids . . . Let's see how I can explain this. Within the gloom and stasis . . . no. Within the unhappiness, he took pleasure in the newspaper, gossiping, coffee, his daydreams, his moments of resolute note-taking and the clattering bursts of his garage-sale manual typewriter. Bits of envelopes, torn edges of newsprint stuck out of his pockets. Restlessly he gathered and sorted the materials for his geological layers. He never gave up. I love him "like a brother"—what an ambiguous expression that is.

Sid was presented with gifts of sympathy, humor, understanding, and concern, but what he needed to understand, narrate, laugh about, and care for was too much for him to manage. He emitted opinions, often stubbornly wrong, distracted by his melancholy. He had lost pride. He had found grief early. His life was a long retreat. His sadness grew more intense as time went by. I want to think he never lost hope, although alone one morning, choking on his blood, struggling to sit up, he must have understood that his fifty-year-long unfinished novel was finally done with. The weather didn't permit.

In my bedroom sit these four crates of my brother's life, the uncharted universe of his dreaming. I carry the boxes into a sunnier room and try to read some of the mass of manuscript and then put the papers in their boxes and carry them back into the dark where he still lives in his geological layers.

Gregory Orr

the accident

What were Jonathan and Peter doing up at this hour? It was only six in the morning, still dark out. They should be asleep; they didn't have to get ready for school for another hour yet. Bill, who was fourteen, and I, twelve, wouldn't be going to school today—the first pleasure of a day that promised many more. Already, the two of us were bundled up in sweaters, coats, and hats, with flashlights stuffed in our pockets. Padded like that, we looked fat as snowmen in the small front hall. But why were Jon and Peter standing there in their pajamas, getting in the way? They were only kids, ten and eight—Dad had promised this adventure to us older kids. As Dad came down the stairs with his rifle, Peter yelled out:

"Why can't we go? Its not fair"

"What do you mean it's not fair?" Bill snapped. "Go away."

I did my best to bat Jon out of the way, as if he were a small, yapping dog, but the room was too crowded for anyone to move easily. Mom was there too, retying Bill's bootlaces.

"Why can't we go?" they both howled at once.

"Because this is for grown-ups, and you're just kids," I said with utter contempt. And as if to prove my point, they both began crying. By now, Bill and I were both shouting that they were just crybabies and should shut up and get out of our way. Dad had stopped on a lower step of the stairs and surveyed the chaotic room as if it was a puddle he'd meant to cross, but suddenly had the thought that it was deeper than he'd antici-pated and maybe wading in wasn't such a good idea. Bill's and my screams weren't having the desired effect of silencing Peter and Jon, and it looked as if they might go on indefinitely, when Mom looked up at Dad and said: "Jim. Maybe they could go just this one time."

At that suggestion, Bill and I were even more furious. As if there would be a "next time"—wasn't this our only chance to have a first day of deer-hunting season? Wasn't it something so special that Dad, a country doctor who never took a day off from morning house calls, had done so today? Why should we share it with them?

But we could sense that shift taking place that so often resulted when Mom entered into our bickering with her reasonable justice that tended toward compassion for the weaker party. Bill and I had no choice but to start whining ourselves, as if we were the more righteous and injured. Dad cut it short: "OK, they can go. But everyone pipe down. And the two of you—get dressed pronto."

They whooped their way up the stairs, while Bill and I muttered and shared one of our rare moments of communion and agreement: the kids, we were certain, were bound to ruin the trip. With them along, we might as well invite Mom, too, and even Nancy, who was only four. Why not bring the dog and cats, too? Why not have a picnic?

It had been a clear night and was still dark as the five of us started our march along the dirt road and then out over the frosted field grass that made a crunching sound underfoot. It was bitter cold. I tightened my parka hood into a small, fur-bordered porthole and kept my eyes on Dad's boots silhouetted in his wavering flashlight beam. Even so, the frigid air felt like a thin mask of ice over the exposed parts of my face. I carried my .22 rifle cradled in both arms, its familiar weight gone vague with the muffling layers of glove and coat.

A faint, gray light was just seeping up from the eastern horizon as we arrived at the trench. Two weeks before, we'd walked this slope with Dad. He'd picked a spot on the bare hillside above the field where we'd often seen deer grazing, and Bill and

I had returned with pick and shovel to dig a hunter's ambush. Now, the five of us paused above our shallow trench, while we three hunters removed our gloves and each loaded a single shell into his rifle. My hands trembled with cold and excitement as I slid a bullet into its chamber and clicked on the safety catch that would prevent accidental firing. We put our rifles on the ground as we clambered awkwardly down into the space that had been dug to hold three and was now being asked to accommodate five. We were packed in so tight that what we lost in mobility we gained in body heat.

All was silence broken only by our whispers and the occasional distant caw of crows. As the gray light grew, I watched my breath rise up in wisps. I watched the frost flowers scattered across the dirt mound a few inches from my face melt like the stars going out overhead. And then we saw it: a deer slowly working its way along the trail through the power-line swamp and out into the field below us, where it paused to browse the short grass. An antlered buck! Dad whispered that Bill could shoot first. I was stunned. What could he possibly mean? Was this another one of those "you'll have your chance when you're older" routines? Did he mean that if Bill missed, I could shoot? Or did he imagine that our luck would be so extraordinary that if Bill killed this deer, a second one would appear this same morning? Surely he couldn't imagine that I would wait for another day. There was no time to explain to Dad how wrong-headed he was. No time to tell him I had to take part. As Bill put his rifle to his shoulder and took aim, I, too, lifted my .22 and sighted along the barrel. And when Bill fired, I fired too, at the exact same instant, so that our two rifles made a single harsh sound that echoed off the woods as the deer collapsed in the green field.

The five of us scrambled down the brush-grown slope and raced to where the deer lay. Now our excited shouts and calls went silent as we stood in a loose circle of awe around the dead animal. I was delirious with glee. Against my father's orders, I'd pulled my trigger at the same moment Bill had fired. I was certain I too had killed the deer and the pride of it thrilled me and filled my whole being to bursting. My father calmed us down.

"Check your chambers," he said.

This was the order to make sure your gun was empty. Each of us was supposed to point his rifle straight down at the ground and pull the trigger. If a bullet had misfired, then the gun would discharge harmlessly into the dirt.

I was certain I'd fired my one and only bullet into the creature that now lay at our feet. I was certain that pulling the trigger would produce only the dull mechanical click of a firing pin in an empty chamber.

I was wrong. My safety must have been on all through the shooting so that I never actually fired the bullet, which was still in my gun. But I thought my gun was empty and so instead of pointing it at the ground, I causally directed it back over my right shoulder toward the woods and never even looked as I pulled the trigger.

Peter was there, a little behind me, not more than two feet from where I stood. In that instant in which the sound of my gun firing made me startle and look around, Peter was already lying motionless on the ground at my feet. I never saw his face— only his small figure lying there, the hood up over his head, a dark stain of blood already seeping across the fabric toward the fringe of fur riffling in the breeze. I never saw his face again.

I screamed, "I didn't mean to, I didn't mean to!"

My father yelled to us to run for help. I ran across the field toward the house as fast as I could. I ran straight across the swampy stream that split the field and scrambled up the bank and through the barbed-wire fence. I heard Bill and Jon running behind me. I was trying to get to the house first, as if somehow that could help, but what I had done and seen was racing behind me and I couldn't outrun it. I wanted to run so fast that I would outrun the horror and reach some place where it had never happened, where the world was still innocent of this deed and word of it might never arrive. But even now I was running toward more horror, toward the moment when I would reach the house and when, no matter how exhausted and out of breath I was, I would still have to tell my mother that I had shot Peter.

I hid in my room. I lay on my bed, curled up in a ball, moaning and crying. I never saw Dad cross the lawn carrying Peter in his arms. But an hour later, I got up and went to my window at the sound of the siren and saw a pale green ambulance backing up to our front door. I glimpsed the stretcher being slid inside, but Peter's body was hidden by blankets and the white-coated backs of the ambulance people.

I couldn't leave my room. I returned to my bed and curled up, clutching my pillow and sobbing into it or crying and biting it. I kept my eyes closed, as if by doing that I could hide from my family and the horrible new reality I had brought into the world. I kept seeing Peter's body on the ground and I found myself pleading with my parents in my imagination, begging them to forgive me for what I had done. But at least it was taking place inside the privacy of my own mind. I thought I would die if I had to actually look at my parents or anyone in the family.

Several hours after the ambulance left, my mother entered my room.

"Greg," she said.

"I'm sorry. I'm sorry. Please, go away." I begged.

"Greg it was an accident. It was a terrible accident. It wasn't your fault."

I started to sob again. What she said made no sense. Of course it was my fault. Did she think I was stupid—that I didn't know what I had done, didn't know that I had done it? You could say that spilling soda was an accident, but you couldn't say that killing your brother was an accident. That was something far more horrible than an accident. Nothing in the word "accident" offered me any hope. But what she said next was even more disturbing:

"Something very much like this happened to your father when he was your age."

"What do you mean?"

"When he was your age, he killed a friend of his in a hunting accident."

Her deep-set eyes were red from her own sobbing, and she stood with her arms crossed on her chest as if she were trying to hold herself together, to keep from bursting apart with grief. She was speaking to me about this strange and awful coincidence, but her voice was numb and distant, as if she were repeating it to herself to simply hear it spoken aloud, to see if it sounded believable. It didn't. Not to me. That is, it sounded unbelievable and terrible, but this was exactly the world I had now entered: the world of the terrible and unbelievable. I had killed my own brother. Why not learn this also—that my father had once killed someone, too? I heard what she said. I wanted to ask what she meant, but I couldn't speak. She stood for a while by my bed and then she left the room, closing the door behind her.

I had wanted her to hold me, but I couldn't say that. I had wanted her to forgive me, but I couldn't ask. I knew I'd lost her love forever.

Hours later, early in the afternoon, there was a knock on the door of my room. It was Bethany, my father's receptionist, with a tray of soup. My hunger overcame my shame, and I sat on the edge of the bed with the tray on my lap, slurping the soup down. Bethany must have brought the soup from her own home, because it had a taste I didn't recognize. While I ate, she stood far back by the door and waited.

"This is an awful thing, Greg, but you should know that right now Peter is in heaven with Jesus."

I stopped eating. I sat there, unable to believe I had heard her say that. I covered my face with both hands, but I was too exhausted or dehydrated to cry anymore. When I closed my eyes I saw Peter and he was not sitting on Jesus' lap and gazing up into Christ's mild countenance as the lamb did in the stained glass window in our church. Instead, he was lying face down on the cold ground in the field. I knew she was only trying to comfort me and to tell me what she believed, but I thought she was crazy.

I wanted to say: "What's wrong with you? Didn't you see his body? Don't you know what happened? Don't you know he's dead?" I wanted to scream at her: "This isn't Sunday school! My brother was just killed by a bullet and I fired it. What kind of nonsense are you saying?"

"It may not make sense now," she continued, "but its all part of God's plan."

I hadn't thought much about God, but when Bethany dredged up out of her rural heart the strongest consolation she could imagine, she inadvertently ended forever any hope I had of conventional religious belief. What she said seemed like a simple-minded mockery of what I had seen and done. Maybe if she hadn't spoken so soon after Peter's death, I could have found comfort in what she said. Maybe if my mother had held me when she visited, had given me some reassurance, I would have been more receptive to Bethany's story of supernatural resurrection and a benevolent though mysterious plan that governed the universe. Instead, I felt rage and despair. Either this was a meaningless and horrible universe and this woman's ideas were a lollipop she sucked in the dark, or else there was a divine plan, but it was not benevolent. What had my mother meant about my father having killed someone too? How could my father and I have done the same horrible thing at the same age? Certainly that coincidence represented some mysterious, even supernatural pattern, but who could imagine it being a happy pattern, a pattern that showed there was a God and he cared about us humans?

I had one last visitor that day. A state trooper arrived to complete the investigation into Peter's death. While he waited downstairs, my father opened my door:

"Greg, you should know that he died in the ambulance and that he never recovered consciousness. That means he didn't suffer."

He asked me to come down to his office. It was part of a three-room complex at the back of the house that included a waiting room and a small examining room. The office was an interior room. Its only light came from a brass table lamp with a green glass shade that cast a small pool at its base. We entered the shadowy room. My father moved to a place in a corner. The trooper was seated awkwardly at my father's desk, which was far too small for him. Even his hat was outsized and out of place, flopped down on the desktop like a giant, brooding spider. He was a young man with a blond crew cut and an open, beefy face. He seemed embarrassed and, except for a brief glance when I first entered, he never looked at me. Instead, he sat with his forehead propped on one hand and his face bowed over the forms like a school kid unsure of his handwriting and so concentrating entirely on the act of moving his pen across the paper.

"What happened, son?"

"I don't know."

That was as close to the truth as I could come, but I wasn't going to be allowed to stop there.

"Start at the beginning. How did it happen?"

"We were hunting."

"Who is we?"

I sat hunched in the chair by the desk. My eyes kept blurring. The neat row of bullets wedged into their individual loops on his gun belt became a centipede crawling across his belly. The mahogany swivel chair he sat in had belonged to my father's father, a man who died when I was a baby. There was a brass plaque mounted on its back that said it was the chair he'd sat in when he served as Superintendent of Prisons for New York State from 1915 to 1919. Now it seemed to foretell my own fate as I stared at the trooper's handcuffs dangling over the edge of the seat.

"Tell me what happened, son."

He was here to investigate and file a report on Peter's death—to me, Peter's murder. He was here to investigate a crime I had committed. All afternoon I had struggled to believe that what had happened had not happened, could not happen, was too horrible to have happened. Every time I had closed my eyes I had seen Peter's body on the ground, had felt the rifle in my hands. But that suspended moment had been a private horror. Now this trooper, who represented society and the world of other people, was asking me to publicly acknowledge that it had happened. He was asking me to confess, to admit to the whole world that I had done the inconceivable: I had killed my own brother.

I saw that I was trapped forever. Once I had spoken the words of the narrative that linked me to my brother's death, once they had been written down in an official report, my guilt and shame would be absolute and ineradicable. I had destroyed my family with my careless act, and now I would stand before the world and my monstrosity would be revealed by my own words. I wanted to be silent, to never speak again, just as I wanted to hide in my room forever. But this trooper, with his embarrassed patience, was forcing me to say the words that would make Peter's death real to everyone.

"Try again, son. I know its not easy. What do you remember?"

"We were hunting. We shot a deer. . . ."

Each word I spoke was innocent. Each sentence seemed harmless in itself. Yet each one moved me closer to my brother's corpse. If I could lie! If I could shout: "It wasn't loaded! My gun was empty!" or "I didn't pull the trigger. It must have been someone else." Would that have saved me? Or if I said nothing at all? If I simply sat there in silence and refused to speak, would someone else have been blamed?

I was going to be destroyed for my crime. Revenge was swift and self-inflicted. I would convict myself with my own words. There would be no formal trial: here was judge and jury. Here was my father who stood for our family, and the trooper who stood for the world outside my family—our neighbors, the town, the country, all those who had a right to know a monster lived among them.

In my dream, I heard God's voice demanding, "What have you done with your brother?" His question was like a fiery finger poking a hole through my chest, through my life. I saw the Bible they'd given me years ago in my first Sunday school, with its black leatherette cover stamped at the top in large gold letters "Holy Bible" and at the bottom "Gregory Orr" in tiny font. A slow-motion bullet approached the book from behind and struck the back cover dead center, entering it in a ragged hole but not emerging on the other side.

Now the book was a black wall I was facing and the bullet hole had become the entrance to a cave. I walked through the tunnel, listening to whispers from the tissue-thin pages that had been torn to incoherence. I knew the book's later meanings had been destroyed by the bullet, especially those of the New Testament that offered hope and redemption. The bullet had penetrated all the way to the earliest pages and I had to follow its path. I walked for hours through darkness. The whispering disappeared. I saw nothing and heard only the sound of my own breathing. Then far ahead there was a dim red glow that grew brighter as I approached and suddenly, I was standing in a hollow space stained with ancient blood. I heard our horrified screams as my gun fired, and I saw Cain standing above his brother, Abel, bleeding to death in a field.

Frightening as my dream of Cain was, it offered me hope by offering me the shelter of its story. It's not possible to survive in a world without meanings, and human meanings begin in stories. If I was Cain, I knew who I was and where I was situated in the universe. I was the one who had slain his brother. I was the one God was angry at. But, according to the story, God would not kill me. Instead, he would drive me alone into the wilderness. And wasn't that already true? Townspeople and my fellow students were, like my parents, afraid to speak to me about what had happened. They probably felt sorry for me, but I didn't know that. I thought they were afraid of me, because they saw my brother's blood on my hands.

It was a worse punishment for Cain to live than it would have been for him to die: "a fugitive and a vagabond shalt thou be in the earth."

"And Cain said unto the Lord, 'My punishment is greater than I can bear.'" But God would not let Cain die and he would not let anyone punish me. He knew that my own self-hatred was a far more terrible punishment.

Like Cain, I would be allowed to live and to live in a world of meaning, though it was a meaning that filled me with despair. Child that I was, I didn't know the world was full of stories. I didn't know that other people were making up other stories to explain Peter's death. I couldn't realize my parents had lives and fates of their own, distant from mine. It never occurred to me that they might believe that their own actions had brought them to this place.

Jerald Walker

sacraments of reconciliation

They were speeding along the expressway when he noticed something strange: she suddenly pulled her seatbelt across her body and clicked it into place. *Now* what is this crazy woman up to, he wondered, and a horrible thought crossed his mind a second before she grabbed and yanked the steering wheel, sending his car through a guardrail and ten feet into the air. As Jim and his new girlfriend tumbled toward the earth, my new girlfriend and I lay in his bed, snuggling beneath a warm comforter. More evidence, some might say, that I was the lucky twin.

The first evidence came when we were two. Our mother had just put us to bed and given us strict instructions to stay put. As soon as she left the room, we got up to inspect the riotous noises coming through our second-floor window. A bunch of kids were arguing over a toy. To see better, I leaned hard against the screen, which gave way and landed twenty feet below in the dirt, a second before me. At the hospital I was given a variety of scans and X-rays, but the only injury doctors could find was a small scrape on my left elbow, caused when I brushed against the brick wall during my descent.

Five years later, Jim fell two feet from a swing and broke his arm. Within days of the casts being removed, he toppled off the swings a second time, breaking his arm again.

The following year, when we were eight, I developed a talent for reciting poems. Jim developed a stutter. My parents hoped it was a phase but it got worse over time. I remember us sitting in class one day when our fifth grade teacher asked who wanted to recite Gwendolyn Brooks' poem "We Real Cool." She scanned the room for takers. Five hands inched up, joining the one being swung wildly by a girl who always smelled of pickles. I hoped the teacher would call her. Anyone besides Jim. She called Jim. He looked up from his desk. The students sitting in front of us turned in their seats, already giggling. The teacher called Jim again. I was sitting directly to his right, close enough to see the rapid heaving of his chest, the tremor of his legs. "James," she said once more, "whenever you're ready."

"We . . . We . . . We . . ."

A few students cupped their mouths to hold in the laughter.

"We . . . real . . . *real* . . . *real*"

The teacher huffed.

"Coo . . . coo . . . coo . . . *coo* . . . *coo* . . ."

The teacher said, "Get it *out*, James, for Christ's sake. *Speak!*"

But his throat had fully constricted by then. All he could do at that point was contort his face and gag. Our classmates laughed openly. The teacher shook her head while the pickle-smelling girl continued to wave. I lowered my gaze. The teacher said my name. I rose, recited the poem, and sat back down. When the teacher smiled and declared my recitation perfect, I was seized with a mixture of guilt and pity, as I had been since the third grade, when the onset of Jim's stuttering became theater for our classmates and a key means by which teachers told us apart. Since then we had both tried to talk sparingly in each other's company, unless we were alone, or with immediate members of our family, when his throat magically opened as wide as mine.

I was moved to an honor's class in sixth grade. Jim was moved to a remedial one. It was our first time being separated at school. For the whole year, whenever my teacher wanted something read or recited, I eagerly waved my hand, like the pickle-smelling girl, and other than being compared to her there seemed to be no penalty for it. Except that there was. But I didn't learn of it until one day in my fourteenth year, when Jim was sitting on my chest, pounding his fists into my face. I don't remember what spawned the fight, only that he was yelling, "You think you're better than me! You've *always* thought you're better than me!"

I somehow got us flipped around, and now I was on his chest, pounding my fists into his face. "I *do not*," I yelled back, "think I'm better than you!"

But I did; I understand that now. All of our lives we'd been compared and I'd always come out on top; girls told me I was cuter; boys told me I was more fun; teachers said I was smarter; and, as I kicked his ass that day, it seemed I was the better fighter too. But I didn't want to be better than him at anything; I just wanted to be different, to have an identity other than as one of the twins. And so when people began noting my pros and his cons, I internalized them. So did he. We stopped spending time together, unless it was to get high. There'd always be mutual friends around, though, who would separate us when our banter turned to taunts, taunts turned to threats, and threats turned to blows. Only sometimes our friends left too soon, and things got ugly.

One of those occasions ended with paramedics carrying Jim away after I'd banged his head on the floor until he was unconscious. Another occasion had him chasing me through the neighborhood with a baseball bat and the police looking for us both. They found him first and, at my exasperated parents' urging, took him into custody until he cooled off. Ninety minutes later, when they brought him home, after he'd apologized and expressed contrition, he broke through the barricade of my bedroom door and flung himself at me with a crazed rebel yell. By the time our father pulled him away, he'd bitten off a chunk of my thigh.

"That's *insane*," my girlfriend Brenda said when I showed her the scar, still visible twelve years later.

I laughed and said, "It's nothing. We were just kids. Besides, we were so high all the time then, I mean, everything was just so messed up. It's one of my biggest regrets," I continued, "the way things were between Jim and me. We weren't exactly what you'd call close."

"It's not too late to fix that."

I should have said that it probably was too late, but it was still early in our relationship; I wanted to make a good impression. "You're absolutely right," I told her. "And I *will* fix it."

And so that was the response she reminded me of several months later when I declined to visit Jim's apartment to celebrate our 28th birthday. "Everyone's here," he'd said when I called, although that wasn't exactly true. Missing was our brother Tim, who was in prison for drug possession; Peter, who was in prison for burglary; Steve, who was in prison for manslaughter; and Greg, who was dead. Just Paul, Rob, and Louis were there, and Louis was there in body only, since he hadn't been the same since killing a woman while driving drunk.

If Brenda convinced me to go, I would be there in body only, too. That world was no longer mine, that company no longer the kind I kept. I was a college student at the University of Iowa now, in Chicago for the weekend only to visit Brenda. She was attending the University of Illinois. We'd met eight months earlier when I'd returned for summer break. For weeks I'd been looking forward to spending my birthday quietly with her, and now she wanted me to spend it with my twin. As soon as I'd refused his invitation and hung up the phone, she'd said, "Remember when you told me you wanted to fix your relationship with Jim?"

"I told you no such thing," I said.

"Of course you did," she responded. "We have to go to his party. He's your *twin*," she reminded me. "Besides, I want to meet him and your friends."

"You don't want to do that," I told her.

"Yes I do. It'll be fun!" she said cheerily. "Come on, *Jerald*."

Everyone else I knew called me Jerry. But Jerry, she'd told me when we'd met, was the name of a child rather than a man. I liked that, how the switch of a name could bring maturity

and signify a break with the past. I didn't care much about the
maturity part, but breaking with the past was important to me.
It was that break I intended to honor now. I was trying to think
of an excuse to not go to Jim's when she went to her refrigerator
and took out a cake.

"What the hell is that?" I asked.

"It's a cake," she said.

I laughed.

"What's so funny?"

"It's just, well, these are not exactly cake eating people."

"*What?* Everybody eats cake." She set it on the table. Then
she lifted the receiver off the phone and held it towards me.
"Call your twin back," she said.

Thirty minutes later, we left her apartment and went downstairs to Jim's waiting car. I got in the passenger's seat, and
Brenda sat behind me. After I introduced Jim to her, he pointed
toward the cake on her lap. "What the hell is that?" he asked.

"It's a cake!" Brenda said.

Jim laughed. Then he took a swallow of his forty-ounce and
eased away from the curb.

The stereo was turned up full blast and the air smelled of cigarettes, marijuana, fish and rancid oil. Brenda was in the living
room trying to learn how to play bid whist, while Jim hovered
over the stove, pulling chunks of perch from the bubbling black
liquid. I'd just walked in to get another beer. "Hey, bro'," he
said, "want some coke?"

I shook my head no. I opened the refrigerator.

"Come on, man," he said. "It's our birthday."

"The beer's cool," I said.

"So you like them Iowa boys now?" he said, laughing. "You
just eat corn and go to school and shit? And *bowl?*"

I forced a smile.

"Come on, Jerry. I mean *Jerald.*" He burst into laughter,
just as the others had done every time Brenda said my name.
He put a fresh batch of battered fish into the grease, causing it

to roar. "One little hit, for old time's sake," he said. He wiped his hands on his apron, then reached inside his top pocket and took out a small piece of paper. He held it out to me. I glanced into the living room; Brenda was staring at her cards while Rob leaned over her shoulder, telling her something that brought a wrinkle to her brow. I turned back to Jim. He was still extending the coke. I took it and backed out of Brenda's view. He handed me a dollar bill, already rolled. I took one small hit, but I wasn't getting high, I told myself, so much as taking a sacrament of reconciliation.

At 2:00 AM, the party started to break up. As we were saying our goodbyes, Brenda exclaimed, "Wait, wait, I almost forgot!" She ran into the kitchen and returned with the cake. Ignoring the laughter, she sang happy birthday.

Brenda and I had decided to spend the night and in the morning have Jim drop her off at her apartment and me at the Greyhound Station. He offered us his room before carrying a pillow and spare blankets to the couch. After Brenda and I got in bed, she apologized for the cake, which hadn't turned out the way she'd hoped. "But," she added, "it was kind of everyone to try some."

"They didn't have to spit it out, though. I mean, they could have *swallowed* it. I swallowed some."

"You're sweet," she said. "Everyone was sweet. Especially Jim. I didn't know he stuttered, though."

"A little," I said. "It used to be a lot worse."

She snuggled against me, and the next thing I knew I was being awakened by a ringing phone. I looked at the clock on the nightstand. It was 3:15. The phone rang some more, and I wondered who would be calling at that time and why Jim didn't answer it. Finally it stopped. A second later it started again. Brenda was awake now too; she'd pushed herself up on her elbows. "Somebody keeps calling," I grumbled, "and Jim's not answering. He had a lot to drink, so he's probably out cold." The ringing stopped. Brenda laid her head back on the pillow. The ringing started once more.

Brenda sat up again. "Maybe you should answer it," she said. "Maybe it's an emergency."

I dismissed that possibility, but only long enough for the ringing to pause and resume. I climbed out of bed and went into the kitchen, where the phone was mounted on the wall.

"Hello?"

"Jerry?"

"Yes? Who's this?"

"Jim's been in a terrible car accident."

"*Mom?*"

"Jim's been in a crash. . . ."

"Mom, what are you *talking* about? Jim's asleep on the couch."

I felt a draft of cold air coming from my right. I glanced in that direction and saw that the kitchen door was wide open. My mother was saying something as I set the phone on the counter and hurried into the living room. The couch was empty, the blankets in a heap on the floor. I went back to the phone. "*What happened?*"

"What . . . aren't you listening?"

"*What happened?*" I asked again. Brenda was standing next to me now, wrapped in the comforter.

"Jim was in a terrible crash."

"*Where is he?*" I yelled.

"Cook County Hospital."

I hung up. I told Brenda what I knew and we hurried to get dressed. Except there was a problem: buses didn't start running until dawn, and there were no taxies in that part of the city after dark, and rarely during the day. We put on our coats, left the apartment, and started walking.

Three hours later, just as the sun was beginning to rise, we entered the emergency room doors. The receptionist offered no information on Jim's condition, only that he was about to go to surgery. She directed us to the third floor.

We found him in the hall, lying in a long row of gurneys covered with patients moaning and calling for help. His face was bruised and swollen, but he was conscious. As soon as he saw us, he tried to speak. "My . . . my . . . my . . ." he began, and suddenly we were back in the fifth grade. "They're . . . ta . . . ta . . . ta . . . king . . . my . . . *my* . . . *arm*." I looked at Brenda. Her hand was over her mouth, like our classmates, only she wasn't laughing. I started to reach for Jim but I didn't know where it was safe to touch, so I just stood there, not knowing what to say or do, until an orderly wheeled him away.

I went to call my parents and they gave me the rest of the story. Jim's girlfriend had walked away from the crash, leaving him lying in the street, his right arm trapped beneath the hood of the upended car. He hadn't been wearing his seatbelt. The doctors said he should have died.

Four hours later, when the surgeon came to talk to us, he stressed that point. "How he survived," he said, "is beyond me." They'd managed to save his arm, though only time would tell how much function it would regain.

Soon after the surgeon left, the double doors of the operating room parted and Jim was wheeled through. He was unconscious, with only his bandaged head and IV'ed left arm exposed from the bundle of blankets. Brenda and I followed the orderly as he steered him into a large room filled with a few dozen other patients. They parked his bed in an empty slot near a window and four folding chairs. Brenda and I sat and waited for him to wake. It took an hour. I saw his eyes flutter open, and then they widened with terror as he began clawing frantically at his blankets, yanking off layer after layer. I went to his side. And if I could have spoken at that moment, I would have told him that everything was okay, that his arm was still there, that he was lucky to be alive.

Darin Strauss

———— ✽ ————

chang and eng

"Chang-Eng," the children chanted. "Mutant, mutant."

Now and then the little innocents would spring from the dust cloud chasing our carriage to cry our names. The path we traveled cut through a droughty careworn field, and to either side of us a fast passing scene of blond grass and dead milkweed thirsted under the burnt sky of sunset. My ear tingled with the nearness of my brother Chang, who picked lint off of my shoulder and knew not to bump my head as he did so, his dark eyes showing little reflections of me. I was thirty-two. My life was about to begin: I was entering North Carolina.

My brother and I did not know that love was soon to deliver us to a new life. But twenty-one children and thirty years later, how obvious it seems that everything that followed was a consequence of that evening. When you know your time is running out, self-deceptions fly from your bedside like embers off a bonfire. Alone, looking back in the dark, with a final chance to bind together circumstances that have made you a peasant who sells duck eggs on the Mekong one day, and the South's most famous temperance advocate the next, you see a curtain open onto the landmark moments of your past.

When Chang and I arrived in North Carolina, we were coming to the end of yet another tour, exhibiting the bond that the public could not see without assuming we two were so very different from everybody else.

Our two-seater carriage had kerosene lamps and the legend "The Siamese Twin" in chipping yellow paint on its doors. The halfwit we'd hired drove at a quick pace. The dust of riding whisked us toward Wilkesboro, the last stop on a junket of somersaults and smiles that had spanned the eastern seaboard.

Chang had the driver bridle our two horses to a stop in a large grassy square near the center of town—a little commons that had not yet changed its name from "Union Square" to "Westwood Park." This open space was blotchy with killed grass, its flagless flagpole lacked ambition in the wind. The hot, dry Christmas season had left Wilkesboro anemic. A line of four threadbare trees gesticulated like marionettes behind the flagstaff.

Townspeople rushed at us from every direction. Dozens of unkempt children and their unkempt parents gathered round our carriage, pointing fingers. The rest of the population climbed on the roofs for a better view. My brother grinned at them all. He delivered his patented wave, like a little boy proving with a casual flick that his hand is clean on both sides—the motion Queen Victoria used to greet her masses.

"Come down, carriage man," my brother called out to our driver, wetting my face with spittle. "Will you please open door?"

The driver muttered at us from his buckboard.

I asked this idiot, "Did you say something?"

The driver let us out, his well-shaved cheeks pink as Mekong tuna meat. He said, "Nothing, sirs."

"You are addressing Eng alone." I said, accepting the man's hand and stepping from the carriage with my brother. "Do you hear my twin talking? You must say, 'Nothing, *sir*.'" I was tired and irritable. "When you speak to me, you speak to one 'sir,' not two."

Far away, between the rough corners of Wilkesboro's buildings (small white Presbyterian church with no steeple, narrow white beer-parlor, small white general store displaying all its stock in its window), rows of sleeping blue mountains hid in shadow, each more blurred than the last. And the full moon had begun its crawl across the gloaming sky.

Everything about this environment seemed animated by our arrival: The gathering crowd on every side of us; the bandy-legged old man in a white suit who walked slowly across Union Square with a yellow rose in his lapel, and the pair of young girls who ran over and took him arm-in-arm toward our carriage; the Negro slaves across the courtyard pitching straw and pretending not to look; the dirty little white hands poking our ligament as we stepped from the carriage. Several reached for my face.

"Chang-Eng," chanted the children. "Mutant, mutant."

"Thank you," Chang and I said, as the dust gathered on our identical black suits—tight and crisply English in cut, the very ones Barnum had bought for us. Strolling through the crowd, my brother and I were two complete bodies affixed at the chest by a fleshy, bendable, seven-inch-long ligament resembling a forearm.

"Chang-Eng acknowledge you, good people," Chang said. We crossed Main Street side-by-side, arms over each other's shoulders, in the calibrated rhythm of our united movement. Like Chang, I wore my hair in a black braid long enough to curl around my head. I tied it in a blue silk tassel that fell over my brother's shoulder, as his fell over mine.

North Carolina was a welcome change from Boston, Washington, Philadelphia, New York, that series of East Coast cities that even before the War of Yankee Aggression had become as vulgar as a row of women of easy virtue on a street corner. Some believe the War divided America's history in one stroke, advancing Northern manufacturing and the forward parade of Yankee progress all at once. But by December, 1842, the North had swelled so hastily it'd already simmered with industry and crime and most of all too many people, while the South remained in rural condition, natural as ever. Wilkesboro was among those bygone cheerful hamlets that were so numerous across the map of North Carolina they seemed like stars in the nighttime sky, before Reconstruction hobbled the South.

Meanwhile my brother had not quit waving to the towns-folk; few returned his greeting. A yellow-skinned man and his conjoined twin may be admitted into a village in North Carolina, but will never be adopted by it.

Main Street was rounded, with a humped center and slop-ing sides, and it led us across town. Chang and I were silent as we walked, thinking to ourselves. We almost never spoke to one another. At all times, a wordless debate about the fundamentals of movement traveled across our bond like a message across tele-graph wire, and that was conversation enough.

The people of Wilkesboro had begun to follow us at a dis-tance: Here two blond schoolgirls crouched behind a craggy black oak tree to stare; there, in the Law Office Building, under the pressed metal façade, a few cheerful boys shouted taunts; one brave soul walked near us before scampering off to giggle behind some wagons tethered to the Court House gallery; across the street a woman stopped in her tracks in front of a livery sta-ble to gape at The Twins, her face turning pale as death. A small number of people, however, did smile openly at us as we passed, and let fly a friendly giggle whenever Chang waved.

"Eng," said Chang. "It is exciting, yes?" With his free hand he smoothed the lapels of his jacket. His face was calm and contented.

"Brother, I don't know what you mean."

Chang was slightly taken off guard. My twin and I were very different. His life had followed a smooth path; I was forever touring deep recesses and scaling tall heights.

"Well," he said, narrowing his eyes to search my face, "this, I mean!" Crooking our ligament, he drew himself in front of and closer to me, and he looked over my shoulder at the now large crowd following at our heels. Chang and I continued to walk in this manner—nearly face-to-face, with my brother striding backwards—as he flung his hand in the air and waved at the people. Everyone clapped. Chang swung around to face forward again.

It was this sort of pandering showmanship that I hated, and strove to avoid for most of my career. (Like most everybody, I have certain accomplishments I am proud of: We never participated in, nor were in any way associated with, an American circus; my predilection for reading and learning, which later saved me from the manner of immigrant speech that bound Chang.)

Main Street came to an end at the Yates Inn. A Southern community such as Wilkesboro, not only in its distant relation to the central government, but also to neighboring villages, believes itself an individual, free from all others. And yet, little inns just like this one were features of nearly all minor Southern towns, and by now Chang and I felt at home loitering by inn-yards, waiting to be admitted.

Wilkesboro's version of the Southern hostel was a two-story unpainted log house with eye-like windows and a modest front-yard overgrown with chokecherry. A giant woman sat on the inn's drooping front porch, fanning herself in the skeletal shade of leafless oaks. She was some five hundred pounds, if not more, this innkeeper.

My brother and I came to stand before her, resting our two free hands on the porch railing. Moist patches of the woman's scalp were visible under her thin gray hair—like peat bog spied through the reeds of a marsh; and her hairline gave way to a glistening forehead just as a marsh would open onto a river.

The lady innkeeper scrutinized Chang and me in our unforgiving black. "A charming creature, just about as strange as they say." Her bassy voice wiggled the flesh hanging below her chin. She wore a homemade dress of gray cloth-stuff, a wide loose garment made with no thought to style. Her skin refused contour. Birds shrieked in the trees.

I imagined this woman a courtier in His Majesty King Rama's palace, bejeweled, dressed in silk while four or five husbands danced around her, runty men with short lifespans.

To her left stood a grinning boy in a straw hat with a crooked rim. To her right, a pair of blond women—her daughters, I guessed, though they were not so young—long-faced, flat-chested and each with lip-rouge on her front teeth. I allowed myself to gaze at these blonds, and the taller one's eyes took me. They flickered impatiently—like the wings of little birds. Possibly it was the light at that hour, or my fatigue pressing in, but I believed she was smiling. Under a wild and rustic smell, Wilkesboro was lowering into nightfall, and a wind had risen, carrying dust in itself.

The declining sun acted on the girl's fine hair, cutting it into elements of gold and pink gold and shadow. Strange how lively her clear face had become. She blushed and bowed her head, but she continued to peek at me from under her brows. She bit her lip. Before long she raised her head and looked at me sympathetically. I could not fathom that a woman was looking into my eyes. I returned her stare, I don't know where I discovered the courage. The whole time her face remained very still except for the crinkling brought about by her developing smile—At this point time fell off its rails.

Evidently, only a few seconds passed, though I knew the moment had slipped from the calendar. For the seeming eternity I stood there, my heart pounded only once, a single thunderclap, echoing. A young lady was looking at me, and smiling. I was certain of it. I knew that my brother, too, was captivated by this tall, blond innkeeper's daughter. Was it me the girl was fixing her eye on, or the twin close at my side?

The whole time, the girl's sister stood in shadow, chewed at her nails, and looked at her own feet. And then this nail-chewing sister looked up at me, too, without smiling or frowning. Now the entire town had gathered behind us, watching everything. At this point, the girls' large mother leaned forward in her groaning chair and straightened her dress, patted her hair.

"Jefferson," she said to her boy. "Go get your father." Daintily, the large woman removed a little gnat that had flown into her mouth. "Tell him I found a pair of husbands for your sisters."

I swear the townsfolk cheered.

Nathaniel Rich and Simon Rich

brothers on brotherhood
an interview by andrew blauner

Blauner: As I was putting together this book, I thought it would be fun to include an interview with two real-life brothers. So I'm here today with the Riches: Nathaniel, twenty-eight, and Simon, twenty-four. They've assured me that they're experts on the institution of brotherhood—and they should be. After all, they spent the first two decades of their lives together, eating, sleeping, and growing up side-by-side, under the same roof!

Thanks for being here, guys.

Nathaniel: Of course. I've been looking forward to this.

Simon: Yeah, this will be fun.

Blauner: So Nathaniel, as the older brother, you get to go first. What does Brotherhood mean to you?

Nathaniel: It's great being a brother. The younger brother benefits by learning from the older brother's wisdom, experience, and leadership. And who knows, maybe the older brother learns something from his younger brother too.

Simon: I learned not to make the same mistakes!

Blauner: Ha! Good one, Simon. So how important is birth order in determining who we are?

Nathaniel: That's funny. I'm glad you asked me about that. I recently read a study in a major scholarly journal that addressed that very subject.

Simon: What did it say?

Note: Live transcript, Nathaniel Rich's apartment, Brooklyn, New York, October 4, 2008.

257

Nathaniel: Well, it was written by a group of extremely qualified scientists and it demonstrated, unequivocally, that younger siblings have a higher tendency toward homosexuality.

Blauner: Whoa.

Nathaniel: The theory states that a woman pregnant with a son often develops immunity against male antigens in her womb. Consequently, when she becomes pregnant with a second son, her immune system may interfere with the sexual differentiation in that fetus's developing brain, causing an increased likelihood of homosexuality.

Simon: That's crazy.

Nathaniel: Yes, I know, it's an exciting advance in the field of fraternal sexuality studies.

Blauner: So . . . Simon. What was it like growing up with an older brother?

Simon: [silent]

Nathaniel: The bottom line is that a younger brother has a 33 percent greater chance of being gay.

Blauner: We got it, Nathaniel. Let's move on to my next question. One thing I've noticed is that there are a lot of brothers who work in the same industry. The two of you, for instance, are both writers. And there are many such examples within the worlds of law, medicine, and even professional sports.

Nathaniel: That's true. I'm a baseball fan, so when you said that, the first person that popped into my mind was Cal Ripken Jr. Did you know that he had a younger brother named Billy? A lot of people don't remember Billy. And that's too bad, because he was a pretty reliable defensive second baseman. I'm not sure if he ever made the All-Star team—as his older brother did, nineteen times consecutively. But Billy definitely had heart, which I guess counts for something.

Simon: I have a study for you. It was in a journal last year. It said that if you are an older brother, there is a 66 percent chance that you will have smaller organs.

Nathaniel: Oh, really? Who performed that study?

Simon: It was a joint study by Oxford and MIT. And NASA.

Blauner: If we can stay on sports for a second . . .

Simon: Some organs that human beings have in their body include the brain and the penis. So the bottom line is . . .

Nathaniel: What my brother just said is obviously not a real thing.

Simon: How do you know it's not a real thing?

Nathaniel: First of all, it's preposterous. Second of all, NASA researches outer space, not human anatomy. And finally, when Mr. Blauner was asking you that last question, you were doing that thing you do with your eyes whenever you're trying to think of something clever.

Simon: [*Eyes roll back in his head*]

Nathaniel: See? He's doing it right now.

Simon: Hey, Nat: Maybe if your *brain* organ wasn't so small, you would be smart enough to know more about science things.

Nathaniel: Science things? That's the best you could do? Geez, Simon, this is a professional interview.

Blauner: All right, let me go to the next question. There's a Chinese proverb that says "brothers are like hands and feet." Do you think that's accurate?

Nathaniel: Definitely. It reminds me of the ancient Greek fable of the two brother tigers and the dark cave. The older tiger was strong and wise and the younger was weak and blind. The rest of the pack was going to leave the younger brother to die in the cave alone. But then the younger brother realized that, if he held on to his older, stronger brother's tail, he could manage to make it out of the cave and survive a little longer.

[*Recites a passage in Greek*]

That translates as, "Where the older brother leads, the younger follows, just as the moon follows the sun across the heavens, or a young child follows a man."

Simon: Here's a fable. There were two bears. One was fourteen, one was ten, and they were at an all-boys summer camp in Kents Hill, Maine. This fourteen-year-old bear was going through puberty more slowly than the other bears his age. One night, at a dance with an all-girls camp for bears, the ten-year-old bear snuck in and pantsed his older brother bear. Everybody at the bear dance started laughing, except for the fourteen-year-old bear. He was crying, like a little girl bear.

Nathaniel: Bastard.

Simon: Hey man, it's just a fable.

Nathaniel: OK, fine. Here's another fucking fable.

Blauner: Guys . . .

Nathaniel: Once there was a twelve-year-old lion who hid in his sixteen-year-old brother lion's closet every day after school. He did this in the desperate hope that he would one day be able to watch his older brother have sex with his girlfriend lion.

Simon: I swear to God, Nat, if you . . .

Nathaniel: After weeks of constant spying, the younger brother's pathetic dream finally came true. The older brother came home with his girlfriend lion and they started getting it on. As they were removing their lion clothes, the girl lion suddenly recoiled. "What is that horrible odor?" she said. The odor was coming from the closet.

Simon: Why are you doing this? Why are you doing this to me?

Nathaniel: When the lion couple opened the closet door, they found the younger brother lion cowering in fear. He had been so excited about the prospect of seeing lion sex for the first time in his life that he somehow lost control of his bladder and actually peed in his lion pants. The girl lion said, "Oh my God, is this your younger brother?" And the older brother lion was so ashamed that he had to say, "No, it's just some random twelve-year-old lion. He must have wandered in from the school across the street, which is for mentally handicapped lions."

Blauner: Jesus, Nathaniel. That's a horrible fable.

Simon: Blauner, if you print a word of this . . .

Nathaniel: What, he can't print the facts? He's not allowed to print real-life facts?

Simon: We're talking facts? OK, fine! Fact: My brother Nathaniel is so afraid of crowds, that in order to leave his apartment, he needs to go through a special ritual. Let me tell you about this ritual.

Blauner: Guys! Listen. . . . I want to apologize to both of you. This interview was clearly a mistake. In fact . . . I'm now wondering if this entire book was a mistake. You obviously have some serious issues to work out. I have seven brothers and things have never gotten this dysfunctional. Not even close.

Simon: What are you saying?

Nathaniel: Yeah, what are you getting at?

Blauner: I just wish that the two of you shared the same kind of supportive relationship that I do with my brothers.

Simon: You think the Blauners are better than the Riches?

Nathaniel: Who do you think you're talking to?

Blauner: Come on. Watch your tone.

Simon: Don't tell him to watch his tone. You watch your tone. And your *ass*. That's Nathaniel Fucking Rich right there.

Blauner: Simon, please. We're all adults here.

Nathaniel: Are you for real, Blauner? Are you actually trying to front on my little brother?

Blauner: What? I'm not trying to front on anybody. I don't even know what that means exactly.

Simon: Here's a fable you'll be able to understand, Blauner. It's called "The Two Ass-Kicking Brothers Named Rich."

Nathaniel: They were llamas and they didn't take no *bull*shit.

Simon: And if you went after one llama, you knew damn well the other llama would be coming after your ass.

Nathaniel: Because that's what those llamas were about!

Simon: And you can tell those other Blauner bitches that we'll be sitting right here waiting for them!

[*Blauner exits*]

[*Nathaniel and Simon hug*]

Simon: Was that too much?

Nathaniel: Maybe. Didn't he say that he had seven brothers?

Simon: Oh, my God, you're right. They're probably all grown men too.

Nathaniel: And strong, like that guy.

Simon: Let's leave your apartment and hide at Mom's house for a while. She'll protect us.

Nathaniel: Great idea. Is it cool if I do my ritual first?

Simon: Take all the time you need.

about the editor
and contributors

Andrew Blauner is the founder of Blauner Books Literary Agency. He is the editor of COACH: *25 Writers Reflect on People Who Made a Difference* (with a foreword by Bill Bradley) and coeditor of *Anatomy of Baseball* (with a foreword by Yogi Berra).

Chris Bohjalian is the best-selling author of thirteen books, including *Midwives*, *The Double Bind*, and *Skeletons at the Feast*. His most recent novel, *Secrets of Eden*, was just published. He lives in Vermont.

Ethan Canin is the author of the novels *America America* and *Carry Me Across the Water* and the story collections *The Palace Thief* and *Emperor of the Air*, among other books. A former physician, he is on the faculty of the Iowa Writers' Workshop and lives in Iowa and northern Michigan. His brother is an oncologist in California.

Benjamin Cheever's most recent book, *Strides*, was published by Rodale.

Fred Cheever is a professor of law and director of the Environmental and Natural Resources Law Program at the University of Denver, Sturm College of Law.

Charles D'Ambrosio is the author of *The Point and Other Stories*; *Orphans, a collection of essays*; and *The Dead Fish Museum*, which was a finalist for the Pen/Faulkner Award. His fiction has appeared in the *New Yorker*, the *Paris Review*, *A Public Space*, and various anthologies.

Dominick Dunne is the best-selling author of several books, including *An Inconvenient Woman*, *People Like Us*, and *A Season in Purgatory*. His essays have been collected in the book *Fatal Charm*. A successful producer, his films include *The Panic in Needle Park*, *Ash Wednesday*, *Play It As It Lays*, and *The Boys in the Band*. He is a special correspondent to *Vanity Fair*.

Richard Ford is a Pulitzer Prize–winning novelist and a story writer and has written many essays—most notably for the *New Yorker*, the *New York Times*, and numerous newspapers in Europe. He lives in East Boothbay, Maine, with his wife, Kristina Ford.

Mikal Gilmore has written for *Rolling Stone* since the 1970s and is the author, most recently, of *Stories Done: Writings on the 1960s and Its Discontents*. His first book, *Shot in the Heart*, was a National Book Critics Circle and *Los Angeles Times* Book Award–winning memoir about his family.

Herbert Gold was born and raised in Cleveland and rose to national fame with his roman à clef *Fathers*. His other books include *A Girl of Forty*, *She Took My Arm As If She Loved Me*, *Bohemia*, and *Haiti: The Best Nightmare on Earth*. He has written twenty novels and published thirty-two books in all. His contribution to this book is taken from his recently published *Still Alive! A Temporary Condition*. He lives in San Francisco.

Pete Hamill is a novelist, essayist, journalist, and screenwriter, whose career has endured for more than forty years. He is the author of sixteen books, including the best-selling novels *Forever* and *Snow in August* and the best-selling memoir *A Drinking Life*. He lives in New York City.

James Hurst is a short story writer, best known for "The Scarlet Ibis," which first appeared in the *Atlantic Monthly* in 1960 and won the "Atlantic First" award. After serving in the United States Army during World War II, he studied singing at the renowned Juilliard School of Music in New York. He currently lives in North Carolina.

David Kaczynski is the executive director of New Yorkers for Alternatives to the Death Penalty. He is the brother of Theodore Kaczynski, the convicted "Unabomber."

Phillip Lopate is the author of a dozen books, including personal essay collections (*Bachelorhood, Against Joie de Vivre, Portrait of My Body*), fiction (*The Rug Merchant, Two Marriages*), film criticism (*Totally Tenderly Tragically*), and other nonfiction (*Being with Children, Waterfront*). He is a professor in the graduate division of Columbia University.

David Maraniss is an associate editor at the *Washington Post* and the author of five critically acclaimed and best-selling books: *First in His Class, When Pride Still Mattered, They Marched into Sunlight, Clemente*, and *Rome 1960*. He won the 1993 Pulitzer Prize for National Reporting for his coverage of Bill Clinton, was part of a *Post* team that won the 2008 Pulitzer Prize for Breaking News coverage of the Virginia Tech tragedy, and has been a Pulitzer finalist three other times.

Frank McCourt was born in 1930 in Brooklyn, New York, to Irish immigrant parents, grew up in Limerick, Ireland, and returned to America in 1949. For thirty years he taught in New York City high schools. His first book, *Angela's Ashes*, won the

Pulitzer Prize, the National Book Critics Circle Award, and the *Los Angeles Times* Book Award. In 2006, he won the prestigious Ellis Island Family Heritage Award for Exemplary Service in the Field of the Arts and the United Federation of Teachers John Dewey Award for Excellence in Education. He is also the author of the best-selling books *'Tis, Teacher Man*, and *Angela and the Baby Jesus*. He died in July 2009.

Daniel Menaker, a former editor at the *New Yorker* and executive editor-in-chief of Random House, is the author of two collections of stories and a novel, *The Treatment*. He has written fiction, journalism, and humor for many major American newspapers and magazines and is the editorial producer of Titlepage, an online book program. He lives in New York City and serves as editorial consultant to Barnes & Noble's e-reader, the nook.

Jay Neugeboren is the author of seventeen books, including two prize-winning novels, *The Stolen Jew* and *Before My Life Began*, two award-winning books of nonfiction, *Imagining Robert* and *Transforming Madness*, and three collections of prize-winning stories. His most recent novel is *1940*.

Gregory Orr is the author of ten collections of poetry and several collections of prose, as well as a memoir, *The Blessing*. He teaches at the University of Virginia, where he founded and was first director of its MFA program.

Nathaniel Rich is an editor at the *Paris Review* and the author of *The Mayor's Tongue*, a novel.

Simon Rich writes for *Saturday Night Live*. He is the author of the humor collections *Ant Farm* and *Free-Range Chickens*.

Steven V. Roberts is the author of *From Every End of This Earth* and *My Fathers' Houses*, and the coauthor, with his wife, Cokie

Roberts, of *From This Day Forward*, a *New York Times* best seller that chronicled their marriage and other marriages in American history. After a twenty-five-year career at the *New York Times*, Roberts became the Shapiro Professor of Media and Public Affairs at George Washington University in 1997. He is a political analyst for ABC Radio, a substitute host on NPR's the *Diane Rehm Show*, and coauthor with Cokie of a weekly syndicated newspaper column.

David Sedaris is the author of the books *Barrel Fever*, *Naked*, *Holidays on Ice*, *Me Talk Pretty One Day*, *Dress Your Family in Corduroy and Denim*, and *When You Are Engulfed in Flames*. His essays appear frequently in the *New Yorker* and are heard on Public Radio International's *This American Life*.

Jim Shepard is the author of six novels and three collections of stories, including *Like You'd Understand, Anyway*, which was nominated for a National Book Award in 2007. He teaches at Williams College in Williamstown, Massachusetts.

Floyd Skloot's fifteen books include the memoirs *In the Shadow of Memory*, *A World of Light*, and *The Wink of the Zenith: The Shaping of a Writer's Life*. He has won three Pushcart Prizes and the PEN USA Literary Award.

Darin Strauss is the international best-selling author of the novels *Chang and Eng*, *The Real McCoy*, and *More Than It Hurts You*. The recipient of a 2006 Guggenheim Fellowship in fiction writing, he is a clinical associate professor at New York University's graduate school.

Jerald Walker received his MFA in creative writing from the Iowa Writers' Workshop, where he was a Teaching/Writing Fellow and James A. Michener Fellow, and he received his PhD in interdisciplinary studies from the University of Iowa. His work has been widely anthologized, including twice in *Best American Essays 2007* and twice in *Best African American Essays 2009*. "Sacraments of Reconciliation" is an excerpt from his book, *Street Shadows: A Memoir of Race, Rebellion, and Redemption*.

John Edgar Wideman is the author of more than twenty works of fiction and nonfiction, including the award-winning *Brothers and Keepers*, *Philadelphia Fire*, and, most recently, the novel *Fanon*. He is the recipient of two PEN/Faulkner Awards and has been nominated for the National Book Award.

Geoffrey Wolff has written six novels, among them *Providence* and *The Age of Consent*. His five books of personal memories and biographies include *The Duke of Deception*, about his father. He lives in Maine.

Tobias Wolff's books include the memoirs *This Boy's Life* and *In Pharaoh's Army: Memories of the Lost War*; the short novel *The Barracks Thief*; the novel *Old School*; and four collections of short stories: *In the Garden of the North American Martyrs*, *Back in the World*, *The Night in Question*, and, most recently, *Our Story Begins: New and Selected Stories*. He has edited several anthologies, among them *Best American Short Stories 1994*, *A Doctor's Visit: The Short Stories of Anton Chekhov*, and *The Vintage Book of Contemporary American Short Stories*. His work is translated widely, and he has received numerous awards, including the PEN/Faulkner Award, the *Los Angeles Times* Book Prize, both the PEN/Malamud and the Rea Award for Excellence in the Short Story, the Story Prize, and the Academy Award in Literature from the American Academy of Arts and Letters. He is the Ward W. and Priscilla B. Woods Professor of English at Stanford.

acknowledgments

Great gratitude to my publisher, Jossey-Bass/John Wiley & Sons, and especially to Alan Rinzler, my editor, who was the first to embrace and champion the value and virtue of this book, and whose help and guidance, from the outset, has been critical. And my thanks to Nana Twumasi, Debbie Notkin, Carol Hartland, Sophia Ho, Mike Onorato, Erin Beam, Marcy Marsh, Jennifer Wenzel, Paul Foster, and Debra Hunter, whose assistance and advice have been invaluable.

I am honored to have Frank McCourt's support for this project, and I will be eternally grateful for that.

The word *contributors*, here, does not begin to do justice in describing the writers whose work is in this book. It's akin to calling each of the Beatles *contributors* to the band. They *are* it. Without these writers and their work, there is no book. And I will never be able to express the full extent of my deep appreciation and admiration.

To my friends who have been like brothers (and sisters) to me: Thank you for everything. Special thanks to Maud Bryt for her encouragement and support with this project. And to John and Jim Solomon: Thank you, thank you for being a profound inspiration, for your brotherhood, and beyond.

As ever, my love to my family, all of them, everywhere. And to Steven and Peter, Patrick and Christopher: may we all be together some time soon.

sources and permissions